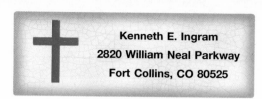
Patterns of
Preaching
A Sermon Sampler

Patterns of
Preaching
A Sermon Sampler

Ronald J. Allen

EDITOR

CHALICE
PRESS
ST. LOUIS, MISSOURI

Cover: Michael Foley

Interior design: Elizabeth Wright

Art Direction: Michael Domínguez

Visit Chalice Press on the World Wide Web at
www.chalicepress.com

10 9 8 7 6 5 4   06 07 08 09 10 11

Library of Congress Cataloging–in–Publication Data

Patterns of preaching : a sermon sampler / Ronald J. Allen, editor.
　　p.　cm.
Includes bibliographical references and index.
ISBN-13: 978-0-827229-53-2
ISBN-10: 0-827229-53-4
　　1. Preaching.　2.　Sermons, American.　I. Allen, Ronald J. (Ronald James), 1949–
　　BV4211.2.P28　　1998　　　　　　　　　　　　　　　　　98–47291
　　252—dc21　　　　　　　　　　　　　　　　　　　　　　　　　　CIP

Printed in the United States of America

To
Monte Vista Christian Church (Disciples of Christ)
Albuquerque, New Mexico, U.S.A.

A People of the Gospel
Whose Vision of God
Is as the Land in Which You Live:
Loving, Gracious, Clear, Open, Awesome

Your Faith
Is in the Soul of
Linda McKiernan-Allen
Spouse
Mother of our Children
Deepest Partner in the Gospel

Whoever Leads Me to
Faith and Community That is More
Loving, Gracious, Clear, Open, Awesome

Acknowledgments

I thank the president, dean, and trustees of Christian Theological Seminary for the research leave that made it possible to assemble this collection. I especially thank the contributors for giving their best efforts to this project at a time of the year (between Easter and Pentecost) when many were staggering under the weight of life-packs that were already too full. However, to a person, they were congenial, upbeat, responsible, and willing to serve the gospel through this project. I thank Jon Berquist for prompting this idea. I also thank Joyce Krauser, faculty assistant at Christian Theological Seminary, who again testified that wise editorial counsel and extraordinary efforts in manuscript production are ministry.

Table of Contents

Introduction

A tremendous new energy has captivated the field of preaching. Preachers are generating new patterns for sermons. Many preachers are rediscovering freshness in older ways of preaching. *Patterns for Preaching: A Sermon Sampler* aims to contribute to this energy by presenting 34 models of preaching—some new, some old.

This collection is distinctive in three ways. First, each sermon demonstrates a particular approach to preaching. This book exposes preachers to thirty-four different ways of conceiving sermons from both the contemporary and classical periods. Second, this book accompanies a textbook on preaching: Ronald J. Allen, *Interpreting the Gospel: An Introduction to Preaching* (St. Louis: Chalice Press, 1998). Each book can be read independently, but when taken together, they form a broad interplay between theory and practice. Third, each sermon is annotated with comments about the congregation in which the sermon was preached and the purposes of the sermon. Readers thus can sense the sermon as part of a living conversation in community.

Several times in this book I refer to the gospel. With my colleague Clark M. Williamson, I take the gospel to be the news, revealed to the church through Jesus Christ, of God's unconditional love for each and every entity and of God's will for justice for each and every entity.[1] The gospel can be formulated differently, but all expressions of the gospel known to me include or imply the elements of unconditional love and call for justice.

The preacher helps the congregation interpret what God's unconditional love and will for justice offers each person and situation and what it requires of each person and situation. The sermon is critical reflection. The preacher helps the congregation name the world from the

---

[1] For this way of formulating the gospel, see Clark M. Williamson and Ronald J. Allen, *A Credible and Timely Word: Process Theology and Preaching* (St. Louis: Chalice Press, 1991), 71–90; idem., *The Teaching Minister* (Louisville: Westminster/John Knox Press, 1991), 75–82; and especially Clark M. Williamson, *A Guest in the House of Israel: Post-Holocaust Theology and the Church* (Louisville: Westminster/John Knox Press, 1993), 18–16, 22–23.

standpoint of the gospel. The sermon can become an experience of divine love and a call to justice.

I also refer to sermons on biblical texts, doctrines, Christian practices, and other topics (e.g., personal and social issues). All these elements may be present in any sermon, but a sermon can also focus on a single one of them. Most preaching centers on encounter with a biblical text, doctrine, a Christian practice, or a topic of a personal or social nature. For fuller explanations of these categories, see the introductory remarks in chapter 22 (topical preaching), chapter 24 (preaching on a Christian doctrine), chapter 25 (preaching on a Christian practice), chapter 27 (preaching on a personal issue), and chapter 28 (preaching on a social issue).

We can understand sermons along two axes: (a) *content* and (b) patterns of *movement*. From the point of view of *content*, a sermon tends to be either *exposition* of a biblical text or interpretation of a *topic*.

In *expository* preaching, the purpose of the sermon is to help the congregation interpret its situation from the perspective of the gospel through the lens of a biblical passage or theme. The sermon centers in the exegesis, theological analysis, and hermeneutical appropriation of the biblical material.

In a *topical* sermon, the preacher helps the congregation interpret a topic from the perspective of the gospel. Topical sermons are typically sparked by a Christian doctrine, a Christian practice, a personal situation, or a social situation. The topical sermon may draw upon the Bible, as well as on materials from Christian history and theology, from the human and physical sciences. However, topical preaching does not center on the exposition of the Bible in the same way as the expository sermon.

With respect to *movement*, a sermon tends to be *deductive* or *inductive*. While philosophers use these terms in tight definitions to refer to specific forms of logic, preachers use the words more generally to describe patterns of movement.

In a *deductive* sermon, the preacher makes the major point of the sermon near the beginning of the sermon. The preacher then develops that point. The preacher can do so in any number of ways, e.g., by drawing out the implications, by considering its effects in different spheres of life (e.g., in the world, in the nation, in the state, in the community, in the church, in the home, in the individual life), by articulating reasons that the major point is compelling. Directness and clarity are major strengths of deductive preaching. A deductive approach is particularly useful when the congregation already agrees with the major point but needs to expand its implications. Such preaching is also helpful when the preacher needs to spell out in precision the reasons for a point of view. Deductive sermons can help the preacher respond to a question or issue that is burning in the congregation's heart, and for which the community wants a straight response.

However, since the congregation knows the direction of the sermon from the very beginning, deductive sermons run the risk of being dull. They do not create suspense and tension that keep many congregations involved in inductive sermons. Deductivity may not serve occasions when the congregation is at odds with the point of view of the sermon. At the beginning of the sermon, the congregation may hear a viewpoint with which they disagree and simply stop listening.

In *inductive* preaching, the pastor does not come to the major point or conclusion until the latter part of the sermon. The message begins with questions or issues that need to be interpreted from the viewpoint of the gospel. The sermon then gathers and evaluates resources from the Bible, from Christian theology, and from other arenas that help the community understand the biblical text, situation, or issue that is the focal point of the sermon. The sermon is a journey of exploration and discovery. Inductive preaching creates tension: The congregation recognizes unresolved qualities in understanding a biblical text, doctrine, practice, or situation and seeks to know how those tensions can be resolved. Inductive preaching is itself an experience of discovery. The congregation joins in the preacher in exploring the text or topic and arriving at a conclusion. In this respect, inductive movement reflects the movement of many human experiences. Inductive preaching is especially useful when the congregation is bored by a text or topic. The inductive movement creates tension that helps the congregation want to be involved in the sermon. Inductive preaching can particularly serve occasions when the congregation is at odds with the viewpoint of the sermon or when the sermon needs to help the congregation change its perception of a text, topic, or situation. The preacher does not alienate the congregation by voicing at the beginning of the sermon a perspective with which the community disagrees. The sermon attempts to develop trust in which pastor and people think together about a vexing text, topic, or situation.

When we put these categories together, we can speak of four kinds of sermons:

- expository–deductive
- expository–inductive
- topical–deductive
- topical–inductive.

These patterns can be combined in a single sermon. A sermon may begin inductively and reach a conclusion that is then developed deductively. A sermon could begin with an exegesis of a biblical text, but conclude with a more general, topical, consideration of an idea or image that is suggested by the text.

Contemporary patterns tend to be inductive in character and to rely heavily on story and image. Classical patterns tend to be deductive and to be linear and propositional. However, all elements are found in some contemporary and classical forms.

One of the most permeating emphases in contemporary preaching is that a sermon ought to be contextual and never generic. The preacher needs (a) to interpret the situation of the congregation from the standpoint of the gospel, (b) find a form or genre of preaching that is congenial to the theological claim and orientation of the preacher and the community, and (c) that gives the sermon a good opportunity to fulfill its purpose.

In these respects, a major shift in emphasis is taking place in contemporary preaching. Whereas preachers formerly concentrated on what they wanted to *say*, preachers now emphasize how *listeners receive* the sermon. The preacher shapes the sermon in view of how listeners will likely process it. Of course, what the minister wants to say and how the congregation receives it are intimately related.

The emerging discipline of congregational studies teaches us that congregations are social worlds with their own patterns of receiving and processing communications. Studies of faith development reveal that within each congregation, listeners receive and process communications in different ways. The sermon needs to take into account the world of the congregation and the different ways in which members of the congregation take messages on board. While a minister may have a preferred style of preaching, a minister needs to be able to make use of multiple approaches to preaching in order to help a sermon have an optimum opportunity to be received positively by a given congregation on a given occasion. This book provides examples of leading approaches to sermon form that are in use today.

In this book I sometimes use the terms *Beginning* and *Ending* instead of the designations Introduction and Conclusion. *Beginning* refers to the beginning of the sermon, the purpose of which is to invite the congregation into the world of the sermon. The first part of today's sermon is seldom a formal introduction. A sermon usually arises from a conversation that is already taking place explicitly or implicitly in the congregation. The subject does not need to be introduced so much as identified and focused. The beginning typically helps preacher and community engage one another in the sermonic phase of the community's conversation about the text, doctrine, practice, or situation.

Ending refers to the end of the sermon. The purpose of the ending is to encourage the congregation to continue reflecting on the sermon and its implication for the everyday world. The term conclusion suggests something that the preacher does not want to happen. The preacher does not typically want the congregation to think that the community's conversation regarding the direction of the sermon is concluded when the preacher stops talking. The preacher hopes that the mode of conversation shifts from the preacher talking and the congregation listening to the congregation reflecting among themselves. The preacher does stop talking, but the preacher hopes that part of the sermon will encourage continuing conversation.

The following types of sermons are represented in the book. The first part of the book, *Traditional Patterns*, contains historic models of sermon structure that can still help congregations encounter the gospel. The next division, *Contemporary Patterns,* contains approaches to preaching that have emerged in the last twenty years and that seem especially suitable to preaching today. Some of these patterns are quite well-known, others less so. The messages in *Patterns for Subjects* demonstrate how different subject matters and different foci can lead to particular approaches in the sermon. The final section, *Patterns for Theology*, illustrates how different theological methods (e.g., evangelical, liberation, postliberal, revisionary) result in sermons that are faithful to the gospel, but that are nuanced according to the theological proclivities of each method.

These four divisions of the book are somewhat arbitrary. The categories mix apples and oranges. The categories also overlap. For instance, a distinctive theological viewpoint can be expressed in any one of a number of patterns of movement from the traditional or the contemporary scene. A sermon on a social issue could body forth from evangelical theology or liberation theology. A teaching sermon can be inductive or deductive; it can be in the Puritan Plain Style, the simple inductive approach, or traveling from Oops to Yeah. The permutations are too numerous for each to be represented in any one volume.

The thirty-four kinds of sermons mentioned in this book are not exhaustive. We could identify many other approaches to preaching in the contemporary church. For example, Thomas H. Troeger mentions the following: creating a parable, assuming there is more to the biblical story, playing with an image, writing the sermon as a movie script, using flashbacks, reframing sacraments, letting children lead in the process of sermon preparation, playing a game, listening to muffled voices, and comparing translations.[2] Eugene Lowry envisions distinct ways of developing narrative sermons: running the story, delaying the story, suspending the story, alternating the story.[3] However, the sermons in *Patterns of Preaching* represent leading movements in preaching today.

[2]Thomas H. Troeger, *Ten Strategies for Preaching in a Multi-Media Culture* (Nashville: Abingdon Press, 1996).

[3]Eugene L. Lowry, *How to Preach a Parable: Designs for Narrative Sermons* (Nashville: Abingdon Press, 1989).

PART 1

Traditional Patterns

1

Puritan Plain Style

As the term "plain" implies, this approach to preaching is simple and to the point. The purpose of the style is to help the congregation encounter the gospel as directly as possible. The Plain Style has been (and is) used by preachers in several theological movements.

The elements of the sermon in the Plain Style are *Beginning, Exposition of the Biblical Text, Theological Analysis of the Text, Application of the Interpretation of the Text* to the situation of the congregation, *Ending*. This style can be adapted to sermons on Christian doctrines and practices and other topics. In the latter instances, the *Exposition of the Text* would be replaced by *Exposition of the Doctrine, Practice, or Topic*. The *Theological Analysis* would focus on the doctrine, practice, or topic.

The *Beginning* helps the congregation focus on the subject of the sermon. The preacher may include a short *Statement of the Direction of the Sermon*. This statement alerts the congregation to the claim of the sermon. In the *Exposition of the Biblical Text, Doctrine, Practice, or Topic*, the preacher gives a brief exegesis of the biblical passage, doctrine, practice, or other topic. When turning to *Theological Analysis*, the sermon reflects theologically on the theological claims of the text, doctrine, practice, or other topic from the perspective of the gospel. Is the witness of text appropriate to the gospel? intelligible? moral? What can the congregation believe about the subject of the sermon? When *Applying* the text, the preacher helps the community articulate the implications of the congregation's understanding of the text, doctrine, or practice for its everyday life. When

7

Ending, the preacher tries to help the congregation continue the conversation that started in the sermon.

Some sermons in this style do not contain a separate component for theological analysis. When a text, doctrine, or practice is appropriate to the gospel, intelligible, and morally plausible, the preacher sometimes moves directly from exegesis to application.

As Thomas G. Long's sermon below illustrates, this style need not be wooden or mechanical. It can have a dynamic quality. The preacher makes excellent use of imagery and story in the service of clarity of communication. The application, while direct and clear, leaves room for the imagination of the listeners to extend its implications into their own everyday worlds.

Listening to a sermon in the Puritan Plain Style, the congregation has every opportunity to get the preacher's point. This type of sermon is easy to prepare. While the preacher must consider what to say, the preacher doesn't have to wrestle with how to say it. The task of each part of the sermon is clearly defined. Further, this style helps the community consider forthrightly the implications of the gospel for their everyday world. Some preachers, however, find this approach unimaginative, tedious, and predictable (especially if the preachers uses it weekly). The Plain Style can violate some materials. Our perception of a poem, for instance, does not always conform to the linear flow of exposition-theological analysis-application.

THOMAS G. LONG, one of the most prolific and influential figures in contemporary preaching, is director of Geneva Press. His *The Witness of Preaching* (Louisville: Westminster/John Knox Press, 1989) and *Preaching and the Literary Forms of the Bible* (Philadelphia: Fortress Press, 1988) are fulcrum works in contemporary preaching. He assembles useful collections of materials, e.g., with Edward Farley, *Preaching as a Theological Task: World, Gospel, Scripture. In Honor of David Buttrick* (Louisville: Westminster John Knox Press, 1996); with Cornelius Plantinga, Jr., *A Chorus of Witnesses: Model Sermons for Today's Preacher* (Grand Rapids: Eerdmans, 1994); with Gail O'Day, *Listening to the Word: Essays in Honor of Fred B. Craddock* (Nashville: Abingdon Press, 1993); with Neely Dixon McCarter, *Preaching In and Out of Season* (Louisville: Westminster/John Knox Press, 1990). He has also written biblical commentaries on Matthew and Hebrews. He preaches and lectures in congregations and conferences throughout the United States and Canada.

THOMAS G. LONG

The Difference Between Brown and Green

Jeremiah 17:5–8

(Beginning) This passage of prophetic wisdom from the book of Jeremiah sharply contrasts the life of faith—a life that trusts the ways of God—with the life that most of us are tempted to lead, a life that relies on its own wits and places its bets on the ways of the world. To be a person of faith, says Jeremiah, is to be like a deep-rooted tree standing on the banks of a flowing river. To be otherwise is to be like a scrub plant, wilting in the fierce desert heat, fighting for its life in a parched and thirsty wasteland.

It is easy to admire the poetic images here—shrub versus tree, desert versus oasis, parched wilderness versus moist and fertile land. However, Jeremiah is not mainly interested in making poetry, but in making souls. This word from the prophet exercises its true power only if its poetry winnows its way into the deep places of our experience. To be grasped by this passage, we must do more than touch its surfaces with our fingers. We must feel the dry heat of the waterless places in our throats. To put it bluntly, we must know about drought, and quite honestly, about drought most of us know very little.

One summer a few years back, we went thirty-seven days without rain, and we called it a drought. My neighbors and I paced our front yards, pawing at the yellow spots, and raised our fists to the merciless heavens because we had lost a few boxwoods and patches of Zoysia. "We sure could use some rain," we would call to each other in the heat. "Yes, we could," the neighbor would call back. "My tomatoes are burned up." But then we would retreat to the air-conditioned cool of our houses and pour glasses of iced tea. About drought we know little.

A kid in line at the theater concession stand orders a tub of popcorn and a soda pop. "What size soda?" the clerk wants to know. "Gimme a giant size," the kid replies. "I'm *dying* of thirst." About drought we know little.

(Statement of the Direction of the Sermon) But about drought, Jeremiah knows much. And Jeremiah has much to teach us—about drought in the human heart.

(Exposition of the Biblical Text) In Palestine, drought is not merely a threat to backyard tomatoes and Zoysia lawns. It is a threat to all of life—human, animal, plant. When the harsh Judean sun turns its blazing wrath upon the land, fields are scored and cracked, cisterns become dry as sandpaper, towns grieve, farmers cover their heads in morning, the crops shrivel,

the doe abandons her fawn, and donkeys pant like dogs in the torrid and killing heat (Jeremiah 14:2–6). About drought Jeremiah knows much.

Jeremiah knew not only about the drought that affects the land, but also about the drought that afflicts the human spirit. "The sin of Judah," he warned, "is written with an iron pen," and that sin was idolatry. "Idolatry" sounds, of course, like an entry in a Bible encyclopedia, a remote description of strange and ancient practices, of Baal and Ashera, of fertility cults, and gods of stone and wood. But the idolatry of Judah sprung from a source very familiar to us—the human thirst for life, full and joyful. The fertility religions of the ancient world, so seductive to the Jewish people, were about the richness of life, the abundance of the land, the human desire not to miss a single pleasure, to celebrate life, to eat the sweet fruit of existence, and to allow the succulent juices to flow freely down one's face.

The advertising copy over the photo of a sexy-looking luxury sports car reads:

"You've made a statement. Here's the exclamation point.

This is exhilaration, period"

That's what we all want for our lives, of course—something to break the tedium, an exclamation point, exhilaration, excitement, the wind in our face. And wanting to lift high the cup of life and drink it down to the bottom is not wrong in and of itself. The arts, the dance, the game, laughter, the feast, the tender touch—all of these are expressions of the human thirst for life, abundant. Indeed, such a life is a gift from God.

But how do we become fully alive? To this question Jeremiah speaks a hard word: The human heart, left to its own devices, chooses the wrong path. What seems to us to be the place to be, what seems to us to be a lush field of joy, what seems to us to be the obvious way to wring every satisfaction from life is, in fact, a mirage. And what seems to us to be a perilous, costly, even foolish way of life—the life of sacrificial faith—is, in truth, the fertile and joyful oasis we weary travelers are seeking.

(Theological Analysis) Many years ago, a biblical scholar, Johannes Pedersen, wrote a book on the geography of Palestine. He was struck by the fact that three of the major world religions—Judaism, Christianity, and Islam—all spring from this same small patch of unpromising land. Pedersen wondered if this were true partly because the inhabitants of that land know the difference between brown and green, between the killing desert and the life-giving oasis, between the scorching wind that burns the skin and the cool oil that heals. Brown and green...death and life...trusting in ourselves and trusting in God. Jeremiah wants us to know the difference.

An old joke tells of a rabbi on his deathbed who called to his side his oldest son. "Itzak," the dying man whispered, "I want to tell you the secret of life." Itzak placed his ear next to his father's trembling lips, the better to hear his parting wisdom. "Itzak," said the old man urgently, "an angel appeared to me in a dream last night and showed me two bridges to the place of glory. One bridge is built of human cunning. It is wide and strong and made of iron and stone. The second bridge is built of Torah, the instruction of God. It is narrow, seemingly frail, dangerous to cross, and made of the woven strands of Moses' beard. Itzak, my son, take my advice. Travel over the first bridge."

And we do, of course. "Blessed are those who hunger and thirst for righteousness." But we hunger and thirst for a comfortable lifestyle. "Blessed are the peacemakers," says Jesus, but we are ready to punish anyone who challenges our national pride. "Blessed are the merciful," Jesus teaches, but if we don't look out for ourselves we will get taken advantage of at the office. We know the way of God, but we choose the bridge of human cunning.

Ironically, the gospel violates common sense. What looks to the human eye like life, Jeremiah tells us, is really a killing desert. What looks like a wilderness, the way of faith, trusting in the promises of God, is really a verdant field of joy.

In 1931, the Midwest experienced a bumper crop of wheat. Cash flowed freely, and times were good. Farmers bought land and machinery. Only a fool would not place trust in the unending richness of the land. "A sort of madness pervaded the atmosphere," one of those farmers wrote years later, "and I fell for it like ever." The next year there was little rain; indeed, the rains failed to come year after year, and the seemingly fertile fields became parched and withered, the famous Dust Bowl of the 1930s. "The summer of '36 was one of the hottest ever," said Oklahoma farmer Lawrence Svobida. "Hundreds of square miles of bare fields absorbed the sun's rays like fire brick in a kiln. The wind was like a blast from a huge, red-hot furnace, causing my face to blister and peel off.... I found myself hardening to disaster. Words are useless to describe the experience when the thin thread of faith snaps. My youth and ambition were ground into the very dust itself."[1]

(Application) Jeremiah would have known well how the youth and ambition of a people could be ground into dust. "Those who trust in mere mortals and make mere flesh their strength, whose hearts turn away

---

[1]Lawrence Svobida, as quoted on the public television program, *Surviving the Dust Bowl*. Produced and written by Cana Gazit, WGBH Educational Foundation, 1998.

from the Lord…shall be like a shrub in the desert." But Jeremiah also knew of another way. "Blessed are those who trust in the Lord….They shall be like a tree planted by water…. It shall not fear when heat comes, and its leaves shall stay green in the year of drought." The difference between brown and green.

There is a person named Wayne who lives in an urban homeless shelter. Wayne has a psychological disorder severe enough to prevent him from keeping a job, but not severe enough to allow him to receive disability payments. So, Wayne is condemned to wander the wasteland of the city streets. But Wayne has also found a green place, an oasis. Wayne has joined a church, and he is present for every service, every meal, every event. "When I go outside this church, I'm a homeless guy, a bum, a transient," Wayne says. "When I'm with [the church] people, I'm just another person." Ask Wayne what the church and its life of faith has meant to him, and he will quickly reply, "These people saved my life."[2] Wayne knows what Jeremiah was talking about. Wayne knows the irony of the gospel, the truth that makes for full and joyful life does not look at life-giving from the vantage point of the wisdom of the world. But Wayne and the church people who honor him know—the difference between brown and green.

Maybe, then, we must know of the drought. Jesus once said that only those who humble themselves could know the rule of God. And Jesus taught that only those who lose their lives for the sake of the gospel could find them. Jesus told the story of a prodigal whose wandering in a wasteland made him hunger for the joys of home. So maybe when we have tasted the dust of the desert, felt the heat of foolish choices, and wandered once-promising paths that led to places of loss and pain, then we can look to the sky and pray for rain and look to the horizon of our hope.

Recently there was an exhibition at New York's Museum of American Folk Art of the drawings of an obscure San Francisco artist named A.G. Rizzoli, who died in 1981. He was the son of poverty-stricken Italian immigrants, and his work would be completely unknown had it not been rescued from a dumpster by a great-nephew. Rizzoli was shy and withdrawn. He lived by himself, working by day as a draftsman and toiling at night drawing pictures of those he loved: his mother, God, and the few people who were ever kind to him.

One day a year, Rizzoli would arrange his drawings in a room in his house and invite his neighbors in for a showing. He would spread

---

[2]Brant S. Copeland, "Scripture as Metaphor and Lens," in *The Register of the Company of Pastors* (Summer 1998): 5.

homemade signs announcing the exhibition throughout the neighbor-hood. But his neighbors were occupied with their own lives, and few of them took the time to come. Mostly, it was children, curious about this strange person who lived in their neighborhood, who would wander into Rizzoli's home and gaze at his drawings. "Those who did," writes Frank Rich in *The New York Times*, "would later themselves be adoringly en-shrined in his pictures—though they never knew it. Love was for him its own private reward. 'No longer any reason for feeling lonely,' was the inscription he put on a portfolio."[3] Love is stronger than loneliness. Faith is more enduring than flame. The difference between brown and green.

(Ending) Jeremiah wants us to hear again the good news of the God who is. To those who wander in desert wastes, God is the oasis of compassion. To those whose lives are scorched by the noonday heat, God is the shade of rest and restoration. To those who are perishing from the thirst of meaninglessness, God is the fountain of living water, the rain that turns the dry places into fields of life. "When the rain finally came," said a Dust Bowl farmer, "it meant life itself. It meant a future. It meant there would be something ahead of you. And…we'd go out in the rain and just feel it hit your face. It was a very emotional time when you'd get rain because it meant so much to you. You didn't have false hope any more…"[4]

The difference between brown and green.

---

3 Frank Rich, "Journal: Valentine's Day Massacred," *The New York Times,* February 14, 1998, A13.
4 Floyd Coen, as quoted on *The American Experience: Surviving the Dust Bowl.*

2

Sermon as Journey to Celebration

This approach to preaching is perhaps the oldest one represented in this book. According to many historians, it preserves patterns of movement derived from traditional African religions. Brought from Africa to the United States by the enslaved, this approach was adapted to the service of the gospel as slaves became Christian. While this pattern has historically been characteristic of African American preaching, preachers in other communities are increasingly incorporating aspects of it. Professor Henry H. Mitchell is one of today's leading interpreters of this mode of preaching.

The pattern may be characterized as a journey to celebration. It is similar to a journey in that it moves from one point to another. This model has many possible ways to lead into the celebration and many varieties of celebration. Indeed, African American churches tend to value an individual preacher's distinctive adaptations of this model. The sermon is comprised of several blocks of material. The blocks of material and their relationship to one another are similar to the plot and moves of David Buttrick's approach to preaching (see chapter 12). According to Mitchell, Buttrick names aspects of this type of preaching that have been prominent in the African American community for centuries.[1]

---

[1] Henry Mitchell, *Celebration and Experience in Preaching* (Nashville: Abingdon Press, 1990), 50.

The last block of material is a celebration. This part is indicative in tone: Preacher and congregation celebrate what God has done, is doing, and will do. The celebration is intended to empower the community with the good news of God's activity in their behalf. It is not exhortatory. The celebration is ecstatic reinforcement of the witness of the text and of the behavioral purpose of the sermon. At its best the celebration is good art in the service of gospel witness. The celebration makes up 10 percent to 25 percent of the message.

To prepare the sermon, the preacher identifies a behavioral purpose: what the preacher hopes will happen in the congregation as a result of participating in the sermon. The preacher determines what kind of journey has a good opportunity to help that behavioral purpose. The preacher develops the blocks of material that move from one to another in such a way as to get from the beginning of the sermon to the celebration. These materials should appeal to both intellect and emotion, providing an imaginative experience of the gospel as the congregation identifies with the movement of the sermon.

Two aspects of this pattern are difficult to represent in print. One is the vocalization of the sermon. The sermon starts at a very low level of intensity. At the outset, the preacher tends to speak slowly. As the journey continues, the preacher's rate of speaking and intensity increase. When the sermon reaches the celebration, the energy of the preacher overflows. Some preachers celebrate with a singing-like quality in the voice (sometimes called whooping, intoning, or tuning). The other aspect is the give-and-take between the preacher and the congregation. Sometimes referred to as call and response, the preacher states a part of the sermon—a paragraph, a sentence, a phrase, or even a word—and the community responds. At its best, call and response is a living dialogue between pastor and people. The pastor may even redirect the journey of the sermon in response to the people's reactions to the sermon.

Mitchell preached the sermon that follows at an annual meeting of the Academy of Homiletics held in Decatur, Georgia. The behavioral purpose is to encourage ministers to manifest integrity between what we say about the gospel and our day-to-day lives. In the language of the text, Mitchell wants us to become living epistles whose lives testify to the message we carry. After beginning the sermon, Mitchell leads the congregation on a journey through four blocks of material. (I) The text points to the necessity of us being living epistles. (II) The letters that we write with our lives can manifest integrity between what we say and who we are and what we do, or they can show a contradiction in those arenas. (III) Showing love for all people is the acid test of whether our message and behavior are continuous. (IV) God's saving work in Christ empowers us to speak and live with integrity. The celebration takes the form of an original poem. In the sermon, Mitchell mentions Roberta Bondi, a professor at Candler School of Theology in Decatur, who also spoke to the Academy from her book *Memories of God*.[2] The conference took place shortly before Christmas.

HENRY MITCHELL, now semiretired, served as a pastor and executive in the American Baptist Convention, and a theological educator, most recently serving as dean of the School of Theology at Virginia Union University, Richmond, Virginia. He is now visiting professor of preaching (with his spouse, Ella Pearson Mitchell) at the Interdenominational Theological Center, Atlanta, Georgia. His most recent book is written with Emil Thomas, *Preaching for Black Self-Esteem* (Nashville: Abingdon Press, 1994). His *Celebration and Experience in Preaching* (Nashville: Abingdon Press, 1990) and *Black Preaching* (Nashville: Abingdon Press, 1990) are widely used in seminary classrooms. He has written several other influential books, including with Nicholas Cooper-Lewter, *Soul Theology: The Heart of American Black Culture* (Nashville: Abingdon Press, 1992). He preaches and lectures in a wide variety of settings—seminaries, clergy and church conferences, seminaries, and colleges.

HENRY H. MITCHELL

Living Epistles

2 Corinthians 3:1–4

The sermon title for tonight is "Living Epistles," in keeping with the theme of this session. "You yourselves are our letter of recommendation written in your hearts, to be known and read by all people (2 Corinthians 3:2, RSV amended).

When one applies the methods of market analysis to the alarming decline of the established denominations in the U.S.A., the possible explanations involve conditions not easily cured. According to a first theory, many downtown, flagship "First Churches" are dying just like the downtown shopping centers, due to the urban exodus of the middle class. A second theory is that bigger is better. The small church has gone the way of the mom-and-pop corner grocery store. Needs are now met at the

---

[2]Roberta Bondi, *Memories of God* (Nashville: Abingdon Press, 1995).

megastore and megachurch. The rise of megachurches has led to a third theory: pleasing the crowd. It blames shallowness and showmanship for megachurch success and growth.

But there are enough effective small-to-medium sized churches to prove that there can be a successful and biblical mode of ministry that saves folks and matures and motivates them to serve God. These effective small-to-medium congregations are not engaged in radical new approaches to ministry. They just witness holistically by kindness, patience, and support networks. This holism is suggested in Paul's self-defense in our text.

I.

The heat is on Paul here for a number of supposed reasons: Mighty as he is with the pen, he just simply cannot preach, at least by comparison to great performers such as Apollos. The mushroom effect of rampant Corinthian criticism spreads even to the matter of Paul's having no preaching credentials. Paul is deeply sensitive to all of this, and in his Corinthian letters, especially the second one, he finds it impossible to resist defensiveness. Our text has him saying, in effect, "How dare you say I have no credentials? Hard as I worked and as much as God has blessed you through my preaching? You must be out of your mind. *You* are my papers, my certificate of ordination, my official recognition by the church of Jesus Christ. What I have wrought is written on the very tablets of your hearts, to be known and read by all humanity. It is written not with ink, but with the Spirit of the living God; not on tablets of stone but on the tablets that are your heart."

Paul's defensive outburst, like much of his writing, is used of God to set forth a major insight, a principle of human communication—a law, if you please, about how the gospel is shared most effectively. It says that a person's *life* is her or his main message. This is true for all of humanity, but it has intensified implications for preachers of the gospel.

In an age of image projection and prophets cosmetically concealed and camera-conscious, Paul would declare, "I may be bald and bowlegged and short of stature. My voice and my oratory may not be slick and bewitching. I may seem beside myself at times, but it's all the real me, and it's all poured out for God. Furthermore, I'll settle for letting the work I've done speak for me. Let *my life* be my letter and my only message. When I think of all the sermons I ever preached with *and* without words, I give God the glory for using both. Like when God used our attitude of praise in the dungeon *and* my words of witness to save the jailer at Philippi. We didn't know all of this was preaching. But Silas and I figured it out when the warden said with amazing sincerity, 'What must I do to be saved?' "

II.

I have always heard about the need for integrity of Christian character. But Paul has helped me to see that my life is on candid camera, communicating something *all* the time, even when I don't have the slightest intention of being on the air.

Come to think of it, I had an experience just recently that really drove this point home. We were at a national convention. A former student I hadn't seen in 23 years invited us to lunch. The love he expressed was rewarding, that is, until he went to reminiscing.

The first thing he recalled was not my lecture on a Black theology of history. Nor was it any of my presumably popular insights on preaching. He had to go and remind me of that day I blew up worse than I *ever* have, before or since. It was the day this woman said, "Suppose all these new discoveries on Black history are in error. Suppose they are lies." I answered, "But they aren't!" But she kept pressing, "Just suppose—suppose— just suppose." My jaws got tighter and tighter, and I finally blurted out, "If you suppose, you don't belong here. You're wasting your time and your money."

It sounded like I was kicking her out. I wasn't, but I was preaching the worst sermon of my life. And just think, for this now-veteran pastor, it was his most memorable. I wish I could preach a *good* sermon that memorable every time I stand to preach.

Now, of course, this has awesome implications for all of us as living epistles. Everything we preach has to stand the test of our living. For instance, we men are tested every time we have an opportunity to take unfair advantage of a woman, profiting from the vicious traditions of society. The homiletical and theological force of such mistreatment is powerfully illustrated in Roberta Bondi's *Memories of God*. Here the life of a woman was literally crushed for more than four decades by allegedly respectable males.

We are deeply indebted to Dr. Bondi for a candid confession of how, in the highest of academic and theological circles, she had to endure being stripped of self-esteem. For instance, an affable and witty college professor once said of her probing questions, "Just like a woman! No wonder women can't think!" Many of her instructors' living epistles were constantly proclaiming, for her and for all women, a mindless, minor role in society. Not until she was well into middle age was she able to over-record these deep, false, lifelong intuitive tapes regarding her diminished value as a woman in the sight of God.

III.

Here's another test: do we show love for people? If, like so many, we *love* to preach but can't stand to be close to people, our actual message on *koinonia* is miles removed from the gospel. People don't want to hear us preach about love, if they sense that we do not actually reach out to them in love.

In regard to letting people know we are loving and caring, I am reminded of Harry Emerson Fosdick's description of the apostle Paul, author of our text. It was done in one of Fosdick's unforgettable Wednesday evening Bible lectures at Riverside Church. He talked for nearly an hour on how closely attached Paul was to the folks with whom he worked.

Fosdick read from Romans 16, in which Paul sent warm regards to Phoebe, Priscilla, Aquila, Epaenetus, Mary, Andronicus, and Junia, these seven and, would you believe, twenty more! Paul took the time and made the strenuous effort to greet everybody by name. And he didn't have a PC, nor a typewriter, nor even a ballpoint pen. He was dipping a quill! He understood the need to express warmth to all. Is it any wonder that he planted churches so well, even without the preaching skills of an Apollos? God used the talents given to Paul.

So although the responsibilities of being living epistles are awesome, we have the comforts of knowing that God will use what we have, and that God has yet to call a perfect person to preach—not perfect in love nor in most other aspects. So God gives us the glorious option of seeking, constantly and in sincerity, to be changed by the Holy Spirit into a person in the likeness of our Lord and the Word.

IV.

Since God knew our personalities so well, long before we were called, God will gladly help us to become what God wants us to be. From profane, impulsive Peter, to every one of US, God has set apart and used flawed human vessels.

I am reminded of something I heard from Adam Clayton Powell, Sr. He was trying to get his congregation to make their magnificent new building available to the neighboring youth gangs of Harlem. His admonition about gangs concluded with a personal confession: "Don't shoot them. Don't send them to reform school. Don't brutalize them, but brotherize them." This man who led in the building of the Abyssinian Baptist Church and Community House, and the author of this testimony was a former hoodlum. So also were lots of us, hoodlums and worse.

Knowing us all to be flawed vessels, God still calls us all and uses us beyond anything we could ask or think.

God called Jesus and used Jesus also as a living epistle, the very Word of God Incarnate. Advent season was drawing near, and I pondered how I might celebrate its meaning. I remembered James Weldon Johnson's sermon-poem, "The Creation." Then I thought of a sermon-poem, and I entitled it "The Incarnation." With a little help from Zora Neal Hurston, this is what it says:

> And God convened the Hosts of Heaven
> In solemn assembly and said,
> I done made me a world,
> And I done made me some women and men,
> But I'm lonely still.
>
> These people don't love me like I planned.
> I made them in my own image;
> And I gave them free will,
> But they done run off with it.
>
> I gave them powerful patriarchs,
> And passionate prophets,
> And they almost killed Elijah,
> And threw Jeremiah down a well.
>
> I gave them judicious judges,
> But they had to have a king.
> Solomon built me a temple, and
> Then ran off chasing after other gods.
>
> Then from the majestic mercy seat
> God paused, and with hand-held head
> And furrowed brow, God toiled
> And God thought and God toiled.
>
> The angels hung their harps on the willow tree.
> Ev'ry eye 'neath heaven's canopy
> Peered up to gaze upon the throne.
>
> Then after just about one eternity,
> God rose and severed the silence.
> The energy of sacrifice
> penetrated the universe, and then
> the Great I Am spoke.

God decreed, I'll send my Son,
Birthed by a maiden poor,
To be my Word made plain,
A loving letter sent from me.

Ol' Gabriel went to bring the news
To Mary, afraid and young,
But when she seen the wonder unfold,
She rejoiced and sang,
My soul doth magnify the Lord.

God waited and watched, and watched and waited.
And when sweet little Jesus boy was born,
God, the mighty God, God, the holy God,
God, the loving God, rejoiced.

Then the choir began a Hallelujah chorus
That resounded throughout the precincts of heaven.
Hallelujah, Forever and Ever!
and Ever and Ever, Hallelujah, Hallelujah!
HAL-LE-LU-JAH!! Amen.

3

Sermons That Make Points

Sermons can be structured to make points. A point is an idea stated in a plain, direct, even propositional way. The preacher settles upon a focus for the sermon and identifies several key ideas about which to converse with the congregation. The beginning of the sermon reveals the subject matter of the sermon. In deductive preaching, the preacher states the claim of the sermon. The heart of the sermon is the enumeration of the points that relate to the major claim of the sermon. Usually a preacher makes from two to five points. The sermon ends by helping the congregation continue reflecting on the relationship of the points to their worlds.

The points can be arranged in any number of ways. For instance, when preaching from a biblical text or a doctrine, a preacher might highlight key lessons. In the sermon below, R. Scott Colglazier articulates three aspects of the doctrine of God. The points in a sermon might be arranged in a spatial order (e.g., world, nation, city, church, household, individual). The points could follow a time sequence (past, present, future). The points may support the main claim, as in, "Here are four reasons for making a pledge to support the church budget." The points can help the preacher talk with the congregation about natural subdivisions in the subject. The points can build on one another. "The first thing we need to know about this subject...the second thing we need to know...." The preacher might use an eliminative pattern: The gospel is not found in number 1; the gospel is not found in number 2; the gospel is found in number 3.

In an earlier era, some preachers liked to use a poem in the last part of the sermon that developed points. This kind of preaching gave rise to the caricature of the sermon as three points and a poem. This approach could still be meaningful, so long as the points have vitality and the poem bespeaks the depths of the gospel and life.

This approach is clear. It gives the congregation every opportunity to get the point. It is especially useful when the congregation is sympathetic to the major claim of the sermon and needs to have its understanding of that claim amplified or explained. However, this approach can have drawbacks. Some subject matters and some aspects of life and the gospel, cannot be reduced to "points" without violating their complexity. Furthermore, philosophers and educators quickly point out that knowledge cannot always be expressed propositionally. Some knowledge is sensory, intuitive, imagistic, and resists propositional formulation. Furthermore, preachers sometimes develop points that are unrelated to one another or to the subject at the center of the sermon. To be honest, some preachers develop points that are simply boring.

The sermon below was the first of a series of six sermons in which the preacher joined the congregation in a theological journey revisiting basic aspects of Christian faith. In succession, the sermons focused on God, Christ, the Holy Spirit, humankind, the church, the eschaton. Though Colglazier's tendency is to preach expository sermons, the topical approach works well for this particular message. The preacher articulates three aspects of God that are most important to him. In a sense, the preacher's doctrine of God is the "text" on which the sermon is based.

R. SCOTT COLGLAZIER is senior minister of University Christian Church (Disciples of Christ), Fort Worth, Texas. Colglazier is the author of *Finding a Faith that Makes Sense* (St. Louis: Chalice Press, 1996) and *Circling the Divine: Spiritual Reflections for the Journey* (St. Louis: Chalice Press, 1998). Colglazier is currently writing a book on touchstones for becoming spiritually alive.

R. SCOTT COLGLAZIER

I Believe in God

I had a strange experience last summer. We were on vacation, and I decided to get up early on a Sunday morning and attend a little Presbyterian church that had an eight o'clock service. I thought, "This will be perfect. Worship at eight. *New York Times* at nine. Brunch at ten. Tee time at eleven. A perfect morning." I arrived at the church a few minutes late, and they were singing the opening hymn. It was a familiar service. We sang. Recited the Lord's Prayer. Had a pastoral prayer. Scripture readings. A sermon.

But one part of the service both delighted and disturbed me. We repeated the Apostolic Affirmation of Faith. Ancient words. Definitive words. Words that have been uttered by Christians for centuries. It begins, "I believe in God, the Father almighty, creator of heaven and earth." (I was sitting on the back row. "Hey, everybody else sits there," I thought. "I'll try it, too.") But even though I was sitting in the very back of the sanctuary and on vacation, too, something about the force of all those people saying, "I believe in God" caught me up. Touched me. We seldom say such affirmations in our congregation. Maybe the strangeness of saying the affirmation created a running theological dialogue inside my soul.

I found myself thinking "Yes, I do believe in God, but *what* do I mean when I say those words? I know other people who believe in God, but I'm not sure I believe in the God they believe in, or at least I would use different language to understand God. I know people who believe that God gives people illness as punishment. I don't believe in *that* God. I know people who believe that God only loves their particular denomination. I don't believe in *that* God. I know people who preach on television promising that God will make them prosperous. I don't believe in *that* God. I believe in God. True. But *what* do I believe about God?"

That's the inner dialogue that happened to me in that little Presbyterian church last summer. My hunch is that all of us, at one time or another, have that swirling dialogue about God inside our heads and hearts. If we haven't, well, we should. What do *you* believe about God?

For a few minutes, now, I want to talk with you about three things that I believe most deeply about God. As I think about all the things that I believe about God, I find these three to be absolutely compelling.

The first one is that God is the creator of the world. God created, and God continues to create. "In the beginning God created the heavens and the earth…." That beginning is also the beginning of my faith in God. God relates to the world through creativity. As the Statement of Faith of the United Church of Canada says, God "has created and is creating."

God is not just *out there* somewhere, or *up there* somewhere, or *under there* somewhere. It is not just that a long time ago, once upon a time, God created the world. I know you can read the Genesis stories of creation and get that literalistic idea—God did it all in six days—but I want to suggest that is simply a narrative way, a story way, of describing the creativity of God. The affirmation of God's creativity is what is most important. No one really knows how the earth formed, how the universe came together, how human life finally started or developed. There are theories. Some more likely than others. We obviously know more about the natural world today than when the Bible was written. However, it seems beyond question today that there was and is a dynamic, evolutionary quality to the world. In that sense, I still believe that God is in the process of creating the world, calling the world into being, offering the world new possibilities to constitute itself. As far as I am concerned, this dichotomy of science and religion is a false one. In fact, the more we understand science, the more we draw near to mystery and chaos and creativity. Therefore, that which we name as God is the ground of all being, the source of all life, the pervasive quality of all meaning.

The mystics in the Christian tradition appreciate God's creativity, perhaps more than anyone. Listen to these words by the mystic Meister Eckhart: "If we said that God created the world yesterday or tomorrow, we would be entertaining a foolish notion. God creates the world and all things in a present now."[1] That's a stunning summary of the creativity of God in the world.

God relates to the world as a creator relates to his or her artistic creation. And what should never be forgotten is that you are part of God's creation. When you, as one of God's creatures, live with openness, love, and joy, you bring joy to God the creator. This weekend Kathleen Battle was in town for a performance. Have you ever heard her voice? It is exquisite. It is the voice of an angel. Can you imagine, if you wrote a piece of music, labored over it, gave birth to it, and finally someone like Kathleen Battle performed it, how glorious you would feel? That would be ecstasy! Nothing brings a creator more joy than when a creation becomes everything it can be.

I believe that God as creator wants you to be everything you are supposed to be. God wants you to live with joy. God wants you to live in healthy relationship to others. God wants you to live in meaningful relationship with God. And not only does God want that for human beings, God wants that for the whole world. That's right, the whole world. That's why it's morally right to have clean air, and clean rivers, and beautiful forests. That's why we need to love the oceans, and the sea otters that swim in them, and the funny looking pelicans that fly above them. The whole creation, not just human life, but the whole creation is the living canvas of the living God. God is forever creating the world.

---

[1] Meister Eckhart, "Sermon 10," in *Meister Eckhart: Preacher and Teacher*, ed. by Bernard McGinn. The Classics of Western Spirituality (New York: Paulist Press, 1986), 265.

Second, God loves the world, and feels the world, and experiences the world more deeply than we can imagine. There's a peculiar line in the story of the great flood in the book of Genesis, but it's one of those lines that is hauntingly unforgettable. "The Lord saw that the wickedness of humankind was great…and the Lord was sorry that he had made humankind on the earth, and it grieved him to his heart" (Genesis 6:6). That's haunting. Yet it defines for me what I most passionately believe about God. God is not a Creator who is disinterested in the world that God made. God is also lover of the world. God is so deeply related to the world that God's heart can break when we as the creation think and talk and feel and behave badly. Your heart can be broken only by what you love.

The songwriter Tracy Chapman captures this divine grief in her song "New Beginning." When she sings it you can almost feel the cracking of her heart. She sings as if everything in the world is broken and is beyond being fixed. Because of all the suffering and pain in the world, she sings that the time has come to start the world all over again, to make a brand new beginning. Isn't that exactly the song that God is singing when God sees the wickedness and waywardness of the creatures?

But the fact that God sings this song of grief is what finally draws me to God. Because like a moth drawn to the flame, I am drawn toward and circle around this creator of my existence. "It grieved God's heart." That means that God cares. You can only be hurt by what you care about. That means that God is related to the world. That means that God loves the world. That means that God is affected, moved, grieved by gang violence, and AIDS, and racial prejudice, and poverty, and abuse, and depression, and war, and floods, and earthquakes—all of it, from our most personal feelings of pain to the most widespread agony of the human condition. And that means that God is at once transcendent and beyond the world, while at the same time being intimately involved in every detail of the world.

Third, God's creativity and God's love makes it possible for us to live in hope. To believe in the creativity of God means that every day is new. We are not imprisoned by the past or the present. To believe that God is love is to believe that God intends for every day to be new. Every day, God offers us and the world a deeper, richer, fuller experience of love.

The past is past. But God takes the past, sculpts it into the present, and then offers each of us a new possibility for the future. This is hope. And at the heart of my faith is hope. If my past was damaged, my today and my future do not have to be damaged in the same way. I was angry yesterday. I don't have to be angry today. I was bitter yesterday. I don't have to be bitter today. I was hateful yesterday. I don't have to hate today. I was hurt yesterday. I don't have to hurt someone else today. With God every day is new, for me, for you, for this world. God is in the business of creating, and that means hope, and hope makes life worth living.

Now, does that mean there are no guarantees in life? To be brutally honest, there are no guarantees that every situation will turn out just the way we want it to turn out. Because we're free. Those around us are free. I do not romanticize the creativity and freedom of the world. We can misuse these gifts. Someone draws a mustache on the Mona Lisa, spray paints graffiti across a Picasso. Someone topples Michelangelo's David. With our freedom, we can create situations of jealousy, bitterness, anger, betrayal, hate, fighting, murder. Nature can even work against the harmony and beauty of the world. Diseases. Natural disasters. These do not result from human freedom. But they result from the fact that even the elements of nature are free to pursue their own course. Even they can turn away from God's purposes of creativity, love, and hope.

There is no guarantee that every situation will turn out the way we want. But, we do have one guarantee. It's the guarantee that no matter what you experience, God will be with you in it, and through it, and even beyond it. That's not optimism; that's hope. And that's why, for me, not even death stops the creative work of God in my life.

God's creativity makes each day new, and I hang on to that because it gives me the power to live with hope. God's presence, God's energy, God's love makes each day meaningful and charged with hope. The apostle Paul said in the book of 1 Corinthians that "If I do not have love, I am nothing" (1 Corinthians 13:2). Or maybe we could say, "If I don't have love, experience love, feel love, know love, then I have nothingness in my existence." Love is ultimately what matters. And I think we know that. I really think we do, but something happens to us, I don't know what it is, but we somehow forget it, or lose sight of it, or maybe we even get afraid of it. But giving love and receiving love is ultimately what matters.

I heard the other day a little quip about Warren Buffet who is currently locked in a tight race to be the second wealthiest man in the country. Bill Gates is evidently still leading the pack. Go Microsoft, right? But someone asked Warren Buffet, "Now that you've become one of the wealthiest people in the country, what is your next goal?" He answered, "To be the oldest."

Well, I can appreciate his answer. But I also know, you know, that true meaning in life is found not in accumulating, but in deepening the love in our lives. That's the treasure. That's the gold. That's the pearl. And yes, it comes from God. The One who is forever creating and forever loving and forever suffering is the one who is forever with you and me. What is my life's purpose? To be open to the creativity, the presence, the love of God in the next minute of my life. And to live every moment in the fullness of that awareness.

Well, I left that little Presbyterian church that morning. When you sit on the back pew, you get out quickly! I headed down the street to buy the *New York Times*. Stopped by the bakery to get a coffee and croissant. I kept walking down the hill. Down toward the ocean. I sat on a little bench above the beach. Looked at the ocean. As far as the eye can see. So deep. So full of life. Sat there a long time. A long time. I thought about my faith, about the kind of God in whom I really do believe. I looked at the waves ceaselessly moving. Something about the ocean—its vastness, its mystery, its majesty, its power—filled me with the sense of God's presence, and with awe and wonder and gratitude. I do believe. I believe in the God who creates, who loves, and who fills us with hope. As the affirmation says, "I believe in God." Do *you*?

4

Preaching Verse by Verse

This approach to preaching first appeared in full dress in the community that wrote the Dead Sea Scrolls at Qumran. Several of the scrolls are in this form. Early in the Common Era many of the rabbis employed it. Origen (185–253 C.E.) was the first Christian preacher known to us to use the model extensively. Since then, it has frequently been a staple of Christian preaching.

The title "verse-by-verse preaching" is somewhat misleading. The preacher moves through the text meaningful unit by meaningful unit. Sometimes these units follow the versification in English. Frequently, however, a meaningful unit is comprised of a sentence or even a scene that stretches across two (or more) verses. At other times, the biblical material is so dense that you can move through it only phrase by phrase or even word by word.

A sermon in this mode typically begins by helping the congregation recollect the historical, literary, or theological setting of the text. The heart of the sermon is exegesis of the text coupled with hermeneutical interpretation. After the beginning, the sermon moves back and forth between the world of the Bible and the contemporary world. The preacher offers exegesis of a segment of the biblical text, then makes a hermeneutical connection between that segment and the world of the congregation. The preacher moves to the next segment of the biblical text, then offers a hermeneutical connection of that part of the text with the congregation. The sermon continues in this pattern until the whole text is discussed. In the last part of the sermon, the preacher helps the congregation clarify the significance of the exposition and hermeneutical reflection as a whole. The preacher does not leave the community lost in a maze of detailed comments, but helps the community discern the big picture of the text.

In the sermon that follows, Professor Fred Craddock first focuses our attention on prayer as the main theme of the passage. He then helps us recall occasions when we have wondered about how to react to prayer, whether to pray, or how to pray. The beginning of the sermon creates an atmosphere in which to hear the verse by verse exposition of Luke 11:1–13. Following the exposition itself, Professor Craddock helps us think about the implications of the text. In this sermon, direct running commentary comprises about 60 percent of the sermon, with about 40 percent of the sermon devoted to drawing out the implications of the commentary for the life of prayer. Some sermons in this mode devote a greater percentage of the sermon to the exposition.

The text was assigned by the Revised Common Lectionary. The sermon was preached in North United Methodist Church in Indianapolis, Indiana. Professor Craddock was a guest preacher in that middle-class and upper-middle-class urban congregation on a Sunday morning when the General Assembly of the Christian Church (Disciples of Christ) was meeting in the city. Several hundred members of the Assembly (including many clergy) were visitors in the congregation. The Disciples immediately recognized the name of the revered G. Edwin Osborn (whom Dr. Craddock mentions in the sermon). The preacher knows that many in the congregation have experienced failure in their ministries, congregations, and other endeavors. Many have found success. Many feel both failure and success. Professor Craddock hopes for the community to deepen their confidence in God and to broaden their Christian experience and witness through the prayer for God's reign that Jesus taught his disciples.

PROFESSOR CRADDOCK was Bandy Professor of Preaching and New Testament at Candler School of Theology, Emory University in Atlanta, Georgia, for many years before retirement. He is the author of one of the pivotal books in preaching in the last fifty years: *As One Without Authority* (Nashville: Abingdon Press, 1979). This book, more than any other, helped move contemporary preaching in the direction of inductivity, story, and image. His *Overhearing the Gospel* (Nashville: Abingdon Press, 1978) is a contemporary classic. His introductory textbook, *Preaching* (Nashville: Abingdon Press, 1985), is widely used. Professor Craddock has written several other biblical commentaries and resources for interpreting the Bible in preaching. He preaches and lectures internationally.

Lord, Teach Us to Pray

Luke 11:1–13

(Verse 1) This is an awkward moment for Jesus and the disciples. They are together—thirteen of them—when one begins to pray. What do you do when one person in a group starts praying? Do you leave? Do you keep one eye open? Do you wish you were somewhere else?

It's awkward for them. They don't want to be disrespectful. It's awkward for Jesus. He must continue his own prayer life (a motif frequently called to our attention by Luke), but he doesn't want to use prayer to browbeat the disciples. "Lord, bless these fellows and help them get the point of what I'm talking about." He doesn't want to use prayer as an evangelistic tool or to make announcements.

What do you do when you want to pray, and you're in a room in which people are not praying? It happens in restaurants. I know people who want to pray every time they go out to eat. They don't want to make a big deal of it, but they don't want to be intimidated. My wife and I joined a couple for dinner. We had just met them. We didn't know them well, but we wanted to get to know them better. They had heard I was a minister. They said, "Would you sit here?" I said, "Sure." He put sugar in his tea, and stirred it, and stirred it some more. She fixed her napkin. She fixed it again. After a long time, one of them finally said to me, "We thought you were going to pray, or something."

I was in a Pizza Hut. At a table behind me, an older man in a very loud voice said, "Lord, bless this food to our bodies, and us to thy service. Amen." In the Pizza Hut. I spilled half my nachos in my lap. I'm not opposed to prayer, but, well…in the Pizza Hut?

So this is an awkward moment in the text. Jesus usually removed the awkwardness by going by himself to pray alone in a desert place or on a mountain. Sometimes he prayed all night. But there were occasions when he prayed when the disciples were with him. That was true when they were near Bethsaida. When he had ceased praying, he said to the disciples, "Who do the people say that I am?…Who do *you* say that I am?" And he began to talk to them about his death.

The situation in our text for today is different. While Jesus was praying, the disciples were near. One of them speaking for the group said, "Teach us to pray. We're not asking to pray like you pray. We've observed you praying. We know that's special. But John the Baptist taught a prayer to his disciples. Would you teach us to pray?"

This is what Jesus said. *(Verse 2a)* When you pray, the beginning point is always reverence for God. Hallowed be God's name. If you don't have reverence for God, if you talk glibly and casually about God, how can you pray? Hallowed…sacred…holy…sanctified…is the name of God. No wonder they couldn't pronounce the name of God in Judaism in the first century. That name is hard to say. When I was a child, my mother would play word games with us in the evening by the fire. She taught us phonic spelling. If you can say it, you can spell it. And she led us into the deep waters of *oviparous, ovoviviparous,* and *hypotenuse.* I once knew how to pronounce and spell *asafetida.* But one word she never put on the list, because she knew we were just children. She never put on the list: *God.*

(Verse 2b) When you pray, you must have one burning desire, "Let the reign of God come." This burning desire will purge your mind of all pitiful, selfish requests. This burning desire will relativize every other value in your life: the kingdom of God, the reign of God in the lives of people, between people, nations, everywhere. Love, and justice, and peace! The one waking thought. The one sleeping thought.

There's nothing here of praying for new luggage or of praying for a parking place near the entrance to Nieman-Marcus. Nothing here of praying that the flat tire will inflate itself. Nothing here of a prayer for a Caribbean cruise. "Let the reign of God come."

(Verse 3) Now the beginning commitment to that, he said, is to live simply. Just pray each day for that day's bread. This will be your first gift to the hungry of the world: to resolve before God in prayer that you will just take your share of food.

(Verse 4a) Now don't get to feeling righteous about this, he said. Everybody lives in sin. And even when we're doing good, we bump into, and bruise, and hurt each other. And there's misunderstanding and miscommunication. So always forgive.

(Verse 4b) You know how frail you are. How will you stand up in the great eschatological struggle, the final temptation and test, if you can't handle the little things? "Lead us not into temptation." Don't put me to the test. I don't know if I can make it. I even know some ministers who have yielded to temptation. I said, "Whatever happened to them?" Lead us not into temptation.

Now, this is a very brief prayer, but praying is not brief. You continue to pray, and pray, and pray, and pray.

(Verses 5–8) He said, "Which of you has a friend, and will go to that friend at midnight, because you've had company arrive, and say to that friend, 'I need some bread. The cupboard is bare. I need some bread to fulfill my responsibilities as a host?'" The person inside says, "Our house

is shut down for the night. The door is barred. The kids are asleep. It took us three hours to get the youngest one to sleep. Quit knocking on the door. If you wake that child up, you'll have to get the child to go back to sleep. Please, leave." "But, look, I've got to have bread." Bang. Bang. Bang. The person in the house thinks, "This neighbor is driving me up the wall. I'll get some bread just to get rid of the noise."

(Verse 9) Now, if that happens among us, we shouldn't tarry long at the door. Ask…seek…knock. Notice how Jesus repeats it. Ask…seek… knock. Ask…seek…knock. What is Jesus talking about? We don't know what prayer is until we stand before a locked door with bloody knuckles. Then, we know. Ah: ask…seek…knock.

(Verses10–13) But don't let that discourage you. All your prayer will be bathed in your trust in the goodness of God. For if you as parents know how to give a child good things, think how much more God gives. A child doesn't come to you and say, "Can I have an egg," and you give the child a scorpion. A child wouldn't say, "Daddy, can I have some bread?" and you give a rock. No. Not at all. You trust in goodness.

(Drawing out the Implications of the Verse-by-Verse Exposition) Why they come to Jesus now, asking for instruction in prayer, I don't know.

It may be that they did not think that you need to *learn* to pray. There are a lot of people who don't believe you teach prayer. You catch prayer. It's natural, they say. You just pray. "We just thank you for this…we just pray for that." I once thought that myself. Teaching, I thought, got in the way of the Spirit. Then, when I went to seminary, Dr. G. Edwin Osborn— bless his memory—had us write prayers. *Write* prayers? When you come out of the back country of Tennessee, as I did, you don't write prayers. "A written prayer is not from the heart. A written prayer is not sincere." [Craddock makes knocking sound on the pulpit.] "Dr. Osborn, could I talk to you about prayer?" "Come in." "Now, this writing prayers…I think all of that just interferes. I believe that prayer should be spontaneous." He was patient. "Can't the Holy Spirit help you prepare the prayer? Can't the Holy Spirit be with you in the study?" He went on and on. By the end of our conversation, I felt like two cents waiting for change.

I now believe that preparation for prayer does not interfere with the Spirit. I believe that spontaneity interferes with the Spirit. Spontaneously, I just think, and feel, and say the things I think and feel. By contrast, the reign of God demands that I do things that I do not want to do, and say things I do not want to say, and go places I do not want to go. Spontaneity gives me a way to hide from that.

The disciples had experienced a little failure. That'll prompt prayer. There had been a child that threw itself in the fire and then in the water.

Jesus was on the mountain with three of them. The others were down below. The parent asked, "Can you help my boy?" The disciples could not do a thing. Maybe that's what turned them toward prayer.

For a brief time, I was acting dean at Phillips Seminary. It was fifteen months. That's similar to fifteen years. The secretary said, "There's someone here to see you." A woman asked me to come out to the parking lot. I was a little nervous, but I followed her to the parking lot to her car. She opened the back door, and slumped in the back seat was her brother. He had been a senior at the University of Oklahoma. He had been in a bad car wreck. He had been in a coma eight months. She had quit her job as a schoolteacher to take care of him. All of their resources were gone. She opened the door and said, "I'd like for you to heal him." I said, "I can pray for him. And I can pray with you. But I do not have the gift of healing." She got under the wheel, and said to me, "Then what in the world do you do?" And she drove off. What I did that afternoon was to go to my study...and stare at my books...and try to forget what she said.

The disciples had also succeeded. Success can be even more difficult. They had been casting out demons and doing all kinds of things. They ran to Jesus crying, "Look at what we've done." But Jesus replied, "Cool it. Don't rejoice that you were successful. Rejoice that your names are written in the book of life." Watch success. It can kill you.

I don't know why they request for Jesus to teach them to pray. They started quarreling. Maybe that's it. Just before this, they got into an argument over who is the greatest apostle. What a thing to say! Maybe they want to learn to pray because they are headed toward Jerusalem. They hadn't planned on the talk of death that had so recently come into their circle. Rejection. Being spat upon. Suffering. They hadn't planned on that.

On the other side of the ledger, maybe they are just overwhelmed with the profound joy of the life they have found in Jesus Christ. Sometimes people pray not because everything is out of joint and everything is broken apart, but because they are so overwhelmed by the favor of God that they can't do anything else. A young mother spoke this way when the nurses brought her newborn baby, and it had all ten fingers and all ten toes. The child was healthy. The doctor said, "What a fine baby." The mother said later, "That's when I began to pray. You've got to have someone to thank."

Some ministers forget that. They hang around overhead, like vultures, waiting for people to drop. "*Now* you need the gospel." They wait for the person of wealth to go broke. "Now, can I help you?" They wait for the healthy person to get sick. Many of us ministers are intimidated by people who are healthy, and wealthy, and doing fine. We circle overhead saying, "Things may be fine now, but one of these days...."

We forget. The person who needs prayer, the person who needs to pray, is not just the person in the wheelchair. It's also that young woman standing on the center pedestal at the Olympics receiving the gold medal. It's not just the old man stumbling in the front yard looking for the paper. It's also the young man at the peak of his power. It's not just the old person leaning in the window at the post office asking, "Did the check come today?" It's also the person at the peak of the economy. Fast lane or slow, it's the same. Whether you are illiterate or just received the hood for the Ph.D., we all need to pray.

Maybe the disciples were just overwhelmed with the joy of this marvelous life. When they were fishing, they never expected to have such a life. I don't know. But whatever the reason, they came. And they said, "Teach us to pray."

Things will never be the same with them. You know that. They had done a lot of good things. They ushered. They were involved in crowd management. They had Jesus get in a boat and put out a little way. "OK, folks. If you'll just stay where you are, you'll get to hear him." They went out two by two, and when the people were not at home, they slipped a little leaflet behind the screen. They had done a lot of good things.

You know how it is. You've worked in the church for years. You've taken your turn with the young people on Sunday evening. You've taught a class. You've helped with the fellowship dinners. But sometime in those years…the dishes are done, or the young people are gone, or the meeting is over. You want people to think you have other things to do. But you have only one thing to do. You want to slip into a darkened sanctuary. "I'd like to go out a little farther…I'd like to probe a little deeper…I'd like to give a little more."

Teach us to pray. That's what they said. And the beautiful thing is that they did not even realize that their request was their first—and perhaps most important—prayer.

5

Thesis-Antithesis-Synthesis

Preachers can develop a pattern for the movement of the sermon by adapting an aspect of the thought of the philosopher G. W. F. Hegel (1770–1831). This pattern conceives of the sermon as containing three major parts: thesis, antithesis, and synthesis. The sermon consists of dialectical movement among these segments. The sermon often moves from a thesis through its antithesis through synthesis. However, as the sermon below illustrates, the movement can go from antithesis through thesis to synthesis.

In its simplest form, this approach begins with a *thesis*: an interpretation of an aspect of God, the Bible, and the world. The *antithesis* is a statement of why the thesis is not correct. In its strongest form, the antithesis is a counterproposition that makes the opposite claim of the thesis. In its milder forms, the antithesis exposes the inadequacies of the thesis or raises questions about the adequacy of the thesis. The *synthesis* mediates between the thesis and the antithesis. It identifies points at which the thesis is true and answers the questions raised by the antithesis. It identifies points at which the antithesis forces the thesis to be reshaped. It articulates an interpretation of the motif under the discussion that transcends both the thesis and the antithesis.

In James Henry Harris' refinement of this approach, the thesis is an expanded ideal as reflected in the Bible passage on which the sermon is based. It is often a motif that we have not previously noticed. The ideal is juxtaposed with an antithesis—the real life experience or condition of existence of the congregation that opposes the ideal. Moreover, in this approach to preaching, a ***relevant question*** that grows out of the tension created between the thesis and the antithesis must be posed and answered in the synthesis.

Harris, who authors the sermon in this chapter, calls his approach "dialectic textuality." Harris makes use of the dialectic movement, but always derives the thesis and the synthesis from a text from the Bible. The sermon developed in the passage typically has a dimension of struggle in that the thesis often states a proposition with which the antithesis struggles. In the antithesis, the preacher raises theological questions about the thesis, or cites phenomena that counter the thesis, or exposes elements of inconsistency in the thesis.

In "Being Unashamed of the Gospel," the preacher begins with the antithesis. Harris notes the power of shame in our culture. He notes that reading the text brings back memories of shame that have been debilitating in his life. The preacher moves to the thesis and its claim that Christians should not be ashamed of the gospel. In the synthesis, the preacher offers reasons for why we need not be ashamed of the gospel. The preacher helps the community see that the gospel overcomes the shame that we feel.

Harris advocates always preaching from a biblical text. While Harris discourages topical preaching, he acknowledges that a preacher can develop a sermon in the mode of "dialectical topicality." In a topical sermon, the thesis articulates a Christian interpretation of some aspect of the topic. The antithesis raises questions about that interpretation. The synthesis offers a way of understanding the topic that is consistent with the gospel and that makes sense of the contrast between the thesis and the antithesis.

This approach to preaching is useful (as in the sermon that follows) when Christian tradition and human experience are in tension. It is also helpful when the subject of the sermon is debated. The preacher can articulate two sides of a disputed interpretation. It helps the preacher resolve the tensions inherent in the dispute. Its clear structure helps the congregation follow the logic that the preacher uses to overcome the difficulties between the thesis and the antithesis. The inductive quality of the movement creates a certain suspense that helps hold the congregation's interest in the sermon.

JAMES HENRY HARRIS is professor of pastoral theology and preaching at The School of Theology of Virginia Union University, Richmond, Virginia. He is also senior minister of Second Baptist Church in the same city, the congregation for which this sermon was prepared. He has served as a professor of philosophy. In his *Preaching Liberation*, Fortress Resources for Preaching (Minneapolis: Fortress Press, 1995), Professor Harris develops and illustrates the homiletical method of dialectic textuality. He is also the author of *Pastoral Theology: A Black Church Perspective* (Minneapolis: Fortress Press, 1991). He has been Visiting Lecturer in Homiletics at Princeton Theological Seminary.

JAMES HENRY HARRIS

Being Unashamed of the Gospel

Romans 1:16–17 (Good News Bible and King James Version)

(Antithesis) Over the past twenty years, I have realized that there is very little consistency of intellectual thought regarding the interpretation of this scripture text. There is, indeed, a kind of mystery to the entire book of Romans—a mystery that seems to escape not only the likes of some of the most famous scholars of this generation, but most of all, me and some of my comrades in theology and ministry. To be honest, I am a little ashamed to admit the degree to which I have wrestled with the gospel in this text for the past fifteen years. Moreover, I am somewhat ashamed by the fact that this wrestling has not yielded greater clarity and profundity in Christian thought and action.

Nevertheless, I have recently come to a new insight concerning this text that allows me to postulate in the negative sense what it means to be ashamed. This text is literally translated, "I have complete confidence in the gospel," or "I am proud of the gospel." This text is a public testimony to the power and working of the Lord in the life of an individual. This is why I can now talk about my understanding of shame in my earlier life.

I remember quite vividly an incident that took place when I was in the second grade. It was during the 1959–60 school year, after the Christmas break. The teacher asked each person in the classroom to stand and tell what he or she had received for Christmas. As soon as the teacher asked the question, I knew I was in trouble because my self-esteem was burdened by comparing myself to other children in the class. We lived fairly close to Virginia State University and attended school with some students whose parents were professors, physicians, and other professionals. Hearing the other children's lavish descriptions of gifts that I had never heard of, I was ashamed of what I received.

I was embarrassed by the simple air-filled circle of resinous elastic material—a bouncing ball—that I received and had to share with my brothers and sisters. Accordingly, I refused to speak when the teacher asked me to share with the entire class what I got for Christmas. My silence manifested shame and embarrassment. Unfortunately, and to my chagrin, the teacher in her lack of wisdom punished me by making me stand in the corner facing the wall all day. That was one of the longest days of my life. And I know many of you have felt ashamed at times in your lives, too.

So, whenever I encounter this text, it brings back memories of some things of which I was ashamed. These memories, however subliminal and uncollected, reside in my collected unconscious. Many of us have things of which we may be ashamed.

(Thesis) Maybe in reflecting upon his own experience, Paul is compelled to compile some of the most powerful words in scripture. Maybe the whole letter to the Romans is so intriguing and influential to me personally because I feel that beneath the veneer of its often strong and jarring words is a word of comfort and joy. Beneath the harsh, tangled language of argument is a word of simple truth—a word of faith and love, a word that speaks to me when I am ashamed. This is the gospel. The good news in the text represents the ideal for which the Christian strives. This simple word, leveled against a backdrop of puffed up intellectualism and unbelief, is an audacious attestation of faith.

When we understand the context of this propagation we grasp the bold, "in your face," quality of this Pauline assertion. Rome was a very sophisticated city, a citadel of misplaced pride and wealth. It was devoid of abiding interest in the gospel of Jesus. Rome was known for its gods and goddesses, for its intellectual curiosity, and culture. I can imagine that there was a great temptation to say nothing about one's faith, nothing about being a Christian, nothing about redemption and salvation, nothing about the name of Jesus. After all, Jesus died on the cross. It would have seemed strange to the sophisticated Romans to hear that a crucified Jew was the Savior.

Yet in this city, the capital of the Roman world; in this city, this haven of libertinism, where Christians were tempted to keep quiet and silent about their faith, the apostle Paul writes to these few bold people who had already started a church. These few folks were devoted to a Lord whom the masses of people did not recognize. In Rome, Christians were persecuted, beaten, and talked about as a direct result of their faith in Jesus as Lord and Savior. In the midst of all this philosophy and theology, Paul makes a socially and politically incorrect exclamation. "For I am not ashamed of the gospel of Christ: for it is the power of God unto salvation to everyone that believeth: to the Jew first, and also to the

Greek. For therein is the righteousness of God revealed from faith to faith...."

Here we are in the city of Richmond, Virginia, the former capital of the Confederate South and now the capital of the Commonwealth of Virginia. Many are ashamed of the South's position on slavery while simultaneously espousing freedom from England. Some in our society should be ashamed for using the language of liberty and justice to establish their own independence while structuring a system of chattel slavery for African Americans. Our city today is much like Rome was in 54 C.E.: a place of culture, the home of many prominent universities, the center of education, commerce, research, and politics. But there is also oppression, poverty, crime, waywardness, drug abuse, and apathy. Like the Romans, those of us in this city and in this Christian community are tempted to ignore everything around us. We are tempted to hide or keep silent about our freedom and faith. We may be ashamed. But I am here to tell you today that every time we are tempted to silence, we must say, like Paul, "I am not ashamed of the gospel."

(Relevant Question) Why should a Christian not be ashamed of the Gospel?

(Synthesis) We should not be ashamed because it is the power of God for salvation. The gospel, the good news about Jesus Christ, has saving power. The gospel lets us know that Jesus came from a home in glory, through forty-two generations, to save us from eternal damnation. Jesus reconciles us with God. Nothing else has the power to save from sin—no scientific theory, no philosophy, no pill in a box, no ideology, no sociology. This gospel is the most cataclysmic and transformative power that I know. This gospel is the treatment that can make us love our enemies, forgive those who spitefully use us. The gospel can do these things because it tells us about Jesus, and if we trust in Jesus, our heavy burdens become easier to bear. There is something joyful about the gospel that obviates shame and makes you hold your head up and be thankful for what God can do.

To be unashamed of the gospel and to know it is the power of God gives you joy in your soul. The spiritual song of the black church tradition captures the spirit of this joyous gospel. "This joy I have the world didn't give it to me, the world didn't give it and the world can't take it away." Don't be ashamed of the gospel because it is the power of God for salvation!

Also, this event of salvation through the gospel is unlimited and non-discriminatory. The gospel does not differentiate on the basis of class, national origin, race, social status, church affiliation. It is offered to everyone who has faith. "This gospel represented no break in the history of salvation...it was fulfilling the promise made to the fathers in Christ."[1] This gospel is not exclusionary, but inclusive. The power of the gospel is not a narrow construct, motivated by an effort to satisfy cliques of Jews or Gentiles. No, it is a liberating, powerful event open to everyone who has faith. Paul doesn't believe that Israel has rejected the good news—though some have hardened and stumbled.

The power of the gospel results in salvation. It leads to final deliverance, salvation, and ultimate victory. For the believer, salvation is ultimately an omega point, a convergence of ultimate becoming. It leads to a kind of eternal "nowness." Jesus corrects Martha on this point. She says that resurrection will take place only on the last day, but Jesus says, "I am the resurrection and the life. Those who believe in me, even though they die, will live" (John 11:25). Salvation is not simply a future hope, but is a present reality.

The gospel teaches us about faith in God. This faith is something of which we cannot be ashamed. It reveals the righteousness of God and provides life to those who have faith. For the Christian, the gospel is as necessary as the air we breathe because it produces faith. A Christian without faith is an oxymoron. In philosophy, we would say it is an ontological negation.

Paul didn't mind saying what he said because he knew what Jesus had done for him. Now his life was in line with the gospel. He wasn't always willing to say what he says now in Romans. But he had learned that the gospel brings us into closer relationship with the power source. The Christian knows that she or he has no power on his or her own. The Christian knows that the ability to "live and move and have our being" (Acts 17:28) comes from God. The Christian knows that when she or he laid down last night, the only way she or he got up the next morning was by the grace and goodness of God. The Christian knows that there is no place for egotism or self-adulation, no place for boasting of our own strength, because without God we would be nothing. The more we learn about God, the more we trust God; and the more we trust God, the closer we get to God, the better we treat our brothers and sisters, the more we are able to share the good news with others. We are no longer ashamed of ourselves or of the gospel.

Paul had a dramatic experience of the gospel. One day he was "breathing threats and murder against the disciples of the Lord." He was ashamed

---

[1] Mark D. Nanos, *The Mystery of Romans* (Minneapolis: Fortress Press, 1996), 36.

of Jesus and wanted to persecute Jesus' followers. As he journeyed to Jerusalem, extraditing Christians, one day near Damascus, suddenly a light from heaven flashed about him, and he fell to the ground and heard a voice saying, "Saul, Saul, why do you persecute me?" Paul asked, "Who are you Lord?" The voice replied, "I am Jesus, whom you are persecuting" (Acts 9:1–5). This experience left Paul blind and fasting for three days. But since that day, he was no longer the same. That which he hated, he now loved. That which he tried to destroy, he now proclaimed. That which he did not trust, he now trusted with all his heart and soul. That of which he was formerly ashamed is now his source of pride.

When I think back to that day in the second grade, I realize now that I should not have been ashamed. Christ Jesus had already died and rose for me. My father and mother were honest, devoted Christian people who did the best they could for their family. I should not have been ashamed of me. I should have been ashamed that the wealthiest nation in the world permits such poverty. I was embarrassed by my social and economic predicament, by my poverty, and by the fact that everybody else in the school had running water and electricity, and we had to read and study by a kerosene oil lamp as late as 1965, when I should have been ashamed that these things were permitted in the most democratic and industrialized nation in the world. I was ashamed of our meager subsistence—feeling guilty about being born on the wrong side of the tracks, on the underside of the culture in the rural backwoods of Virginia, when I should have been ashamed that our society today even thinks in terms of "the right side" and "the wrong side" of the tracks.

I think about the cross, symbol of pain and suffering. I think about how Jesus lived a blameless life, yet took the blame for our transgressions. I think about that journey from Bethlehem to Calvary. I think about how even his own disciples denied him, how Judas betrayed him, how Pilate and Herod treated him with scorn, indifference, and hate. Oh, when I think about what Jesus did on the cross and what he has done for me, how can I be ashamed of him? How can I be ashamed of myself? How can I quell the emotions that well up in my soul? How can I keep back the tears of joy that I feel? How can I not be happy and completely unashamed about the gospel, that saving message, that act of suffering and shame that Jesus took upon himself for me? Jesus died on the cross for your sins and mine, so I can say today, that, like Paul, I am not ashamed of the gospel!

6

From Problem through Gospel Assurance to Celebration

Sermons can move from a description of a problem to the problem's resolution. Frank A. Thomas adapts this movement to take account of an insight from the approach to preaching by Henry H. Mitchell (chapter 2). Thomas advocates a sermon that moves from the description of a problem, through its resolution, to the celebration of the resolution. Thomas refers to the problem as a complication, and he speaks of the resolution as gospel assurance.

In the first part of the sermon, the preacher describes a problem that **complicates** the world of the congregation. The complication might be a life situation that raises questions for the community. It might be a theological problem raised by a biblical text, a doctrine, or a Christian practice. The preacher would typically describe the problem, helping the congregation recognize how they are implicated or affected by the problem. The preacher helps them identify how the problem touches them intellectually, emotionally, and behaviorally. The sermon may need to help the congregation identify both the symptoms of problem and its deeper causes.

In the phase of **gospel assurance**, the preacher helps the church recognize how God's unconditional love and God's universal will for justice help the church interpret the complication and determine how to respond to it. The preacher helps the community to meditate on how the gospel calls them to think, feel, and act with respect to the problem. The preacher brings together exegetical insight, doctrine, and aspects of Christian practice in the service of speaking to the mind and the heart. The preacher helps the congregation identify with the gospel's resolution. The gospel assurance is not always a salve that immediately makes people feel good. At times the resolution calls for a change of thinking, feeling, or behaving on the part of the congregation or the wider community. This change can be difficult, even painful. For instance, the resolution to a particular problem may be possible only through honest, painful repentance.

In the phase of *celebration*, the sermon celebrates God's empowering presence that brings about the resolution. The preacher engages in ecstatic reinforcement of the good news. The celebration is just that: a strong statement in the indicative mood of what God has done, is doing, and will do that makes the assurance possible. The celebration draws on core beliefs in the Christian community and shows how those beliefs lead to regeneration or renewal. This part of the sermon is never exhortatory. It celebrates the news that God is working toward resolution. The celebration may encourage the community to join God, but the preacher needs to make it clear that God is the primary initiator and actor.

In the sermon below, Frank Thomas identifies a complication that he finds in both the biblical text and in life. When serving God became difficult, Jeremiah decided not to continue in divine service. When faced with difficulty, we, also, are tempted to abandon our witness. The gospel assurance, however, is that in the midst of suffering, God is present and redemptive. The occasion of suffering can become an occasion of witness. In the celebration, the preacher creates an imaginative experience of being arrested. Through that experience, the preacher finds the truth of the text confirmed. Indeed, the arrest becomes a surprising occasion of spiritual renewal and a time of testimony (service). The congregation leaves the sermon celebrating the fact that in every circumstance, God arrests us.

FRANK A. THOMAS is senior pastor of New Faith Baptist Church in Matteson, Illinois. This sermon came to life during a time of deep pain and trial in ministry. He is the author of *They Like to Never Quit Praisin' God: The Role of Celebration in Preaching* (Cleveland: United Church Press, 1997). In this book he gives a comprehensive account of the role of celebration in preaching. He also contributed to *Atonement: The Million Man March*, edited by Kim Sadler (Cleveland: Pilgrim Press, 1996).

FRANK A. THOMAS

Arrested by the Lord

Jeremiah 20:7–9

(Complication) The prophet Jeremiah has just come from a major confrontation with Pashhur, the chief priest charged with the responsibility to maintain order through the temple police. Jeremiah told the people that the Lord would bring disaster to their nation because of their stiff necks. When the chief priest heard Jeremiah, the chief priest had the prophet arrested and whipped with many lashes. Following the beating, the prophet was placed in stocks. False prophets were placed in stocks as a sign that their messages were invalid. The stocks also inflicted excruciating pain through slow torture. The prophet was placed in the most conspicuous place in town, so that everyone could see his humiliation and shame.

When Pashhur released Jeremiah, the prophet this time spoke against Pashhur himself. "The Lord will make you a terror to yourself and to your friends." Jeremiah told him that God changed his name from Pashhur to "Mr. Terror All Around." Because of his opposition to God, Pashhur would be exiled to Babylon and die there. Jerusalem would fall. The Israelite people would also be exiled.

Jeremiah then went to a lonely place. In the quietness of soul and feeling the violence done to his person, he doubts. He is mangled, cut, bruised, sore. His soul is battered. We walk in on conversation between the soul of the prophet and God in verse 7 of our text. Have you ever had a conversation between your soul and God? When a soul talks to God, it is not always theologically pretty. Sometimes when a soul talks to God, there is complete honesty about what one really feels, what one really thinks. Sometimes, the soul pulls its gloves off. Jeremiah blames God. "O Lord, you deceived me, and I was deceived." There are several different translations of this verse because the word deceived is offensive. The meaning of the Hebrew "deceived" signifies that Jeremiah accuses God of seducing him. God has placed a divine compulsion on Jeremiah's spirit so that Jeremiah could do nothing other than respond to the Holy One. Jeremiah accuses God of not giving the prophet real options. For that reason, I like to substitute another term that better captures the spirit of the text—arrested. "O Lord, you arrested me, and I was arrested."

In the latter part of verse 7, Jeremiah continues to blame God and says, "O Lord, you deceived me and I was deceived; you overpowered me and prevailed." Jeremiah claims that a part of him wanted to be arrested, but in the end, God overpowered him and prevailed. And because God ultimately overpowered him, Jeremiah had no responsibility for his plight and condition. Jeremiah admits that a part of him had resisted the role of prophet. (The preacher reads Jeremiah 1:4–8.) Jeremiah resisted the call and did not want to obey God. He uses the excuse that he was young and could not speak. But the Lord overpersuaded, overpowered his resistance and prevailed. The Lord told Jeremiah not to worry. The Lord would be with the prophet, would tell him what to speak, would rescue him. At that time Jeremiah believed God's promises, but now, after the stocks and the beating, Jeremiah believes that God has abandoned him. The prophet thinks that God overpromised and underdelivered.

(Gospel assurance) However, what is dangerous about being a victim is that we are often so busy complaining that we forget the resources of God. The Lord had told Jeremiah that Jeremiah's ministry would be difficult and people were going to be against him. God had told Jeremiah not to worry, because God had made provision for him. "Today, I have made you a fortified city, an iron pillar, and a bronze wall to stand against the whole land, against the kinds of Judah, its officials, its priests, and the people of the land. They will fight against you but will not overcome you, for I am with you and will rescue you,' declares the Lord" (Jeremiah 1:18–19).

God tried to tell Jeremiah the reality of Jeremiah's situation and the greater reality of God's help. When we are victims, sometimes we cannot see that God is larger than our enemies. We sometimes think of our problems as large and our God as small.

But, let us be fair to Jeremiah. At the beginning of his ministry, he could not conceive of the magnitude of the opposition. He did not mind a little verbal abuse, but he never thought he would take a whipping, the stocks, the torture. He is a full-scale victim in verse 8. "I am ridiculed all the day long; everyone mocks me. Whenever I speak, I cry out, proclaiming violence and destruction. So the word of the Lord has brought me insult and reproach all day long." The burden got so heavy that he finally decided he would no longer deliver the message. He decided he had the right to remain silent.

I have noticed that church members decide they have the right to remain silent. Many people believe they have the right to decide whether or not they come to church, sing in the choir, work in the Sunday school, or give.

Concerning his decision to remain silent, Jeremiah says in verse 9, "But if I say, 'I will not mention [God] or speak any more in [God's] name,' [God's] word is in my heart like a flame, a fire shut up in my bones. I am weary of holding it in; indeed, I cannot." He came to know that he had been arrested by the Lord. He learned that his call was irreversible, and

God's word was irrepressible. What does it feel like to have fire shut up in your bones?

The best analogy that I can draw in response to that question took place recently at dinner. I unexpectedly ate a jalapeno pepper in an already spicy dish. It was so hot that it ruined the meal for me. It took several large glasses of water to restore my senses. Maybe fire shut up in the bones is like that five-alarm fire in my mouth. We could paraphrase Jeremiah. "The word of the Lord is like jalapeno peppers shut up in me." Water does not quench this kind of thirst. This fire can be quenched only one way: by preaching.

Jeremiah realized how deep this call was in him. He realized how much God had hold of him. He realized that he did not make the choice, but the choice made him. Michael Jordan is made to play basketball. Picasso was made to paint. Frederick Douglass was made to protest. Martin Luther King, Jr., was made to march. Jeremiah was made to preach. I imagine that God tired of Jeremiah's victim-based complaining and said, "Quit if you can. Go ahead. See if you can quit."

In some respects, if we can quit, we might not have been called. If you get mad in the choir, and you quit singing because you are mad, you may not have been called to sing. If you are a deacon, and someone hurts your feelings, and you quit deaconing, you may not have been called. Quit, if you can. Jeremiah says, "I have been arrested by the Lord. I cannot quit." Jeremiah is under house arrest by God.

(Celebration) All of us know some of what Jeremiah feels. All of us have decided that we are not going to serve God anymore. Once, I said I was not going to preach anymore. I was going to take charge of my life, and so I got in my car, heading in the opposite direction of my call. I decided to speed down the interstate highway of my own life—traveling fast and free in the four-lane highway of my direction on cruise control on the speedometer of my own will. The music of my own imagination was blasting in my ears when, all of a sudden, in the rearview mirror, I saw a car with red flashing lights. I must pull over. The officer comes up to my car and asks for my license. The officer says, "Pastor Thomas, I hate to inform you that you are under arrest." "Arrest?" I retort. "Yes. The judge signed a warrant for your arrest and put out an all points bulletin that whenever you were seen, you were to be arrested."

I protested. "But I have not done anything wrong. I was just speeding down my own life. At worst, I should get a ticket. But be arrested?" But I knew who the judge was, and I knew that he had issued a heavenly search warrant, and I knew God put out the all points bulletin. "Sir, please step out of the vehicle, and I will read you your rights," said the officer. "You no longer have the right to remain silent. Whatever you do not say will be used against you in a court of law before the judge."

They take me in. I am allowed one phone call. I call my wife and say, "I have been arrested." "Arrested?" "Yes, I have been arrested by the Lord." She wants to bail me out, but there is no possibility of bail in this dispute. This is a matter between a soul and the Savior. I tell her, "I am scheduled to see the judge tomorrow morning, and the best you can do is to pray for me."

I hang up the phone. They put me in solitary confinement. They tell me the judge wants me to have some time to think. I am mad. I am upset that I cannot live my own life. I am upset that I cannot make my own career choice. I am upset that I am not the captain of my own ship. But after awhile, a vision comes to me in my cell. My cell wall becomes a screen. I see myself as 8, 9, 10, 13, 15 years old. I see all my friends and me playing baseball, football, and basketball. I see us hanging out and being kids together. The screen goes blank. Then, in 1993, I go to the same street corner, and see some of my old friends. Several have been murdered as they try to deal in drugs. Several others are in jail for other offenses. Several are strung out on drugs or are alcoholics standing on the corner asking for dollars to get some wine. God says, "This is why I arrested you. In your mother's womb, I called you to serve me. Serve me, or serve yourself."

The next morning, they take me to the courtroom to face the judge. I ask to approach the bench and say to the judge, "I would like to save the court time by pleading guilty. I need no jury or attorney, but completely throw myself upon the mercy of the court. I would like to save the court even more time and pronounce my own sentence. Given what I saw in my cell last night, I sentence myself to life. I want life in your dominion, a life sentence proclaiming the gospel. I want a life sentence of choirs, deacons, ushers. I want life in your service."

The judge says, "Life it is. But if you are going to serve for life, I am going to make you a deputy." I respond, "But what does a deputy do?" "A deputy goes around arresting people in my name. I put out all points bulletins, and the deputy brings them under arrest."

As a deputy for the judge, I have been sent to arrest somebody. I know that you are here. I know that you have been running away from a call God has on your life. God has a mission for you. While you were running you may have slipped and fallen—fallen into drugs, into complacency, into the wrong crowd. I have been sent with a heavenly warrant for your arrest. God put out an all points bulletin. God wants you back. God wants to restore you. God wants you to fulfill your God-given purpose in life. All you have to do is say, "I am guilty. But now, I want life in God's service."

7

Bipolar Preaching

Bipolar preaching derives from F. W. Robertson, a preacher in England in the nineteenth century. Robertson believed that truth emerges in the dialectic between two opposite poles. Robertson did not seek a *via media*, a way to mediate between disagreement. He did not try to harmonize the differences in the different ideas. Robertson assumed that almost every text, doctrine, or situation contained an aspect of truth. Robertson also assumed that no text, doctrine, or situation contains all truth. Fuller visions of truth emerge in the interplay of differing understandings.

Within a single biblical text or among different biblical texts, Robertson compared and contrasted different ideas. The preacher calls attention to ways and situations which made a positive contribution to the congregation's understanding and to ways and situations in which each pole had its limitations. A preacher might find the poles within the text itself or within interpretations of the text by preachers and theologians. In the sermon below, Joseph R. Jeter, Jr., takes this approach to the viewpoints of two books in the Bible. The same method can be applied to Christian doctrines, practices, and situations.

Robertson's approach is well suited to an aspect of the contemporary ethos. It helps the preacher take account of pluralism and multiple points of view in biblical texts, in Christian theology and practice, in communities, and in situations. Robertson encourages the preacher to honor the particularity and distinctiveness of a passage, a doctrine, or a setting. This pattern can help the preacher whose congregation is wrestling (or needs to wrestle) with different points of view. It can help when the Christian community is struggling with an important issue. Robertson's bipolar path can help the preacher model critical thinking.

On a cautionary note, however, not all subjects divide conveniently into two viewpoints. Some texts, doctrines, practices, or situations may contain only one real pole. Others may generate three, four, five, or more angles of interpretation. This approach could let the preacher and the church drift into relativity when we need to come to a normative conclusion. While most biblical passages, and most doctrines, practices, and situations contain elements of truth, some elements are more appropriate to the gospel, intelligible, and morally plausible than others. The less appropriate ones need critique.

Joseph Jeter preached this sermon as a guest at First Christian Church (Disciples of Christ) in Eugene, Oregon—a community wrestling with the degree to which it is to be open to fresh impulses in the wider culture and the degree to which it is important to maintain boundaries from the culture. Jeter finds two poles in the choices of Ruth and Esther. The service contained readings from selected passages in each book. However, these readings represent the whole stories of Ruth and Esther. In the sermon, Jeter refers to *The Last Will and Testament of the Springfield Presbytery,* an important document in the history of the Christian Church (Disciples of Christ), the Christian Churches, and Churches of Christ.

The sermon generated considerable response, including that of a woman who said that Jeter missed an important point: Both women were doing what they had to do to survive in a patriarchal world. Jeter observes that her viewpoint states one pole in what would be another sermon.

JOSEPH R. JETER, JR., is Granville and Erline Walker Associate Professor of Homiletics at Brite Divinity School, Texas Christian University, Fort Worth, Texas. He is the author of *Crisis Preaching* (Nashville: Abingdon Press, 1998) and *Re/Membering: Meditations and Sermons for the Table of Jesus Christ* (St. Louis: Chalice Press, 1995). With Cornish R. Rogers, he edited *Preaching Through the Apocalypse: Sermons from Revelation* (St. Louis: Chalice Press, 1992), and he is the author of *Alexander Proctor: The Sage of Independence* (Claremont, California: Disciples Seminary Foundation, 1983). He preaches in congregations and conferences throughout the United States.

JOSEPH R. JETER, JR.

Ruth People in an Esther World

Ruth 1:6–18, Esther 8:3–8

A couple of years ago I was speaking in Lafayette, Louisiana, at the regional assembly of the Christian Church. One of the advantages of being a guest speaker at such events is that you can sneak out during the business sessions and nobody minds. So I walked downtown to a Cajun music festival. I stood on the fringes listening to the music and watching the people. The music was great, but what really touched me was that the people were not only enthusiastic about the music, but that they were also enthusiastic about who they were—their language, their music, their heritage, their ethnicity.

I've seen this at other times and places, too. The feast of Booths in the Orthodox Jewish section of Brooklyn. Protest marches by African Americans in Mississippi. Mexicans at the festival of the Virgin of Guanajuato. And I'm told this same thing happens in an Irish pub. But I cannot recall having had this same kind of visceral experience myself. I come from French Huguenot and Scottish stock, with a Mexican great-grandmother mixed in for flavor. But I cannot remember ever being exuberant about who I am, about my ethnicity. And I suspect that many of you are in the same boat.

This is echoed in our religious experience as well. We Disciples of Christ have as one of our bywords that "we are not the only Christians, but Christians only," while some other groups will say that if you are not a part of that group, you're doomed. We seek to be open, inclusive, ecumenical, and we're not terribly demonstrative about our faith. I haven't heard an "Amen" yet this morning. Our patriarch, Alexander Campbell, was a cold-blooded rationalist if ever there was one. Oh, there was one occasion when Walter Scott was preaching that Campbell got so excited that the jumped up and said "Glory to God!"—but he quickly realized what he had done and quietly slipped back into his seat.

Maybe this helps explain our fascination with the story of Ruth. Disciples have a fondness for this story. I've heard scores of sermons and even more devotionals on Ruth, and the Christian Women's Fellowship holds the story especially dear, as if Ruth were a matron saint. This makes sense. Ruth was a Moabite who married a Hebrew. The man died. Ruth's mother-in-law, Naomi, lost her husband and decided to go back to Israel. Naomi encouraged Ruth and her sister-in-law, Orpah, to remain with their people, the Moabites. Orpah decides to return to her people and her religion, but Ruth responds with the touching soliloquy that, like many other poetic texts, reads better in the King James:

> Entreat me not to leave thee, or to return from following after thee: for whither thou goest, I will go; and where thou lodgest, will lodge: thy people shall be my people, and thy God my God: where thou diest, will I die, and there I will be buried; the Lord do so to me, and more also, if aught but death part thee and me (Ruth 1:16–17).

This is very special. It's not only lovely; it's a prime example of openness and inclusivity. Ruth rejects her own ethnicity, her own heritage, to embrace another. We feel good about that. It is a tintype of the way we think about ourselves. We are Ruth people, not demanding that others see things the way we do, and even, as one of the primal documents of our movement, *The Last Will and Testament of the Springfield Presbytery,* says, willing to die, to sink into union with the church at large. We are willing to give up who we are for the greater good of the gospel.

We like that. We feel good about it. The only problem is—we are Ruth people in an Esther world. Esther is Jewish, married to a king. Because Jewish people are out of favor, she hides her ethnicity until her people are in danger. Esther has a good life with King Ahasuerus and she's queen over all the land. But she risks everything: her life, her possessions, her throne, everything. She schemes, she plots, she deceives—all to save her people. She says to the king, "If I have won your favor, then save my people....How can I bear to see the calamity that is coming on my people? How can I bear to see the destruction of my kindred?" When the crunch comes, what really matters is not her relationship with the king or even her own life. As Esther says, "If I perish, I perish." The only thing that really matters is that she is Jewish and her people are in trouble.

Well, Esther prevails in this confrontation and the people are saved, but that's not the point I wish to make. The point is that this is a very different story from that of Ruth. Ruth rejected her ethnicity. Esther claims hers as the prime datum of her life. And the fact is that Esther's way is the way of the world right now. We live in a time of raging ethnicity. We see it on the TV in the Middle East, and the crumbling Soviet empire, and at Wounded Knee, and in the inner city, and we're very uncomfortable with it.

The truth is that I have not tended to define myself as a SWAM, which is the new parlance for straight, white, American male. The most enthusiastic I have been about my identity has been my identity as a Christian. I remember many times at young people's activities and in congregations where being Christian brothers and sisters became the prime datum of our existence. Whenever someone would raise the question with which we began this sermon—"Who are we?"—we were quick to reply, "No, the question is '*whose* are we?'" And I can remember, for many years, whenever I filled out an application or questionnaire, I always wrote in "Christian." This is consistent with being a Ruthian disciple. Our motif is immigration, amalgamation, the melting pot, the many become one.

The problem comes when we see the other side of this motif. In the desire for the many to become one, there is the danger of defining "one" in terms of the majority. In order, therefore, for there to be unity, everyone should be like "us." And the world is saying a loud and unmistakable "No!" to that. African American students have made it clear to me that they have no intention of preaching white, and women have made it clear that they will not preach male. Ruth may be willing to give up her identity, but Esther has no intention of doing so, and right now the voice being heard in the world is Esther's.

My intention this morning is not to claim that either of these great women was wrong. I simply point out that both voices are real, both are givens of our world, that we have tended to prefer and be defined by Ruth's voice, and that the exploding pluralism and recovery of ethnicity of our world require us to come to terms with Esther's voice as well. What shall we do about this situation?

Choosing either voice alone cannot, I believe, be an option for us. We can no longer call on people to give up those critical realities by which they define themselves, to sink into a melting pot and become like everyone else. Nor can we embrace ethnicity as the final word or goal of the human project. Once again, we have to choose the hard way. We have to find a way to honor the needs and identity of the individual and the subgroup, and the needs and identity of the whole.

We have heard plenty of stories in church about people who found themselves by helping others. Let the stories of James Cone and Kwok Pui-Lan speak for many who help others by finding themselves. Cone writes, "The more I read about black history, the more I became proud of being black. A person without a past is a person without an identity. And the absence of an identity is very serious, because without self-knowledge others can make you become what they desire." [1]

---

[1] James H. Cone, *My Soul Looks Back* (Abingdon: Nashville Press), 28.

Similarly, Kwok Pui-Lan says,

> It is not easy to be both Chinese and Christian. Out of this most trying experience, I have come to face both my cultural heritage and the Christian tradition with courage and hope. My Chinese foremothers brought their experience to bear on their interpretation of Christian faith and dared to challenge the established teaching of the church. It is because of this history that I can claim to do theology from a Chinese woman's perspective...and realize that all people must find their own way of speaking about God, to generate new symbols, concepts and models for expressing their religious vision. As a Chinese Christian woman, I have to critically reassess my double heritage, to rediscover liberating elements for building my own theology.[2]

This double heritage—which we might call the way of Ruth and the way of Esther—is hard to live with, but in one way or another we all do. Paul told the Galatians, "It is no longer I who live, but it is Christ who lives in me" (2:20), but on another day, at least according to Luke, he claimed his right as a Roman citizen and said, "I appeal to the emperor" (Acts 25:11). Maybe it all boils down to this: Do we live in one world or two? Some say strongly one; some say strongly two. Maybe what we should say is that we live *in* two, but *toward* one.

The best way to do that in the face of raging ethnicity and/or sectarianism is to know ourselves, to learn our stories, individual and corporate, to hold tenaciously to that heritage that honors the word of God, the waters of baptism, and the table of grace and judgment...and then to watch and listen to the stories of others, individuals and groups, watching for the points of contact between stories where we might find a place to stand together and listening, always listening, for the word of God. This congregation should be a powerful witness for the Disciples' faith stance and, because of its strategic location hard against a major university and its creative membership, should be a place of particular hospitality to new ideas and new people.

I had a student once when I was teaching in Claremont, California, a beautiful young Korean woman named Chung Hyun Kyung. She was very bright and articulate. She was assigned to preach from Luke 1:46–55, the Magnificat of Mary. But when the time came for her to preach, she

---

[2] Adapted from Kwok Pui-Lan, "Mothers and Daughters, Writers and Fighters," in *Inheriting Our Mothers' Gardens*, ed. by Letty Russell et al. (Philadelphia: Westminster Press, 1988), 26, 29, 31.

walked to the front of the chancel, stood silently, and then slowly began to dance. The dance was awkward and halting at first, but slowly gained grace and power, until she finished in a fortissimo of motion. And then she sat down, never having said a word. The class and I were transfixed. But I gave her a bad grade. When she asked why, I said, "because you were assigned a text and you didn't exegete the passage." She left downcast and disappointed.

Years passed and I recently came across a chapter in a book by Hyun Kyung. In this book, she tells her own story and it begins like this.

> When I was seven, my mother and I traveled to a small remote village in southwestern Korea to visit my aunt. No bus or train service was available. We had to go over the mountain and cross the river. I was exhausted from walking so long on the dusty road under a hot summer's sun. Mom had been telling me about how she and her sisters swam in the river when they were children. So when we came to the river, she jumped in. I was shocked. We were respectable people. How could she do this? I looked to see if there were any other people around. I did not approve of my mother's behavior at all. At last she got out of the water, but the situation got worse. She began singing a song I had never heard. And she danced while she was singing. Humiliation and confusion made me cry. "Mom, stop it! Stop it!" I screamed, but she kept on dancing until finally, because of my continuous crying, she stopped.[3]

Hyun Kyung's mother is long since dead, but she finishes her story with a plaintive letter, in which she says, "Dear Mom, come and dance again. I'll join you this time, not crying but laughing. And Mary will sing the Magnificat for our dance."[4]

"My God!" I thought, and I quickly hurried to the end of her story to see if she mentioned the idiot professor who had seen her reclaim the dance of her mother and of the mother of Jesus, bring them together, and then gave her a bad grade. But she was more gracious and wise than I.

The coming age, friends, is one of pluralism. There are a lot of Ruths here today and I'm happy to be one of you. But I tell you there are going to be more and more Esthers and Hyun Kyungs among us as the days go by. And the test of this fellowship will be the creativity of the encounter

---

[3] Paraphrased from Chung Hyun Kyung, "Following Naked Dancing and Long Dreaming," in *Inheriting Our Mothers' Gardens*, 54–55.

[4] Ibid.

between the one and the other. Last week I wrote a letter to the registrar of the School of Theology at Claremont and told them to change Hyun Kyung's eight-year-old grade to an "A." That was one fantastic sermon. It's just that some sermons take longer than others to get through. I wonder why Jesus never gave up in his quest to make us all one, even as he was with God. And I wonder if my Mexican great-grandmother ever danced.

8

Sermon as Theological Quadrilateral

Preachers use the term "quadrilateral" to describe John Wesley's notion that Christians draw on four sources for the knowledge of God:
scripture, tradition, experience, reason.[1] While the word "quadrilateral" is
associated with Wesleyanism, nearly all preachers use these sources when
preparing a sermon. The quadrilateral can directly serve as a structure for
a sermon in which the preacher turns to each of the sources. The sermon
would likely have a beginning that helps the congregation focus on the
subject of the sermon. It might include a statement of the direction of the
sermon. The sermon would discuss each of the four sources.

A sermon in this model can be either expository or topical. An expository sermon focuses on how a biblical text or theme is understood in
the Bible and how the church interprets the material in tradition, experience, and reason. In a topical approach, the preacher helps the congregation understand how each of the four sources helps the community
interpret the topic.

When discussing *scripture*, the preacher turns to biblical perspectives—
key texts, themes, and images. When the Bible contains a plurality of
viewpoints, the preacher needs to respect the pluralism of the Bible. The

---

[1] For the notion of quadrilateral in Wesley, see Albert C. Outler, "The Wesleyan Quadrilateral—
in John Wesley," *Wesleyan Theological Journal* 20 (1985): 7–18.

community may need to wrestle with which biblical viewpoints are more (and less) authoritative today.

When turning to *tradition*, the preacher considers how major voices in church history understand the focus of the sermon. The tradition is huge. Consequently, the preacher frequently refers in the sermon to representative voices. The preacher needs to respect the pluralism of the tradition and may need to help the congregation wrestle with which viewpoints are more or less authoritative today.

Reason is both medium and source. It is always operative in considering how the Bible, tradition, and experience work together in helping us come to the knowledge of God. Logic can also sometimes help us conclude what we can and cannot believe.

Experience is the full range of thought, feeling, and behavior through which the pastor and people encounter the subject of the sermon, including both rational and transrational elements. Like reason, it is both a medium through which we come to the knowledge of God and a source for the knowledge of God. The preacher helps the congregation name ways in which experience interacts with the subject of the sermon.[2] Experience is ambiguous. It contains elements that reveal the divine presence and purposes. It also contains elements that frustrate our perception of that presence. Therefore, when turning to experience, the preacher needs to have norms by which to gauge those aspects of experience that point us to God and those that do not.[3]

The quadrilateral is precise and comprehensive in identifying the sources of the knowledge of God on a particular subject. It is especially suited to doctrinal preaching (as in the sermon that follows). Its block-by-block approach helps the congregation recognize the particular contributions of each source. Of course, the preacher must not overwhelm the community with the many perspectives that turn up in the various sources. The categories (scripture, tradition, experience, reason) are sometimes arbitrary.

RONALD J. ALLEN is editor of *Patterns of Preaching* and the author of its companion volume, *Interpreting the Gospel: An Introduction to Preaching* (St. Louis: Chalice Press, 1998), as well as more than a dozen other books

---

[2] Wesleyans often refer to experience as specifically religious experience. However, I use the term the to refer to general experience as a theological source.

[3] In *Interpreting the Gospel: An Introduction to Preaching* (St. Louis: Chalice Press, 1998), I suggest three such norms: appropriateness to the gospel, credibility, and moral plausibility. These norms are also discussed in the books cited in note 1 (page 1).

on preaching and ministry. This topical sermon interprets the breaking of the loaf in the Christian Church (Disciples of Christ). The elders and deacons, to whom the preacher refers, are lay leaders in the congregation.

RONALD J. ALLEN

The Breaking of the Loaf: God's Every Sunday Assurance

(Beginning) Our church gathers for the breaking of the loaf every Sunday. The elders stand behind the Table. The deacons line up along each side of it. The elders pray over the elements. Those prayers are usually short and simple, but they often resonate with depth. The deacons carry the trays with the bread and the cup into the community.

This meal is a little strange. We tear a piece of bread about the size of your thumb from the loaf. We drink a cup of room temperature grape juice that is about the size of a thimble. We sometimes call these two tiny pieces of food the Lord's supper. But how can you have supper at 10 o'clock in the morning? Some of our congregations don't eat real bread. They use wafers about the consistency of cardboard. One of my friends calls them "fish food." Not exactly a real meal deal. Yet, this meal is the central act of worship. For many of us, it is one of the most important acts of the week. How can this be?

(Statement of the Direction of the Sermon) This morning, I want to think with you about the breaking of the loaf. What are its roots in the Bible? How did our ancestors understand it? How does it help us?

(Bible) The story of the breaking of the loaf in the Bible begins with the ways in which people understood meals in Israel. Meals were symbolic. Eating together represented commitment to one another. Food was scarce. To share your food with another person was to say, "Your life is so important to me that I share with you this food that is necessary for my own life." Eating together was also a part of sealing a covenant. Sharing a meal while making or renewing a covenant was a symbol of making a promise to one another.

This symbolism goes a step further in bespeaking relationship with God. Special meals remind the community of God's promises to the community and the community's promises to God. The act of eating and drinking on a sacred occasion helps the congregation realize God's presence. A sacred meal brings the power of past and future events into the present. The Passover meal, for example, prompts Jewish people to see themselves as those whom God delivered. "*We* were Pharaoh's slaves in Egypt, and the Lord our God, brought *us* forth from there with a mighty hand and an outstretched arm."[4] A meal can also anticipate a future event.

These associations are the background of the references to this meal in the Second Testament. Different writers emphasize different qualities. To over-simplify, the stories of the Last Supper emphasize Jesus' promises to keep covenant with the church. John emphasizes Jesus' presence. "I *am* the bread of life" (John 6:35). For Paul, participation in this meal anticipates Jesus' second coming. "For as often as you eat this bread and drink the cup, you proclaim the Lord's death until he comes" (1 Corinthians 11:26).

The early churches used different elements in order to partake. Bread and cup became the norm. But some communities used fish and bread. In the feeding of the 4,000 and the 5,000, we hear that Jesus *took* bread, *blessed, broke,* and *gave* it. That's the technical language that is a part of this meal. Luke's church may have used bread only—"the breaking of bread." Yes, the cup is missing in some ancient manuscripts of Luke's story of the Last Supper.

The roots of our understanding of participating in the loaf and the cup are in the Bible. But no single text in either testament expresses all the dimensions of the Jewish tradition or of the breaking of the loaf as we think of it and experience it today.

(Tradition) After the Bible was written, there developed a spectrum of interpretation of this meal. At one end, the Roman Catholic tradition says that transubstantiation takes place. The bread and the cup become the body and blood of Jesus. Lutherans teach consubstantiation. While the loaf and the cup do not cease to be bread and drink, they change in the same way that a metal poker changes when it is left in a hot fire and turns from cold and black to hot and red. Episcopalians speak of the real pres-ence of Christ. Moving toward the other end of the spectrum some Chris-tians think of the meal as only a sign that points us to Christ. A few Christian communities do not observe this rite.

Our church draws the inspiration for our understanding of the meal from the Reformed tradition—located midway on the spectrum of in-terpretation. John Calvin, a preeminent Reformed voice, taught that God uses the bread and the cup to assure us of God's love. The bread and the cup remain bread and cup. But through the acts of eating and drinking,

---

[4] *The Passover Haggadah with English Translation, Introduction, and Commentary*, ed. by Nahum Glatzer (New York: Schocken Books, 1969), 23. Preacher's emphasis.

Christ becomes present and communicates the divine promises to us.[5] The bread and the cup are outward and visible signs of inward and spiritual grace.

Our ancestor Alexander Campbell follows Calvin. Campbell did not want to refer to this act as a sacrament, because our word "sacrament" comes from a Latin term (*sacramentum*) that denoted an oath taken by a Roman soldier. To speak of sacrament would emphasize *our* responsibility and would downplay *God's* initiative. Some churches speak of "eucharist" because one of the central words in this meal in the Greek text of the Last Supper is *eucharisteo*, "I give thanks." Again, this term emphasizes our role (*we* give thanks) whereas the emphasis of the Bible is on Christ's action for us. Others speak of "communion." However, communion can take many forms, for example, singing. Campbell is warmer toward the title Lord's supper (1 Corinthians 11:20) because it shows that Christ is the host. But, the church can partake in such a way that the meal is not the *Lord's* supper.[6]

Campbell prefers the title "Breaking of the Loaf," a designation drawn from Acts (e.g., 2:42). Campbell includes both the breaking of the loaf and the pouring of the cup. He insisted that one loaf be on the Table, representing the one body of Christ. The loaf should be broken, showing forth the death of Christ. The death of Christ definitively demonstrates God's love for us. Hence, the breaking of the loaf is intended "to quicken us to God, and to diffuse [God's] love within us."[7] God uses the material elements of bread and cup to create an awareness of the divine presence in the community. "As bread and wine to the body, so it strengthens...faith and cheers [the] heart with the love of God."[8]

My colleague, Clark M. Williamson, a Disciple who teaches systematic theology, puts it this way. Immersion and the breaking of the loaf "confirm, proclaim, and seal the promise of God to be gracious." They are not the only means whereby God communicates divine love to us, "but they announce, show, and ratify what is given to us by the grace of God."[9]

---

[5] John Calvin, *Institutes of the Christian Religion*, ed. by John T. McNeill, tran. by Ford Lewis Battles (Philadelphia: Westminster Press, 1950), 14.17.1–10, 1359–1371.

[6] Alexander Campbell, *The Christian System* (St. Louis: John Burns Publisher, 1866), 307–309. I an indebted to D. Newell Williams for this interpretation of Campbell.

[7] Ibid., 311.

[8] Alexander Campbell, *The Christian Baptist* 3 (1834): 176–77, cited in Richard L. Harrison, Jr., "Early Disciples Sacramental Theology: Catholic, Reformed, Free," in *Classic Themes of Disciples Theology*, ed. by Kenneth Lawrence (Fort Worth: Texas Christian University Press, 1986), 75.

[9] Clark M. Williamson, "The Lord's Supper: A Systematic Theological View," *Encounter* 50 (1989): 57.

(Reason) This understanding of the loaf and the cup makes sense. The bread remains bread. The cup remains the cup. But God uses them to communicate with us analogously to the ways in which we communicate with one another with a hug.

It is also consistent with what we most deeply believe about God. "Grace is what God is....Grace is not one attribute of God among others...Rather, it is God acting out of God's deepest being."[10] The breaking of the loaf re-presents God's grace to us.

Members of our church say that the breaking of the loaf functions as such an assurance. When my spouse and I were co-pastors of a congregation in Nebraska, we called on a woman who said, "When we come to the Table, I get a full feeling. When I'm sitting in the pew, it's like God is beside me." She had come into our congregation from another denomination that does not keep the feast each week. She said they do not to partake weekly because they think it would not mean as much to them if they take it too often. "But," she says, "I have found just the reverse to be true. Receiving the bread and the cup every week deepens my appreciation."

I once insensitively declared that worship without the breaking of the loaf is like taking a shower without turning on the water.

We do not always *feel* God in our hearts when the loaf is broken. Sometimes *we* are broken. Sometimes we are alienated from others. Sometimes we come to worship with enervating questions about God. Sometimes we doubt God.

When I was a child in a Disciples congregation, our pastor said, "Our faith in God is based on facts not on feelings." I did not know then that our pastor spoke firmly in the Disciples tradition. By "fact," we mean God's action in our behalf. Our faith is not based on our feelings about God. Feelings come and go. Feelings can be deceptive as well as revealing. Our faith is based on the confidence that God acts *for* us in Christ. When we do not feel God with us at the Lord's table, the breaking of the loaf re-presents God's "facts."

Partaking of the loaf and cup does not magically solve problems. It assures us of our ongoing relationship with God, who rejoices with us in good times and who suffers with us in bad times. Eating together calls to mind and heart that God is with us.

A parent troubled by a strong-willed child comes to the Table distraught over that child's life choices. An employer told someone, "You've done a great job, but we don't want you any longer." The memory of the

---

[10] Ibid.

physician's words drown almost every other word. "I'm sorry. We can do nothing more." At such times, the bread and the cup assure you that God is for you, even though you may not feel God's presence at the moment.

The Table is not the only place we encounter God. God is present in every circumstance, in every breath. But this meal is a focal moment that helps us recognize God's presence in all times and places. A walk on the beach at sunset. A passage of poetry that runs like electricity through you. Confrontation with agents of injustice. All of these can reveal God. But, the breaking of the loaf is God's every Sunday assurance.

(Experience) This way of understanding deepens our experience at the Table. Our experience at the Table confirms and enlarges our understanding.

I was once a guest preacher at a congregation in conflict. Their cathedral-like building was located in a downtown area. The membership was dwindling. They were conflicted over whether to move to the suburbs. They fought over how to spend limited funds. Whose favorite ministry would be cut? At the most negative point of a board meeting, one member shouted at another, "Drop dead."

The leader of one faction, an older woman who looked like Lillian Gish, was an elder. And the leader of another faction, a red-faced man, was a deacon. On the day I was there, these two served at the Lord's table. He was the lead deacon and stood beside her. You could feel the tension at that corner of the Table.

So Lillian Gish prays. She picks up the tray holding the bread. But before she gives it to Big Red she gives him a little touch on the arm. Then she speaks the words of institution. "Take, eat. This is my body, broken for you." She serves him the bread. Before she can move to serve the next deacon, he gives her a little touch.

Not a word passed between them. But what happened at the Table was an assurance that, despite the pain of their situation, they are claimed by a power greater than themselves, a power who transcends their differences.

(Ending) The breaking of the loaf is God's touch for you, for me, for our church. When our lives are positive and full, this sacred meal assures us that all our blessings come from God. When we are in the midst of struggle, the breaking of the loaf is an every Sunday assurance that the living God is here for us. Come, for all is ready.

9

Simple Inductive Preaching

For many years, textbooks on preaching have discussed inductive preaching. However, since the early 1970s, inductivity has moved to the high altar of discussion about preaching. Indeed, most contemporary approaches to preaching have inductive qualities. However, because most of the patterns for the sermon generated by today's church give particular nuancing to their inductive characteristics, this book includes a simple inductive sermon.

As noted in the Introduction, the inductive sermon does not come to the major point or conclusion until the latter moments of the homily. The message begins with ideas, issues, or situations that need to be interpreted from the standpoint of the gospel. The preacher then gathers and evaluates resources that help the community understand the biblical text, situation, or issue that is the focal point of the sermon. These resources may be from the Bible, from historical and systematic theology, from the human and natural sciences, from the arts, and from other arenas.

The inductive sermon creates tension: the congregation recognizes unresolved qualities in understanding a biblical text, doctrine, practice, or situation and seeks to know how those tensions can be resolved. Inductive preaching is itself an experience of discovery. In this respect, inductive movement reflects the movement of many human experiences.

Inductive preaching is especially useful when a congregation initially finds a text or topic to be dull. Inductive tension creates interest that helps the congregation want to be involved in the sermon. Inductive preaching can particularly help the listening environment when the congregation disagrees with the viewpoint of the sermon, or when the sermon needs to help the congregation alter its interpretation of a text or topic. The inductive preacher does not inflame the congregation by speaking at the beginning of the sermon a perspective with which the community is in fundamental disagreement.

In the sermon below, L. Susan Bond takes an inductive approach to one of the texts for the first Sunday after Epiphany in Year A in the Revised Common Lectionary. The sermon begins by noting tension between Isaiah's call to the community to "arise and shine," and the fact that many people today feel overwhelmed by what they are already doing. Isaiah calls the community to shine a light in the world, but the world is so dim and foreboding. The preacher then helps the contemporary congregation identify with the people of Isaiah's day. They, too, felt overwhelmed and frightened. However, we need to look again at the character of what God asks us to rise and do. God asks us to witness to a world that is a renewed community. Fear, anxiety, and separation are replaced with hope, security, and mutuality. Toward the end of the sermon, the preacher describes a congregation in which this vision is already coming to life. That image offers the congregation an experience of the new world. That experience gives us the strength to rise, and shine, and to want to give ourselves to the work of helping God build this community.

L. SUSAN BOND is assistant professor of homiletics and liturgics at the Divinity School, Vanderbilt University, Nashville, Tennessee. She is the author of several articles and chapters in books. Her significant discussion of issues related to preaching Jesus Christ raised by and in feminist theology, *Trouble with Jesus: Women, Christology and Preaching*, is being published by Chalice Press in 1999. She is editing a volume of sermons by Gardner Taylor for the Chalice Library of Contemporary Preaching.

L. SUSAN BOND

Coming Home

Isaiah 60:1–6

Well, here we are, just cleaning up the mess from Christmas, and ready to get on with life at a more normal pace, and we get this call to rise and shine. Rise and shine. The phrase reminds me of a story about a girl whose father, a regular early-riser, would peek his head in her bedroom door and call out, "Rise and shine." The girl would pull the covers even closer around her ears and mutter, "I will rise, but I sure ain't gonna shine!" The call of the prophet to rise and shine doesn't immediately inspire us. We may rise up for the day, but we're not sure we want to put on a shiny face to do it. We don't want to be summoned for another job.

Here's the first problem. We're busy now. There's just too much work to do already. Like a kid who's been waiting for the weekend stretched out ahead, we don't want to fill our hours with work. Hey, Isaiah! Can't we just relax and take it easy? God, we're only human.

Maybe that's the whole idea. We're only human. We resist this constant urge to work and get busy. We're already worn out and fragmented by our daily lives. Pastoral counselors use the phrase "emotional homelessness" to describe our feelings of being alienated or cut off from things. We are psychologically disenfranchised and without a sense of belonging. We are in exile. Part of the reality that we call "postmodern" includes suffering from a sense of discontinuity and rootlessness. We are a nation that tries to escape more demands. We drink more alcohol than we should. We pop more pills and stick more needles in our arms than almost anybody else. Booze and drugs, symptoms of our alienation, are faulty attempts to fill the emptiness or to at least numb it. Children want a safe haven. Parents want someone else to fix things. We are only human, and we feel stretched beyond our limits. We don't want to take on one more mandate.

We come to church to escape the problems of the world. We've had enough of trouble. Every day we see news reports of disaster. Television is full of reports that scare us to death. The TV tells us that our houses are full of toxic synthetics, and our food is pumped full of pesticides. On the evening news we hear stories of children gunned down in the hallways of public schools. We're already convinced that the world is in trouble, but we feel helpless to change things. We want church to be a safe place, a sanctuary in a falling-apart world.

Isaiah's people can identify with us. They are grabbed up and taken into exile in another land. They've been kidnapped by a foreign nation and taken to prison camps hundreds of miles away. They are far from home, and they can't get back. If you've ever traveled to another country or just to another part of this country, you know how they feel. They are in a nation of strangers. The street signs are all in another language, the money is different, the food is not what they know. They have no political power, so they don't have any hope of getting someone in office who will be sympathetic to their situation. The powers-that-be dictate every waking moment.

The children are learning strange ways and forgetting everything about their homeland. Like children everywhere, they react by trying to make their own communities. They just want to hang out with other kids. They play in alleyways and back streets. They make fun of their parents and their old-fashioned ideas. But even underneath their youthful recklessness, they know things are not quite right. They just wish someone would protect them and take care of them. Maybe they're looking for a place to belong. Their folks are tired and grumpy, too caught up in the Babylonian rat race to pay attention to the things that worry kids. The teenagers must be terrified. They are old enough to realize that their folks are not in charge. The terrifying thing about growing up is realizing that adults don't have things under control. Their folks can't really take care of them, can't protect them from the violence of everyday life.

Just the other day, one of the Isaiah kids was slapped in handcuffs and hauled off to the Babylonian juvenile detention center. Who knows what she was doing. Maybe she'd skipped out of school and was hanging around on the street corner smoking cigarettes. Or, maybe she had a knife in her backpack because, well, life is dangerous in Babylon. All she wanted was a little escape from the daily grind. She wanted to feel in control. Belong someplace. Now she's in a holding cell, fingerprinted and photographed, waiting for the judge to make a decision.

In Isaiah's world, everybody is on hold and hopeless. There's no safe place anymore. They're convinced that the world is in trouble, but they feel helpless to change things. They want a place where they can lock the doors and make the world go away. They don't want Isaiah giving them one more program or mission. They're only human. Stretched beyond their limits. They want a sanctuary, a safety zone in the midst of a falling-apart world. They've had enough of trouble. The world is covered with clouds and shadow.

Now, look at what God promises. God's promises are light to a world covered in midnight. Someone says that only from the deepest nighttime does God's promise make sense.[1] God promises a light that will break through the clouds, a glimmer of hope that will dawn on a people in exile. God set up Adam and Eve with a bridal shower of good things. Fertile land as far as the eye could see. Fruit hanging on every tree, animals of every kind, grain, and grapes. God's plan was to give humans a land of abundance. From creation to the New Jerusalem, the people of God hope for a real historical future that is brighter than the current situation.

---

[1] Douglas John Hall, in *Lighten Our Darkness: Toward an Indigenous Theology of the Cross* (Philadelphia: Westminster Press, 1976).

The physicality, the real embodiedness, the concreteness of the vision is critical, since it takes flesh and blood seriously. There is religious meaning in things like food production, farming, organization, and survival. Whether God promises a garden or a city, the divine promise is that Yahweh can use spirit and body, nature and history, politics and the future. Whether in the cities or in the farmlands, God's promise is an inheritance of sufficiency from one generation to another. Land, a territory, a safe place, a religious symbol of "actual earthly turf where people can be safe and secure, where meaning and well-being are enjoyed without pressure or coercion," and it also symbolizes "wholeness of joy and well-being characterized by social coherence and personal ease in prosperity, security and freedom."[2]

In the New Testament, we bump into the same notion in Jesus' teachings about the realm of God: a real place where we belong and can flourish. To have a place means that God hopes for our security and our well-being. Jesus talks about such a place. The realm of God is a new creation where the meek inherit the earth. When you are homeless and alienated, when you are far from home, when you are without a safe place, the idea of a homeland is good news.

Something should be bothering us along about now. All this gathering and homeland and family stuff sounds a little too much like a family reunion, a community of like-minded and blood-related folks. We think about the growing cliquishness of the world. For years now, Israel and Palestine have been fighting over the "homeland." People in Northern Ireland have been fighting a family feud in the streets of Belfast. Black and white Africans continue to mark out townships along racial boundaries. Even here, in the U.S.A., Californians are trying to keep the borders strong to prevent Mexicans from coming into the state. We have racial quotas. Polish Americans, Irish Americans, Italian Americans, Asian Americans. We have schools for boys only. National organizations for women. Colonists came to this country as a pilgrim people wandering in the wilderness to find a freedom home and within 200 years had built up their "sanctuary" into a world-ravaging death machine, wielding power over other countries. The possession of land and wealth or the idea of a "nation for us" can quickly become demonic.

But God's "nation" is not limited to one geographic, or ethnic, or religious, or racial group. God's holy nation is a gathering of all peoples, all nations, and backgrounds.

---

[2] Walter Brueggemann, *The Land* (Philadelphia: Fortress Press, 1977), 2.

The socio-political reality which Isaiah envisions is an earthly reality in which God is in charge, in which earthly rulers have been displaced by Yahweh. Isaiah proclaims a nation ruled by the divine mandate to form a community of justice and inclusion. The nation will be a place in which all the homeless and displaced gather in security, in which violence and destruction are things of the past. Isaiah's vision, like the other prophetic visions, includes provision for widows, orphans, and the impoverished. The vision is that of a just world, where, as verse 17 claims, peace will be the overseer and righteousness will be the taskmaster.[3] There will be neither absolute princes nor absolute paupers.

Isaiah calls for a human community of justice in which all the sons and daughters will be reunited, not just the biological or ethnic sons and daughters. If Adam and Eve are the original parents, then all humans are sons and daughters of Yahweh. "Your sons shall come from far away, and your daughters shall be carried on their nurses' arms." Isaiah's vision of a just world is what Jesus proclaimed when he began his preaching ministry, saying "I have come to proclaim good news! I have come to set the inmates free from the penitentiaries, to provide medical care for the disabled, to proclaim that this year is when God's salvage operation should commence." The good news is good news most particularly to those who have been left out, discarded, neglected, orphaned, and forgotten.

There's a church in a southern city where the displaced and the dispossessed gather every Sunday. The building is small and modest. The churchyard stretches toward poor and working-class neighborhoods and toward a public housing project. But on Sunday morning, folks from the suburbs and folks from the inner city gather on the lawn. Folks of every color, in every kind of dress. A woman from Africa stands in native dress, talking to a white gay couple and their newly adopted South American baby. A middle-aged single mother helps her adopted son struggle up the sidewalk on his walker. An elderly African American woman pushes a wheelchair bearing a Caucasian man. A young Asian woman walks hand-in-hand with her Euro-American boyfriend. A van drives up to unload work-release prisoners free for the day. As we approach the church yard, a young woman laughs with delight. "It looks like a halfway house!" she giggles.

---

[3] Verse 17 is not included in the lectionary passage, but should be included in the preacher's homiletical reflections. It, along with the preceding verse 16, impose serious conditions upon what kind of realm God ordains. Otherwise, we could fall into precisely the kind of triumphalism that Third Isaiah rejects.

Do you see Isaiah's vision? In the darkest hour, when all seems hope-less, there is hope. When our children are at risk, when our streets are not safe, when our daily lives are captive to strangers, God's new world still takes shape. God's people gather, from all corners of the world, to create a promised land of justice, a promised land of safety, an actual earthly turf where people can be safe and secure. Gathering together, they are the dawn of a new day, a light to other nations, a glory to the Lord. God takes on flesh and walks among us, life in the Dominion of Death. "Lift up your eyes and look around; they all gather together; they come to you; your sons shall come from far away; and your daughters shall be carried on their nurses' arms. Then you shall see and be radiant; your heart shall thrill and rejoice." Arise, shine; for your light has come.

PART 2
Contemporary Patterns

10

The Form of the Text Shapes the Form of the Sermon

An exciting development in recent preaching is to let the form (genre), movement, and function of a biblical passage inform the form, movement, and function of a sermon. Genre and meaning work together. The meaning of a text and its form do not exist in the same relationship as a candy bar and its wrapper, in which you can unwrap the candy bar and throw away the wrapper. The phenomenon of hearing a passage from the Bible is a part of the meaning of the passage.

When preparing a sermon so that the form and function of the text can shape the form and function of the message, the pastor must name the genre of the text, its literary and rhetorical qualities, and its intention. The preacher can then meditate on how the genre and its function could suggest a genre, qualities, and intention for the sermon.

This pattern works easily with narratives. For instance, the preacher could divide the passage into meaningful units. The sermon could begin with the setting of the passage, and then help us identify an analogous setting. The preacher turns to the first scene and how it relates to us; the second scene and how it relates to us, etc. This pattern also helps with non-narrative passages. The sermon might follow the logic of the text. For example, a sermon might follow the logic of Paul's reasoning in Romans 4.

Letting the form of the text shape the form of the sermon is more challenging with shorter texts. In these cases, the preacher might develop a sermon that honors the function of the text and incorporates literary features of the text, without corresponding to the structure of the text in a one-to-one fashion. Alyce McKenzie takes this approach in the sermon below. In preparing the sermon, she noted that the proverb (v. 10) at the heart of Matthew 15:1–20 is a paradoxical proverb meant to undercut the way we habitually look at things. Conventional wisdom, whether biblical or contemporary, usually pairs good behavior with good results. "A penny saved is a penny earned." "The righteous will flourish like green leaves" (Proverbs 11:28b). Conventional wisdom usually pairs foolish behavior with ruinous results, as in the contemporary proverb coined by computer operators "Garbage in, garbage out." But Jesus' proverbs at times pair something we would normally view as good with ruinous results. "Those who want to save their life will lose it" (Mark 8:35a). He pairs what we would view as negative with positive results. "Those who lose their life for my sake, and for the sake of the gospel, will save it" (Mark 8:35b). The proverb at the center of Matthew 15:1–20 is intended to shake up our conventional worldview and point us toward new but faithful attitudes and actions. The sermon functions in the community analogously to the function of the proverb in the text.

ALYCE McKENZIE is assistant professor of preaching at Perkins School of Theology, Southern Methodist University, Dallas, Texas. She is the author of *Preaching Proverbs: Wisdom for the Pulpit* (Louisville: Westminster John Knox Press, 1996). She contributes frequently to *Word and Witness* and to other resources for preaching.

ALYCE McKENZIE

Pure Heart, Loving Words

Matthew 15:1–20

In the movie *As Good As It Gets,* actor Jack Nicholson plays an obsessive-compulsive author named Melvin Udall. He lives alone in an exclusive New York City apartment, and he is busy. Several hours a day he writes about love and romance. He also spends quite a bit of time making sure he doesn't step on the cracks in the New York City sidewalks. Another of his favorite pastimes is insulting everyone with whom he comes in contact and fouling the air with his prejudices—against his gay neighbor or the Jewish patrons of his favorite restaurant who dare to sit at his favorite table. When anyone tries to have a conversation with him, he proves to be the world's poorest listener.

Oh, and there's one other pastime for the busy Mr. Udall: his daily handwashing ritual. He opens his medicine chest, and there are row upon row of gleaming amber bars of antiseptic soap wrapped in cellophane, never before touched by human hands. During his daily handwashing ritual, he goes through several bars of soap. He swipes each bar only once across his palms before discarding it and unwrapping another.

Jesus reminds the Mr. Udall in us all that "it is not what goes into the mouth that defiles a person, but it is what comes out of the mouth that defiles." The plot of this movie can be summed up as Mr. Udall gradually living into the truth of this pithy saying of Jesus.

Jesus offers us this proverb for the same purpose that he offered it to his first-century listeners. He handed it to them like a small glowing candle with which to illumine their darkness. He invites us to look out over the expanse of our culture, our church community, our personal lives to see if there are any situations that stand in need of its pithy but powerful challenge.

I have a friend Laurel who is Jewish. She grew up in Trenton, New Jersey. She began her freshman year at Penn State University in State College, Pennsylvania. She had moved her things into the dorm and met several other women. One of her favorite new friends was a girl named Debbie who had grown up in a rural town in central Pennsylvania. One day in the lunchline, Debbie said to Laurel, "Did you know that there are some Jewish girls in our dorm?" Laurel said in pretend surprise, "Really?" "Yes," said Debbie. "I'm kind of glad I didn't get one as a roommate. I never saw one before. I wonder what they look like?" Laurel said, "I'll bet you'd be surprised."

A decade ago, a mother moved her eight-year-old son from Maine to Florida, hoping the warmth would help him feel better. He had HIV/AIDS from a contaminated blood transfusion. Parents in the new neighborhood protested the boy's enrollment in the elementary school with placards, letters, and threatening phone calls. The woman began packing for Maine. "I'd rather brave the Maine winter than the hot Florida hatred!"

A mother, obsessed with her weight and appearance, weighs every morsel that she puts in her mouth, monitoring her fat intake to less than 10 percent of her daily caloric intake. She is outraged that her daughter just entering puberty, is not the willowy creature she would like her to be and continually berates her with the nickname Big Bertha.

When I was a child growing up my brothers and I would get into fights when one of us thought we'd been wronged by another. Someone had cheated us at cards or four-square; someone had borrowed someone else's stilts without asking, or had committed some other offense. What began as a truth crusade deteriorated into an insult contest. Words such as "liar" and "cheater" gave way to things that can't be printed. My mother, walking through the room, would say, "Do you have any idea how you sound? I wish you could hear yourselves. I'm going to record this next time and play it back for you."

It's a funny thing about hurtful speech. Though we're the ones spewing it, we have trouble naming it for what it is. All the while, those around us are picking it up loud and clear! Defiling speech has a certain unmistakable tone, a certain smell.

Thank goodness my mother never made good on her threat and taped my brothers and me at our worst. But in moments of painful self-evaluation, we all remember hurtful words with which we have defiled others. In those moments we wish the childhood saying had been true: "Sticks and stones may break my bones, but words can never hurt me." We wish we could eat the words that it is too late to take back.

Instead, the walls of our homes have words ricocheting off them: some loving, but a lot hateful. And those hateful ones are the ones we regret. If the walls of this church could talk they would remember some hateful words mingled in with the loving ones. The walls of scripture *can* talk, and here are some of their memories of defiling words.

"Am I my brother's keeper?" asks Cain (Genesis 4:9). "Sell me your birthright and you can have some stew," says Jacob to Esau (Genesis 25:31). "Here comes this dreamer. Come now, let us kill him and throw him into one of the pits; then we shall say that a wild animal has devoured him, and we shall see what will become of his dreams," say Joseph's brothers (Genesis 37:19–20). Jephthah rashly promises God, "If you will give the Ammonites into my hand, I will offer up as a burnt offering whoever comes out of the doors of my house to meet me when I come home victorious" (Judges 11:30–31). "If you are the Son of God, command these stones to become loaves of bread," Satan says smoothly to Jesus (Matthew 4:3). "I do not know the man," swears Peter three times in the courtyard of the high priest (Matthew 26:69–75).

In our passage, Jesus insists that harmful words express evil intentions that lead to harmful deeds. Scripture bears him out with its catalogue of murderous, adulterous, false, and thieving words. "It is not what goes into the mouth that defiles, but it is what comes out of the mouth that defiles."

What we eat is processed through our bodies and eliminated. It goes to the sewer. There is a more complicated kind of waste management, one we often oversee poorly, with the result that lots of verbal sewage flows in our streets. What we say comes straight from our hearts. For Jesus' listeners the heart was not a faculty separate from the mind, but the seat of emotions, intellect, will, and spiritual life. Words come from the heart and head for the heart. If the heart is a poisoned well, it has great potential to defile.

Our heart's hurtful words and deeds can take away life, can ruin relationships, can kidnap hope, can twist the truth into a lie, can snuff out life. But a pure heart is a different story. "A person does not live by bread alone," Jesus corrects Satan, "but by every word that comes from the mouth of God"(Matthew 4:4). When we feast on the bread of life, Jesus our savior, our hearts are pure. And from a pure heart loving words come.

"Blessed are the pure in heart," says Jesus, "for they will see God" (Matthew 5:8). The Greek word *katharos* connotes clean—as in the clean linen shroud mentioned in Matthew 27:59. It connotes *pure* in the sense of unalloyed, as in the pure gold of Revelation 21:21. According to Psalm 24:4, access to God's presence during temple worship is for the one who has "clean hands and a pure heart." "Those who have clean hands and pure hearts, who do not lift up their souls to what is false, and do not swear deceitfully, they will receive blessing from the LORD, and vindication from the God of their salvation."

Clean hands by themselves are not enough. Cleanliness may be next to godliness but it makes a poor substitute! The pure in heart are those who are spiritually pure rather than ritually or ceremonially clean. Blessed are those who are innocent of moral failures (deeds) and of evil intentions. Jesus, centuries before the advent of annual health checkups, is recommending that we all get our hearts checked!

No one can achieve purity of heart without the help of God. The habits of judgmental gossip and subtle self-promotion are hard to break. But the pure in heart consistently, repeatedly, allow God to cleanse them of these corruptions. They allow God's light to shine in their hearts to give the light of the knowledge of God in the face of Jesus Christ (2 Corinthians 4:6). They are trees that, out of their goodness, bear good fruit (Matthew 12:33–37). Jesus promises us that the pure in heart shall see God (Matthew 5:8). That is, they will have fellowship with and knowledge of God in the reign that is to come.

The pure in heart recognize their need for God; they empathize with and extend comfort to others; daily they forgive those who wrong them. When our hearts are pure, our words are loving. When our hearts are pure and our words are loving, our deeds usually follow. When our words and deeds are loving, our lives have great power to heal and bring joy. We forgive, and, as Jesus did, we challenge injustice.

Listen to some purifying words from scripture. "I am your brother, Joseph, whom you sold into Egypt. And now do not be distressed, or angry with yourselves, because you sold me here; for God sent me before you to preserve life"(Genesis 45:4–5). "You are the Christ, the Son of the living God!" were Peter's words, before, and after, he denied Jesus. "Father, forgive them; for they do not know what they are doing" (Luke 23:34).

The flip side of Jesus' paradoxical proverb about defiling words is a positive insight about the power of purifying words. It is not what goes into the mouth that purifies a person, but it is what comes (from the heart) out of the mouth that purifies. That goes for both the sender and the receiver.

Remember my Jewish friend at Penn State whose new friend made such offensive comments to her, not knowing she was Jewish? Laurel decided that Debbie was not being malicious, but had just lead a sheltered life. And she let it go at that. When Debbie realized her mistake, she came to Laurel and apologized profusely. "I'm so embarrassed. I wouldn't blame you if you never wanted to talk to me again." Laurel replied, "I just figured this was beyond your experience, and once you learned more, you'd realize we're people just like you." Debbie said, "Thanks for the benefit of the doubt. Still friends?" Laurel nodded, smiling slightly. "But the next time you hear somebody else say something anti–Semitic, you're going to speak up, right?" Her new friend nodded vigorously.

I overheard a young father say to his toddler son in a grocery store checkout line, "I love you. I'm so glad I get to be your dad." As he tousled the toddler's hair and the boy smiled, a millimeter of the pain of the hurtful words I've spoken as a parent and heard other people speak slips away. I felt refreshed and a bit hopeful.

It was January, 1993. New Year's had come and gone. Morrie Schwartz, a retired sociology professor from Brandeis University knew this would be the last year of his life. He had been diagnosed with Lou Gehrig's disease several months before. He was using a wheelchair now and fighting time to say all the things he wanted to say to the people he loved. When a colleague at Brandeis died suddenly of a heart attack, Morrie went to his funeral. He came home depressed. "What a waste," he said. "All those people saying all those wonderful things and Irv never got to hear any of it."

Morrie had a better idea. He made some phone calls. He chose a date. And on a cold Sunday afternoon, he was joined by a small group of friends and family for a "living funeral." Morrie had always been a warm, loving, demonstrative man. And their comments reflected the way his love had thawed their hearts through the years. Each of them spoke and paid tribute to their parent, spouse, friend, cousin, sibling, professor. Some cried. Some laughed. One woman read a poem. "My dear and loving cousin, Your ageless heart as you move through time, layer on layer, reminds me of a tender sequoia."[1]

Morrie's experience raises a good question. Why wait to share the healing purity of our hearts with those around us? My life experience has taught me, among other things, that I should never pass on an insult and should always pass on a compliment. What am I waiting for? What goes into the mouth does not purify, but what comes out (of the heart) through the mouth is what purifies. There is a country song whose rueful refrain is "It's a little too late to do the right thing now." We could tamper with the words a bit and find in it a message for ourselves. "It's a little too late to say the right thing now." And that's true. We have each spewed our share of verbal garbage on the world, and our feet have teeth marks on them from spending too much time in our mouths. It's too late to eat the words others have already digested. It's too late to retract our harmful acts. But, as Scarlett O'Hara once said, after spending several hours of movie time spouting hurtful words, "Tomorrow is another day." There is something called a second chance. There's God's grace to forgive, and there will always be a fresh opportunity to take the high road with the people around us, both those we love without even trying and those we have to work to love.

"It is not what goes into the mouth that defiles, but it is what comes out. It is not what goes into the mouth that purifies, but it is what comes out of a pure heart that purifies." Most people get heart checkups and start watching what goes into their mouths. Jesus recommends that we check out our hearts and then start watching what comes out of them!

---

[1] Mitch Albom, *Tuesdays with Morrie* (New York: Doubleday, 1997), 12–13.

11

Four Pages of the Preacher

Paul Scott Wilson proposes that the preacher think of the sermon as a manuscript with four pages. Each page has a different theological and homiletical task. The motif of "page" is figurative. A page is a part of the sermon. A page usually comprises 20–25 percent of a sermon. Wilson discusses this approach to preaching primarily as a way of preaching from a biblical passage. However, it can be adapted to preaching from a doctrine, a Christian practice, or a personal or social situation.

Wilson mixes metaphors slightly to combine the notion of filmmaking with that of the four pages. Each sermon has one dominant image, and each page is much like a film clip that pictures the theological task of each page. The preacher "films" the central task of each page. A page may actually be a film clip, that is, the purpose of the page may be fulfilled by an image without accompanying analytical discourse.

Page 1 focuses on the biblical text or the topic. This page names the theological problem that gave rise to this text. The preacher describes the manifestation of sin in the world of the Bible for which the text is a response. Often the preacher summarizes the text and acquaints the congregation with aspects of the literary, historical, and theological context of the passage or topic that are necessary for understanding the sermon. In addition to discussing the trouble that generated the text, the preacher films this trouble.

Page 2 moves the action from the world of the Bible to our world. On this page, the preacher helps the congregation identify ways in which we experience difficulties that are analogous to those in the world of the biblical passage. How are we complicit in the sin that gave rise to the text? How do we experience brokenness in ways that are similar to those of the biblical community? The sermon films trouble in the contemporary world.

Page 3 shifts focus to the good news of God's presence and purposes. The theological purpose of this part of the sermon is to help us recognize how God's grace redeems the situation described in Pages 1 and 2. This page identifies God's action in the world of the Bible. The preacher identifies the good news at the center of the text. This page contains a film clip of grace in biblical community.

Page 4 returns to the contemporary world. The preacher helps the congregation recognize, experience, and respond to the good news of God's grace in today's world. How is God at work in our setting in ways that are similar to God's work in the biblical setting? This page films grace in today's community.

In addition, some sermons require a short beginning and ending. The beginning helps the congregation focus on the text or topic. The ending helps the congregation continue reflecting on the text or topic after the sermon concludes.

Most sermons unfold in the sequence just discussed. However, the preacher can arrange the pages in different sequences. For instance, Page 1 could focus on trouble in the Bible. Page 3 might then follow and could articulate the good news of the text. Page 2 could name trouble in our world, with Page 4 correlating the good news of the Bible with us.

In addition, Wilson envisions a practical relationship between sermon preparation and these pages. The preacher can prepare a certain page on a certain day. Monday: researching the text and planning the sermon. Tuesday: prepare Page 1. Wednesday: prepare Page 2. Thursday: prepare Page 3. Friday: prepare Page 4.

This pattern of preaching puts God's grace at the center of the sermon while looking sin in the eye. It can serve almost any occasion. The congregation should find it clear and easy to follow. It incorporates intellectual precision with evocative imagery so that it speaks to head, heard, and will.

Paul Scott Wilson preached this sermon in chapel at Emmanuel College during Lent, as the academic term was coming to a close. The preacher hopes to encourage students in preparation for ministry to name the fact that they sometimes feel that aspects of their ministries—and their studies—appear futile. Yet, Wilson hopes that the congregation will recognize that God's grace can transcend and even transform their service and their study. Indeed, actions that seem futile to them can mediate divine grace.

The preacher refers to "First Nations," a Canadian way of speaking of Native Americans.

PAUL SCOTT WILSON is professor of homiletics at Emmanuel College, University of Toronto, in Toronto, Canada. His complete discussion of this approach can be found in *The Four Pages of the Preacher* (Nashville: Abingdon Press, 1999). He is the author of the important textbook, *The Practice of Preaching* (Nashville: Abingdon Press, 1994), which is noted for its incorporation of literary and rhetorical criticism into the homiletical task, as well as *A Concise History of Preaching* (Nashville: Abingdon Press, 1992) and *Imagination of the Heart: New Understandings in Preaching* (Nashville: Abingdon Press, 1988). He is editor of *Word and Witness*, a journal containing materials to help with preaching from the Revised Common Lectionary. He is also editor of a series of books discussing the relationship of preaching to other theological disciplines, Preaching and Its Partners, to be published by Chalice Press beginning in the year 2000.

PAUL SCOTT WILSON

Futile Acts of Faith

John 12:1–8

(Page 1) Mary walked around the edge of her dining room. Martha was busy in the kitchen. Their brother Lazarus was here, reclining, eating with the guests, their legs radiating from the table like rays of the sun. At last, sure there was enough of everything, Mary paused to study the faces in the candlelight, Judas—now suspected of theft—Peter, James, the others, and Jesus. O the face of Jesus. The conversation continued but suddenly for her it stopped—it was as though it was winter again and a chill came over her, and she realized what was happening. The threats of the religious authorities when Jesus raised Lazarus, Judas breaking rank, Jesus' own words predicting his death: Jesus was approaching his death now.

She really had no plan when she bought the nard. In a scene that the Gospel of John never recorded, only a week ago she had been in the market in Jerusalem buying embalming myrrh and aloes for Lazarus. The merchant had shown her a beautiful alabaster box inlaid, with ivory, containing a pound of pure nard direct from India, brought by camel over a space of months. "It's what royalty use," the merchant laughed. "Costs a year's wage." When she smelled the seal, so beautiful was its fragrance that even in her grief she imagined she was on the green slopes of the

Himalayan mountains in India that he described. After Jesus raised Lazarus from the dead, she had been looking for some gift that would be appropriate thanks to Jesus. Her mind kept coming back to that alabaster box in the marketplace, fit for a king. Then she knew a cheaper gift would not do. She went to a neighbor and sold the field her father had left her then returned to Jerusalem and bought the nard from the surprised merchant. Then with the box clutched tightly in her bag, she rushed from the city and, outside the wall, she sat down, shocked at what she had just done. She did not even know when she would give it. She just knew she wanted Jesus to have it for his ministry.

But now, with Jesus actually present in her house, her gown brushing his feet each time she brought in food and drink, she realized how near his death might be. She brought the box. She might have been remiss: She did not go from guest to guest asking, "Excuse me, do you have any allergies?" But then, in the ancient manuscript of the New Testament that I read, it says that this was hypoallergenic nard. The others at first did not notice anything. In fact, the first they knew, the room was filled with the sweetest fragrance they had ever smelled, not a whiff, but a wave of scent so powerful and compelling that their ears began to boogie, their teeth began to sing, and those who were nearsighted became farsighted—just for a moment. Some said later it smelled like myrrh and frankincense, or flowers from mountain meadows, or orange blossoms and cinnamon with honey. Mary, in tears, was cupping the oil in her palm, spreading it on Jesus' feet and ankles as she would if he was actually dead, in the way that she had done so recently with Lazarus. Only Lazarus had been dead. Now, she did not count the cost—Judas was already frowning. She did not care what he or others thought or would say. And then she was reaching behind her head to let down her hair, biting her lip, and taking her hair and wiping off the extra oil, not caring that she was improper or what anyone thought. Her Jesus was dying. Her Jesus was dying. She would have given anything to save him.

(Page 2) Would that our own ministries could be so extravagant, so spontaneous, so beautiful, so memorable. Every time I think of doing an extravagant thing, like quitting my day job and going to Calcutta to work as a Sister of Mercy, I start thinking of why I shouldn't. That is one of the dangers of education, you start thinking too much. Gregory Baum, the Roman Catholic theologian, once said that he was glad that he had never studied psychology, for in analyzing his reasons for doing what he did, he might never have become a social activist. Some people did a survey some years ago in the United States. The surveyors asked alumni/ae to comment on their schools. The graduates of the best schools, like Yale, Harvard,

Cornell—Emmanuel College—were the most critical of their alma mater. At first this puzzled the people doing the survey until they realized that the alumni of the best schools were most critical because they had been taught to think critically by their schools. It is hard to be spontaneous and extravagant in one's love for Christ if you always have to think about it first.

One could wait one's whole life for exactly the right cause to which to dedicate one's life. Like the man visiting Toronto who kept waiting for a clean taxicab and never found it. In 1986, then moderator of our denomination, the Right Rev. Bob Smith, picked one main cause to highlight his term in office: an apology to the people of the First Nations for the hurt the church native residential schools caused. Some said it was a futile gesture, too little, too late. And maybe it was. But it made an important difference to some people. Then he helped start up the Healing Fund, dedicated to providing funds for First Nations projects to give concrete expression to that apology. Some said that it was a futile gesture, too little, too late. And maybe it is. But it is making an important difference to some people.

When we know this, why is Judas still in us looking on what others are doing and judging them negatively? Perhaps we are aware how little difference in this world we can make to the suffering of others—if you are like me at the end of this term, you are so tired you are not sure if you have anything to offer others. Or perhaps we are afraid to trust that God might make something of whatever small offerings of justice and kindness we can offer to others.

(Page 3) As the disciples lay at the table with Jesus, they must have been as surprised at Mary's action as Mary was herself. There was no mistaking the value of the perfume, apart from the alabaster and ivory box itself. If any of them had been near members of the royal court or attended a royal funeral, they would have smelled this before. And Mary was not measuring it in small amounts—when she was not ladling it with her cupped hands onto Jesus' feet, she was pouring it directly from a height above his feet. It was an extraordinary act of surprising beauty and exceptional dedication, futility and waste. Poor Judas was unable to join in the excess of the moment; he was after all, a treasurer, and treasurers are to be concerned about these sorts of things. If the other disciples in that moment were filled with the Holy Spirit as Mary herself was, they would have seen in Mary the picture of discipleship, giving to the world, giving as a servant, giving up all pride, giving out of love, getting nothing in return but the welfare of the other. Who but God could inspire such an extraordinary act of service? When Judas complained this perfume could have been sold for the price of a Cadillac and the money given to the

poor, Jesus merely responded, "Leave her alone." Jesus did not attack Judas for betrayal. Rather, Jesus blessed Mary. Because he was dying—his own death was at hand. "She bought this…for the day of my burial." Only the Holy Spirit could have told her that.

Judas' question is ours as well: How could such an extravagant gesture be justified? But before we go too far down that road, we might thank Judas. His is exactly the question we should be asking. If we ask how Mary's gesture could be justified, worth say $50,000, how much more should we ask it of Jesus' journey to the cross, for which Mary prepares? How could Jesus' extravagant gesture be justified? Jesus giving his life for the sake of all who seek to know God, dying for the likes of Judas and you and me. God places unlimited value on any human life. Mary knew that her gesture was not too great but too small. Her brother who was dead was alive. God places unlimited value on any human life. Jesus' going to Jerusalem, to the cross, to his death is such a stupid act—so extravagant, such a futile gesture. "Don't do it, Jesus," we shout again in Lent, "your ministry has only just begun. There is too much stupidity in this world. We will kill you." But he is going to Jerusalem to his death. And yet when we look to Christ on the cross we see what Mary anticipated Jesus giving to the world, giving as a servant, giving up all pride, giving out of love, getting nothing in return but the welfare of the other.

(Page 4) By the power of this futile gesture, this wasted life, this stupid deed, this extravagant act of love, you and I have been plucked from death, restored to life. For what purpose have we been plucked from death? Our purpose is also giving to the world, giving as a servant, giving up all pride, giving out of love, and getting nothing in return but the welfare of the other. As St. Paul says, "For we are the aroma of Christ to God among those who are being saved and among those who are perishing" (2 Corinthians 2:15); the Anointed One has anointed us with his perfume. We are the aroma of Christ.

So much in ministry seems futile. Sunday night. The youth group. So often it seems a futile gesture. Some weeks there are seventeen; other weeks there are six. Finding a time to speak of God or Christian ethics is never easy and rarely smooth. It's the embarrassed glances more than the stony silence. They seem to smell religion coming from a long way off. And you speak again of Jesus' love for all, for the Judas in us and the Mary in us. A futile gesture? A thirteen-year-old boy speaks out for the first time: "My daddy has cancer. My Mom says its going to be okay." And suddenly there was a sweet fragrance of perfume in the room.

So much of ministry seems futile. A person came in off the street, foul smelling, just prior to the service. The student minister was asked to escort the person out. The student was preaching that day on "do unto others...." The words of the sermon suddenly seemed futile. With some trepidation he looked into the sanctuary to discover that members of the congregation were already taking care of the person in appropriate ways—the chair of the session was seated talking with him. A woman was just leaving to make him a sandwich. Most moving, however, was a little seven-year-old girl who brought him a pair of socks—her daddy's socks.

And what about you? You are devoting all these years and all this money to education for ministry. You do not even know what will await you at the end. Just getting to the end of this term may seem impossible, a futile act writing useless papers. Is your act futile? It may seem so, especially when you are in the midst of it. And yet yours is an extravagant act, offering your life to God and your neighbor. It has the aroma of Christ and the power of God's love.

12

Sermon as Plot and Moves

David G. Buttrick conceives of the congregation as a community. The congregation is a not a collection of individuals, but is a body of persons who are related. The sermon as an event shared by the body and that is designed to form communal consciousness. Communal consciousness functions more slowly than individual consciousness and calls for certain ways of speaking that differ from the ways in which individuals talk with one another.

In this approach, the sermon is a plot composed of a series of elements called moves. By plot, Buttrick refers to the selection and sequencing of the various parts of the sermons so that they can work together to help the sermon achieve a particular intention. The plot is made up of moves—small segments of the sermon. A move lasts from three to four minutes. Consequently, a twenty-minute sermon would consist of a beginning, four to six moves, and an ending.

While the preacher creates a fresh plot for each sermon, Buttrick proposes three basic plots that form sermons. (a) A sermon may be in the "mode of immediacy." In this plot, the sermon follows one's immediate participation in the world of a biblical text, especially narratives. The sermon is made up of moves that follow the movement of the biblical text. However, the preacher does not simply retell the biblical story. The preacher explicitly helps the congregation relate the biblical and contemporary worlds. (b) A sermon may be in the "reflective mode." In this approach, the plot follows the movement of the preacher's reflection. The moves of

87

the sermon are moments of reflection on a passage. Some biblical passages (e.g., the letters of Paul) are themselves reflective and are especially suited to this mode. (c) In the "praxis mode," the preacher focuses not on a biblical text but on a topic. The plot is comprised of the steps of theological analysis needed to come to a Christian understanding of the situation. The preacher selects a plot for each sermon, and develops the moves for that plot in accord with the content of the text or the situation.

In the sermon below, Buttrick follows a plot of reflective consciousness. Move 1: The church in the United States today is in exile in a culture that is becoming increasingly secular. Move 2: Many in the church long for the church to be rejuvenated and for its exile to end. Move 3: The church, however, should regard the exilic situation as home. Move 4: Moreover, God is involved in creating the exile. Exile liberates us from idolatries and other false loyalties. Move 5: The church is called not to withdraw from the secular world, but to serve God in it.

Each move consists of the following parts. It begins with a **statement**, that is, a clear indication of the content of the sermon. The preacher must make this statement in two to four short, direct, sentences, each one making the same point, but in different words. The preacher then **develops** the statement by explaining it, usually in clear, analytical language. After the development, the preacher offers an **image** that pictures the point made in the move. The move ends with **closure**. Like the statement, the closure is made up of two to four short, direct sentences that make the same point. They summarize the point of the move.

Buttrick's approach can help the preacher and the congregation to interact with biblical texts as well as situations. The movement of the sermon has a contemporary feel to the congregation because the system of plot and moves is similar to the fast pace (with short segments) of television. This mood suggests that God and the gospel are contemporary. For preachers who are immobilized by wondering how to begin sermon preparation, Buttrick's three overarching plots provide a place to begin conceptualizing what kind of sermon to put together. Yet, a fresh set of moves must be developed for each new sermon. Buttrick's model thus provides the preacher with a way to approach the sermon that both provides beginning resources and calls for contextualization of the form of the sermon as well as the content. While I much appreciate the strengths of Buttrick's pattern, I am unconvinced that all sermons must be developed in this way, or they will fail to communicate. My anecdotal experience, coupled with reading in the plurality of human ways of knowing, leads me to think that human consciousness is more pluriform. Furthermore, this approach to preaching is not always well suited to texts, situations, and theological problems that do not lend themselves to analysis in moves of three to four minutes each. Some matters require old-fashioned logic, buttressed by historical, literary, theological, and ethical deliberation.

Buttrick preached this sermon at a Sunday morning service of worship in the chapel of Duke University. This chapel is unusual among college and university chapels in that it has a large Sunday congregation comprised of area residents as well as students and faculty. The passage from Jeremiah was assigned by the Revised Common Lectionary. Buttrick selected this focus because he noticed that the notion of "exile" is used by many these days to justify the church withdrawing from the world. Buttrick seeks to discourage withdrawal and to encourage the church to serve God in the midst of the world.

DAVID BUTTRICK is professor of homiletics and liturgics at The Divinity School, Vanderbilt University, Nashville, Tennessee. A collection of essays has been published in his honor: *Preaching as a Theological Task: World, Gospel, Scripture, in Honor of David G. Buttrick*, edited by Thomas G. Long and Edward Farley (Louisville: Westminster John Knox Press, 1996). His *A Captive Voice: The Liberation of Preaching* (Louisville: Westminster John Knox Press, 1994) is theologically provocative, as is his *The Mystery and the Passion: A Homiletic Reading of the Biblical Traditions* (Minneapolis: Fortress Press, 1992), and *Preaching Jesus Christ: An Exercise in Homiletic Theology.* Fortress Resources for Preaching (Philadelphia: Fortress Press, 1988). His *Homiletic: Moves and Structures* (Philadelphia: Fortress Press, 1987) develops the approach summarized in these paragraphs. Buttrick is the author of several other books and numerous articles.

DAVID G. BUTTRICK

A Letter to Exiles

Jeremiah 24:4–9, Romans 8:35–39

(Beginning) Some years ago *Life* magazine published a pathetic picture. The pictured showed an Arab prisoner of war standing behind barbed wire in a Middle Eastern prison camp. His clothes: a pair of shorts and battered canvas shoes. Around his neck on a chain was a large key, the key to a house in which he had once lived. He stood with his hands spread helplessly, as if saying, "How can I live here?" Well, nowadays the question seems to echo in our churches. "How can we live here?" "How can we live as displaced people in a secular land?" So listen to the prophet Jeremiah writing a letter to exiles. Listen, for perhaps he is writing the letter to us.

I.

(Statement) Exile:"Exile" does seem to be a metaphor for Christians in America these days. We live as exiles in a secular land. *(Development)* Oh, once upon a time America was settled by true believers—Puritans in New England and Catholics down in Spanish Florida. In between there were the Dutch Reformed in New York City, German pietists in eastern Pennsylvania, and aristocratic Anglicans sprawled all over the state of Virginia. But now, to borrow Stephen's Carter's phrase, we live in a "Culture of Disbelief." Church bells used to ring out on Sunday mornings; now we've got champagne brunch in city restaurants. Once upon a time your great grandfather measured his steps by *Pilgrim's Progress;* now we subscribe to *Psychology Today.* At the start of the twentieth century, atheists had to rally to defend their position, but subtly times have changed and nowadays anyone who believes in God must be ready to explain themselves. *(Image)* So Tony Kushner on Broadway pictures American religion as a crowd of old angels clutching a big Bible-sized book, wondering when and if God will come back to America any time soon. *(Closure)* Exile. "How can we live, Christian people in a secular land?" The question troubles us these days.

II.

(Statement) Well, listen to the voices all around; listen to voices in our churches. "How do we live?" There's no shortage of advice. *(Development)* Some Christians are still chasing the bright dream of religious revival. Every now and then *Time* magazine does a feature on baby-boomer faith and churches swoon! But somehow revival never seems to happen anymore—not even down South. Other Christians have joined a militant Christian Coalition to recapture the land from secularists by political power. Although you do wonder how an outfit that favors a fat defense budget, slashing welfare for the poor, wants prayer imposed in school rooms, is anti-feminist, gay-bashing, and eager for the death penalty can claim to be the voice of Jesus Christ anywhere? Of course, most churches are simply trying to hold onto themselves for dear life; these days, survival is the name of the game. *(Image)* Did you see that Doonesbury cartoon some months ago? It showed an almost empty Gothic church with two little old ladies in a front pew with a decrepit old gentleman behind them. And in the pulpit, a young priest with an arm raised up, saying, "Our day will come again!" We laugh but not too loudly because the promise does seem unlikely. *(Closure)* Exiled in our own land. How we can live for the Lord in an alien, secular world?

III.

(Statement) Jeremiah speaks. Jeremiah, the prophet, has a word for us. *(Development)* Listen: Build houses and settle down, plant your gardens and harvest them. Get wives, he writes; breed children, yes, grandchildren and great-grandchildren. For look, even in exile we are still in God's creation—a world filled with good things for human pleasure: Build your house, breed your young, feast on the harvest of earth. Notice you will not get Jeremiah to support Christian ghettos, even stained-glass ghettos on Church Street, U.S.A. For Jeremiah knows that everywhere, yes, even in exile, we live in God's good creation; human beings with human beings on the earth together. *(Image)* A new neighbor moved into our neighborhood recently. A corporate wife, she'd moved too many times in too few years. But she had a picture book with photos of all the houses she had lived in. In every picture there was a same old table and always a flower garden. "I move in my kitchen table," she explained, "and then I plant my garden." "Build and plant your fields and feast on the earth." So Jeremiah writes to the exiles. *(Closure)* Says Jeremiah to us twentieth-century Christian people, "Join the human world!" For everywhere and, yes, anywhere is God's good creation.

IV.

(Statement) Now stop and ask a question: What prompts his faith? How can Jeremiah be sure he's handing out the word of God? *(Development)* Did you hear how the letter is addressed: The Word of the Lord "to all the exiles whom *I* have exiled!" Did you hear? "To the exiles whom I, *God,* have exiled." We talk of the secular world as if it rose up separate from God. But no, somehow God has been involved all along shaping our exile. Was God delivering us from medieval church triumphalism? Perhaps. Or had God decreed that if we insisted on wandering from the divine will, we would end in confusion, the strange confusion of our unbelief? Maybe. But the secular world is still God's world, and incidentally a world God loves! *(Image)* So old Dr. Brown, an early-century Presbyterian leader, stood on a platform before the fledgling National Council of Churches, and shouted his faith: "I do believe," he exclaimed, "beneath the surface of things moves the mighty current of God's eternal purpose." For heaven's sake, secularism began with the Protestant Reformation. In mid-nineteenth century, it became an "ism." And secularism has spread, emptying churches all over Europe and now here in America. The secular world has been shaped by science, by industry and labor unions, universities and political parties, and yes, by churches. *(Closure)*

Nevertheless, somehow God has been involved in all. "To the exiles whom I have exiled." Listen, the secular world is still very much God's world.

V.

(Statement) So, guess what, we can serve God in a secular age. Our calling is to serve God here and now. *(Development)* "Seek the welfare of the city," sings Jeremiah, "Pray for the welfare of the land where you are." Listen, we are Christians who follow Jesus Christ. He lived human in a human world. He healed the sick. He spoke out boldly. As his disciples, we, too, must serve the worldly world, working for the common good. So you will not devote yourself full-time to a church school class, but you will also seek to serve school kids in poverty areas. God knows, we need smart schools for everybody's kids. And you will not become merely a church leader, for nowadays we must speak out in political places. America is having trouble pulling its political act together. The danger now is that we Christian people may clutch our Bibles and retreat into a safe, sweet, sheltered churchiness, pulling the covers of faith over our heads. No, we must speak the word of God to the world, the secular world in which we live. *(Image)* A few years ago there was a big book of pictures done by Sunday school kids. In the middle of the book was a centerfold, a big picture of stick-figure people in pairs bending down toward each other like waiters waiting on tables, all over the pages. Underneath in crayon letters was a caption: "Kingdom of God." Every pagan place is still within the kingdom of God and every moment a usefulness to neighbors. *(Closure)* "Work for the welfare of the city," sings old Jeremiah, "pray for the welfare of the land." Oracle of the Lord!

(Ending) So how do we live in a secular world, exiles in faith? We settle down yes, and breed our children and work for the welfare of all. And we feast—breaking bread, hoisting a cup—yes, feast as the family of God, trusting in the providence that, like a mighty moving current of God-love, surrounds our lives.

13

Preaching from Oops to Yeah

Eugene Lowry sagely notices that the sermon is an event that takes place in time. In events, things happen one after another. The things that happen influence one another. They work together to create a plot. Lowry, then, sees the sermon as a homiletical plot in which a sequence of events work together. As the congregation joins the progression of events, the congregation imaginatively moves from one perception of life to another.

Lowry sees tension as the chief element of the homiletical plot. The sermon begins with a question, an ambiguity, or an unsettled point that arrests the congregation's interest. The sermon helps the congregation move toward an adequate response to the question, a clarification of the ambiguity, or a settlement of the issue. The sermon begins with an itch. The sermon seeks to scratch the itch. Many contemporary sermons do not scratch where the congregation itches. Consequently, the congregation doesn't pay attention.

The homiletical plot has five moments. Each moment has its own function and its own memorable name. (1) *Oops: upsetting the equilibrium of the congregation.* The preacher introduces conflict. The pastor names the problem that is the focus of the sermon. It could be a question or difficulty that arises in connection with the Bible, or with some aspect of Christian practice, or as part of a situation where the congregation needs to feel the itch.

(2) *Ugh: the plot thickens.* The preacher explores the complication. This phase of the sermon is analytical. The preacher helps the congregation

think critically about the manifestations and causes of the situation that upsets the equilibrium of the congregation. What is wrong? Why is it wrong? The community goes "Ugh" as the reasons for the problem come into focus.

(3) *Aha: disclosing the clue to resolution.* A sudden shift appears. The sermon now reveals insights from the gospel that point to ways in which God's love and call for justice can resolve the tension and difficulties articulated earlier in the sermon. "Aha! We see a way forward."

(4) *Whee: experiencing the gospel.* The minister now expands on the clue to the resolution and applies it to the situation of the congregation. At its best, this part of the sermon contains an imaginative experience of the resolution to the tension through the gospel.

(5) *Yeah: anticipating the future.* This phase of the sermon is an unfolding. The preacher anticipates how the discovery of the sermon will affect the future. Community, empowered by the gospel, asks, "Yeah, what next?" The congregation wants to know how the resolution of the tension will affect the future of the congregational life and their life in the wider world. What can the church anticipate from God? What does the church need to do to live into the resolution? Each sermon, then, is an event that develops through time.

This homiletical plot encourages a church to name and analyze a disequilibrium that has taken place in the community. It can also help the preacher when the congregation needs to reconsider an aspect of its life that it had considered settled. The beginning of the sermon creates an itch that the congregation wants to scratch. The sermon urges the community to be alert to ways of understanding the gospel that are more faithful than their present assumptions. Of course, this model even with its permeating tension can become familiar if the preacher follows it every week. Further, some circumstances need less the new discovery of an "Aha" than the patient reassurance that what they believe and do is adequate to the gospel and to their situation.

EUGENE LOWRY is professor of preaching and communication at Saint Paul School of Theology, Kansas City, Missouri, and prepared this sermon when he was invited to fill the pulpit in a local congregation. His *The Sermon: Dancing on the Edge of Mystery* (Nashville: Abingdon Press, 1997) masterfully summarizes contemporary theories in preaching. His other major works include *Living with the Lectionary* (Nashville: Abingdon Press, 1992); *How to Preach a Parable: Designs for Narrative Sermons*. Abingdon Preacher's Library (Nashville: Abingdon Press, 1989); *Doing Time in the*

Pulpit: The Relationship Between Narrative and Preaching (Nashville: Abingdon Press, 1985), and his classic *The Homiletic Plot: The Sermon as Narrative Art Form* (Atlanta: John Knox Press, 1980).

EUGENE L. LOWRY

A Knowing Glimpse

Luke 24:13–35

(Oops) Sometimes, the most fascinating parts of a story may be the parts not said or key moments not shared. With this text, it may be a moment not given.

What I want to know is: What are these two friends of Jesus' doing on the road on the Easter Sunday afternoon anyway? Why are they heading away from the city? Are they going home to Emmaus? Certainly they landed in a familiar dwelling for the evening meal that night. But, all the action was happening in Jerusalem. The women had said the stone was rolled away, and the body was missing. They even claimed to have been confronted with two men in dazzling clothes alleging Jesus to be alive. "An idle tale," concluded the disciples when told the story. Impulsive Simon Peter ran to the tomb—of course—to see for himself. But these two friends seem, instead, to be running away—away from the action.

(Ugh) Could they be afraid that there might be new victims in this story? Or in confusion did they want to take a long walk? We don't know. I can't help wonder if *they* knew. For whatever reason, they are walking to Emmaus—Cleopas and another never named.

They are joined by this stranger. It is Jesus, but they don't know it. They do not recognize him at all. "What are you talking about?" he asks in feigned innocence—and they cannot believe this stranger to town hasn't heard the news of their slain friend, who they hoped might be the promised one. When I first read or heard this story, I found it inconceivable that they would not recognize Jesus. How could they not know it was he?

(Aha) But, I don't wonder anymore, primarily because of an experience I had twenty-five years ago. I was attending a birthday party in my honor at the home of some friends, the Samples. Peggy is a fine canvas artist. Unbeknown to me, she had painted my likeness as a clown and placed the painting above the mantle. They found several excuses for me to have to walk past that mantle during the course of the evening. I never did see the painting.

Eventually, her husband, Tex, asked me how I liked the new painting. I looked, and granted that I thought it a really nice painting—but had no clue whatsoever it was I in the painting. Now I might have recognized the sadness in the face, for I was walking through quite a valley in those days. Or just looked at the face. To this day, twenty-five years later, people always recognize the face. But I didn't. Somehow, I couldn't. Somehow it was beyond my capacity to believe that Peggy would have painted my likeness—so I didn't. I remember the face looking familiar. But it was just too much to perceive—to recognize.

Well, so it was for them. Too incredible, no matter what the women had reported earlier in the day. Way too much to imagine. And so they didn't, and, instead, proceeded to "instruct him" about the events of the last few days.

Finally, he took over the instructing role and filled them in on the significance of the week's events. Once they arrived in Emmaus and as an act of hospitality, they invited him to stay for supper and a night's rest. He moved ahead, as though he was going yet further, but they insisted he stay with them—even invited him to serve as host for the meal.

(Whee) So, he took the bread, blessed the bread, and shared the bread—clearly a sacramental meal, explains Fred Craddock.[1] And as the bread was broken so was the veil of their ignorance. They recognized it was Jesus. It was Jesus who had been walking with them, explaining the scriptures to them all along the road. And the moment they recognized who he was, he disappeared, vanished from their sight. Poof. Just like that.

Seems like divine humor to me. Just when we think we can get our hands on the holy—poof, it is gone, beyond our grasp. We should never imagine any capacity ever to survive more than a glimpse. Not here. Don't press it. Don't try to bottle it. Don't try to preserve it as a possession. That's the way it is, in what Rudolf Otto called the *mysterium tremendum*—that experience of the wholly other.[2] Those folks who speak so glibly of their ongoing relationship with the divine—well, I just don't trust it. If Moses was allowed to glimpse only the back side of Yahweh, why should we think greater capacity for ourselves? I know there are those who claim a nice little conversation with Jesus about a parking place at the mall. But I have my doubts.

Isn't it more a matter of *a knowing glimpse*—the kind of glimpse that takes the breath away? "Were not our hearts burning within us while he

---

[1] Fred B. Craddock, *Luke*. Interpretation (Louisville: John Knox Press, 1990), 286.

[2] Rudolf Otto, *The Idea of the Holy: An Inquiry into the Non-Rational Factor in the Idea of the Divine and Its Relation to the Rational*, second edition, trans. by John Harvey (London: Oxford University Press, 1950).

was talking to us?" they asked. Now, that's more like it—that momentary glimpse that grips the soul.

(Yeah) Well, I'll tell you, it gripped their bodies, too, and literally turned them around—one hundred eighty degrees. The text says that within the hour, "they got up and returned to Jerusalem." By this time, it must have been dark. They had to walk back to Jerusalem in the dark. Oh, no they didn't. Don't think it for a moment. It was during the day—as they walked toward Emmaus—that they walked in the dark. And now, at night, they started walking in the light.

That's the way it can be for us all. If any of us ever get a glimpse—you know, even just a fleeting, momentary, fragmentary glimpse—well, it'll turn you around! Yes, it will.

14

Moving from First Naiveté through Critical Reflection to Second Naiveté

Paul Ricoeur, one of the most influential hermeneutical theorists today, proposes a threefold movement by which the Christian community can engage biblical texts. This pattern can serve as the movement for a sermon. The three moments are first naiveté, critical reflection, and second naiveté. This pattern can also help the preacher and community interact with doctrines, practices, and situations.

In *first naiveté*, the preacher and the community visit the world of the text, doctrine, practice, or topic in a precritical way. The visitors assume it to be true. They do not question its picture of personal, social, and natural realms, its values, behaviors, feelings, ideas, or its portrayal of God, humankind, and the religious life. Preacher and community experience the world of the text on its own terms.

As its name implies, in **critical reflection** the preacher and the community think critically about the text, doctrine, practice, or situation. Do aspects of the text raise questions that we find difficult? Do we experience the world working in the way that it is described in the passage? Do the text's portrayals of God, the church, and the Christian life resonate with our deepest understandings of these things? The preacher compares and contrasts the worldview, values, and claims of the text with those of the contemporary setting. The contemporary community must sometimes critique the text. At other times, the text prompts today's church to rethink aspects of its understanding of God, the world, the Christian life. With respect to the Bible, critical reflection particularly helps the congregation understand how words, phrases, characters, and even whole passages function as symbols that interpret the divine presence and purposes.

In *second naiveté*, the pastor and the congregation return to the text informed by critical reflection but no longer distracted by the questions generated by critical reflection. Second naiveté is a constructive phase in which the preacher helps the congregation identify ways in which the text names the world. For instance, although a miracle story may not appear to be a factual account of an event that took place in just the way reported in the text, that story may help the congregation name ways in which God is at work in their community's world. The congregation is able to enter the world of the miracle story in the same way that it enters any story—recognizing that certain elements may not be factual, but that the story can nonetheless help the community interpret God's presence and purposes. In second naiveté, we can say that God heals.

This way of preaching is similar to many moments of discovery. We encounter something. We explore it and reflect on it. Then we figure out how to relate to it. In preaching, this approach is especially useful when the sermon deals with material in the Bible or in Christian tradition that seems foreign to today's world. It can also provide a good homiletical model when the sermon needs to encourage the congregation to challenge its understanding of a part of the Bible, a doctrine, a practice, or a situation. In such a sermon, the preacher and congregation can enter the world of the congregation's present understanding in first naiveté then reflect critically on that understanding which results in a way of reappropriating the motif in second naiveté.

In the sermon below, Pablo Jiménez takes this approach to the motif of partnership. In first naiveté, he reviews a traditional notion of the way in which partnership has been understood in the Christian community. In critical reflection, he questions this understanding as it has affected relationships between the powerful, especially from Euro-American society in the United States and those who are not so powerful, especially persons from other racial and ethnic communities. In second naiveté, the preacher returns to a notion of partnership now informed by biblical exegesis and theological reflection that can help the church become a community of diverse members in partnership in the gospel. The preacher uses the phrase "Campbell-Stone family" to refer to the Christian Church

(Disciples of Christ) because it is descended from movements spearheaded by Barton Stone and Thomas and Alexander Campbell.

> **PABLO JIMÉNEZ** is professor of preaching at the Episcopal Theological Seminary of the Southwest, Austin, Texas. He preached this sermon at a regional meeting of the Christian Church (Disciples of Christ) in Georgia. The purpose of the sermon is to encourage the church toward a "subversive partnership" of the kind described in the sermon. Professor Jiménez is the author of a number of books and articles in Spanish. His first book in English is *Pulpito* (Nashville: Abingdon Press, 1999).

PABLO A. JIMÉNEZ

Paul's Subversive Partnership

Philippians 1:1–6 (author's translation)

(First Naiveté) The letter of Paul to the Philippians is one of the most poignant documents in the New Testament. Written in and sent from prison, the epistle is the apostle's farewell. The letter was probably written from Rome as implied by the references to the "imperial guard" (Philippians 1:13) and the "emperor's household" (4:22). Paul did not survive this jail term.

The church at Philippi had learned of Paul's imprisonment, and its members were justifiably concerned. At the time, the Roman ruler was Nero, the fifth Emperor of Rome. Although during the first eight years of his government the Empire flourished—due mainly to the influence of the philosopher Seneca—Nero's conduct changed drastically after 62 C.E. He tended toward public brutality—using on occasion Christians as scapegoats. It is believed that both Peter and Paul lost their lives during his rule.

But Paul in this text is still alive and well, preaching the gospel of life even to his would-be assassins. He knows that his life is endangered, but he also knows that life is a mystery that dwells solely in God's hands: "For to me, living is Christ, and dying is a gain" (Philippians 1:21). That is why he even dares to joke about death asserting that he is "hard pressed" in choosing between living and dying: "I don't know what to do! I will be better off if I depart to be with Christ but you still need me. What to do? What to do? Well, don't worry. I am convinced that I will stay with you all a while longer" (compare with Philippians 1:21–25).

Evidently, Paul had an unique relationship with the Philippians. They had supported him in his missionary work (see Philippians 4.15–18). In their generosity they had outdone even wealthier churches, like the one in Corinth (1 Corinthians 9).Yes, they had a close relationship.You only joke about death with your loved ones.The Philippians were his "partners" in ministry (Philippians 1:5).

(Critical Reflection) "Partner" is a mighty strong term.A partner is a person with whom you share some of the most important aspects of your life. No matter whether these aspects be personal, professional, economic, or legal, a relationship implies close cooperation to achieve a given goal. "Partner" is a powerful concept. A partner is an associate, a colleague, a companion…an equal, if you will. There is fellowship, harmony, unity between partners. In a word, there is *koinonia*, that is, solidarity between people in partnership.Yes, "partner" is a mighty strong term.

Paul's relationship with the Philippians is certainly inspiring. So inspiring that I was tempted to expend the rest of my time with you extolling the virtues of partnership; encouraging each and every one of us to bask in the fellowship that the beautiful environment of this retreat center inspires; romanticizing this otherwise subversive story into a theological "Barney song": "I love you, you love me, we're a happy Campbell-Stone family." I almost fell into the trap…almost.

If a partner is an equal, a colleague, a companion, then partnership is dangerous, hazardous, precarious. A person that is in partnership with another recognizes the absolute humanity of his or her partner.

My partner is as human as I am. My partner has the same rights that I have. My partner has the same privileges, the same power.

A partnership is not a relationship defined by one party over the other. It leaves no place for control and domination of the weaker by the strongest. It has no room for the subordination of the powerless to the powerful. In a partnership there is no: top and bottom, center and margin, upper and lower, uptown and downtown, richer and poorer, high church and low church, white and non-white. A partnership is defined by the *koinonia*; by the solidarity of the people involved in the venture. This is what the apostle Paul emphasized in his "last will and testament." [Preacher reads Philippians 2:1–7.] These are powerful words.

The Prince of the Universe became a slave! This word has a chilling effect on me. My grandfather was a black man, the son of freed slaves who toiled in the southern part of the island of Puerto Rico. A slave! This word still has a chilling effect on this nation. Here we are in the state of Georgia a couple of hours from Macon, the former capital of the South. As you wander through its beautiful fields, please notice the cast iron landmarks that remind every inhabitant of Georgia that a bloody fight defiled this sacred land.The blood of thousands of women and men, young and old was shed in a fratricide conflict over the right of some to classify others into top and bottom, center and margin, upper and lower, up-town and downtown, richer and poorer, high church and low church, white and non-white. A battle we lost. A battle humanity lost.

(Second Naiveté) As early as the crib we learn that there are two kinds of people: "Us" and "Them." "Us people" are good. "Them people" are bad. "Us people" are right. "Them people" are wrong. "Us people" do not enter into partnership with "Them people." I learned it. You learned it, too.

Paul, "a Hebrew born of Hebrews" (Philippians 3:5), learned this lethal lesson early in his life. He learned that the Jewish people were the "Us" and that the *goyim*, the non-Jewish people were "Them." "Us people" do not enter into partnership with "Them people," was the motto that steered his life. Then the worst possible thing happened. Some of "Us" (Jewish people) began to preach a gospel that included "Them" (non-Jewish people) in a partnership with God. And Paul, guided by his exclusionary motto, began to persecute, to terrorize the traitors among "Us." Yet, the zealous young Phari-see found—or may we say was found (Galatians 4:9)—by Jesus on the way to Damascus. Paul had a conversion experience when he heard Jesus; the one who became a slave in order to make his fellow slaves into a community of priests, serving God forever and ever (Revelation 1:5b).

Therefore, what we find in Philippians is startling. A former "Us per-son" testifying that he lives in partnership with those he formerly thought as "Them people." Such partnership is subversive, because it joins former enemies in solidarity and affirms their common humanity.

Like Paul, we learned rather early our place in society. I learned that the United States was the greatest nation of all, and that white Anglo-Saxon Protestants were the best people in the whole wide world. I also learned that I was not a genuine "American" and—that no matter how much I strive to—I would never be one. I learned my place in the social power structure. I even learned that I was powerless in some settings and powerful in others. I still have to "unlearn" most of this. We all do.

We—church people—claim to be in partnership with each other. However, we must confess with much sadness that our relations are deter-mined more by our place in the social power structure than by the message of the gospel. I see it everyday. As you know by now, I work as executive director of an organization dedicated to promote and enhance the theo-logical education of Hispanics. And I am both saddened and infuriated each time that I see how denominations—both the long established ones and the pentecostal ones—reluctantly scratch a minimum budget to establish lay schools to license Latino preachers, while, at the same time, others are sent to seminary. The licensed preachers do not have the neces-sary training to climb the "corporate ladder." They will never be bishops, superintendents, regional ministers, heads of divisions, or general ministers and presidents. They will never be more than local pastors of small underdeveloped ethnic churches.

God is calling the Christian Church (Disciples of Christ) to mirror Paul's "subversive partnership" with the Philippians. I yearn to see all levels and constituencies of our denomination united in a sincere partnership.

I know that this can happen. A true story illustrates how. In 1933, a sad episode threatened to cloud the growth of the Christian Church (Disciples of Christ) in Puerto Rico. After three decades of missionary work, our church came of age. Most congregations had Puerto Rican pastors. People began to compose new hymns with local imagery. Guitars replaced the organ in worship. Local congregations became more charismatic.

Do you know what happened? The missionaries from the mainland were appalled. They could not understand why the churches that they had nurtured for so long had abandoned their teachings. On one occasion, they even obtained a restraining order to keep a congregation out of a church building. That night, the pastor broke into the church and kept a prayer vigil.

It took the missionaries almost two years to realize that Puerto Rican Disciples had not deserted the gospel. The Puerto Ricans were just seeking to be faithful to God in their language and in their own cultural context. When the missionaries came to that discovery, they again acted in partnership with the Puerto Ricans, and the church began to grow again.

The unity of the church is not based on cultural uniformity. In order to be in partnership in the gospel, we do not need to look alike, belong to the same social class, or speak the same language. We do not need to sing the same hymns, follow the same order of worship, or preach in the same style.

In fact, the partnership of persons who are different is precisely the subversive partnership of which the great apostle Paul speaks.

I long for the day when our practice of the faith will demonstrate that we affirm that every constituency of this church is as human as mine. Every constituency of this church has the same rights as mine. Every constituency of this church has the same privileges, the same power. We still have a lot to learn in order to achieve this kind of "subversive partnership." We also have a lot to "unlearn." To reach it, we even may have to find Jesus anew on the road to Damascus and convert.

15

Sermon as Movement of Images

Thomas H. Troeger proposes that a sermon can be a movement of images.[1] An image is a picture painted by the words of the sermon and its embodiment. Of course, thoughts and statements can have an important place in preaching. Nevertheless, the electronic media have acclimated many people in today's culture to processing the world and its meaning through images. Consequently, Troeger finds that a sermon itself could be a sequence of word-pictures in which the images communicate the meaning of the message. Because the congregation hears and sees the preacher, the image created in the sermon is multimedia. The sermon can engage the congregation on multiple levels.

When developing the sermon as a movement of images, the images flow from one to another with a minimum of explanation from the preacher. The preacher does not explain the images. The congregation enters into sights, sounds, touches, smells, tastes, and feelings of the image world. An image touches the congregation simultaneously at the levels of mind, heart, and will. When the community leaves the world of the image, they can perceive their everyday world from the perspective of the image world. The sermon also could be a single, extended image.

The movement of the images could be organized in a wide variety of ways. In the sermon below, Barbara K. Lundblad develops images in the

---

[1] Thomas H. Troeger, *Imagining a Sermon*. Abingdon Preacher's Library (Nashville: Abingdon Press, 1990), esp. 44–52.

order in which they are suggested by the biblical text. Indeed, the sermon is made up of the preacher's description of the narrative scenes of the passage. The images could follow the movement of time, e.g., in a human life (childhood, youth, young adulthood, middle age, golden years) or the history of a community. The images could be arranged by space, e.g., a Christian community in central Nebraska, one in Harlem, one in Russia, one in Paraguay, one in Zambia.

This approach to preaching works easily with texts or topics that have rich, sensory associations. In the sermon that follows, the preacher simply brings the imagery inherent in the text into the consciousness of the congregation. A preacher can also use this approach to help bring alive passages and ideas that are more propositional, abstract, or hard to grasp. The sermon describes the heart of the text, doctrine, or practice in an image. The congregation enters the image and experiences the world as shaped by the claim of the proposition or idea. The image paints a word-picture of the proposition or abstraction that touches the congregation in heart and feeling as well as in head and cognition. Sermons that move in images feel like the language of today to many people in the congregation. By developing imagery, the pastor is likely to honor the fullness of meaning in a text and not to reduce a rich, sensual text or practice to a pale statement or idea. The congregation experiences how they would feel, behave, and think in their everyday worlds if the world of the image reshaped their everyday world. Congregations that contain a large percentage of persons who have an affinity for the arts will especially appreciate this approach.

At the same time, Christians, whose thinking patterns are linear and propositional, may be somewhat frustrated by this type of preaching. They want to be able to state the point of the image in a proposition. They want to get "the lesson" of the text and the sermon. And I have heard an occasional sermon in this mode in which the sensory description was so vivid that it called attention to itself. Furthermore, this approach does not suit every occasion in congregational life. From time to time, a congregation needs hard, clear, critical reflection in propositional form.

Frequently, a pastor can combine the notion of the sermon as image with the sermon as critical thought. The preacher might create an image in the sermon and subsequently analyze the image. Or the preacher might develop a gospel claim arising from a text, a doctrine, a practice, or theological reflection on a topic, and then embody the claim in an image.

The sermon below was prepared for The Protestant Hour, a nationally syndicated service of worship carried on the radio. In the sermon, the preacher acknowledges a difficulty in radio preaching: She cannot see the congregation.

BARBARA K. LUNDBLAD is Joe R. Engle Professor of Preaching at Union Theological Seminary in New York City. She has been the Lutheran preacher on The Protestant Hour for many years. In addition to preaching and lecturing in congregations, seminaries, and clergy conferences throughout North America, she is a frequent contributor to resources for preaching.

BARBARA K. LUNDBLAD

Standing Still and Moving On

Luke 24:13–35

In a cupboard in my parent's house there is a treasure: a box of old 8mm movies recording our family history from the time when I was five and my sister was two and my brother was yet to be. Some of the films have been spliced together under a theme—such as "Christmas, 1950–1953." There I am with my sister singing something in silence in front of the Christmas tree, wearing our new red cowgirl hats. These movies are all silent, made before the days of camcorders with built-in mikes. Oh, there's my grandfather throwing ears of corn into the wagon—what a wondrous thing to see Grandpa moving, laughing, so fully alive years after he died. Even without sound, those moving pictures bring people to life as a still photograph cannot.

Yet, I also treasure the hundreds of snapshots stuffed into albums or still waiting inside old envelopes in the buffet drawers. Black and white photos tucked down at the corners, stacks of pictures still waiting to be organized. No sound, no movement, but you can sit and look at a picture for a long time. The photograph doesn't move: It stands still long enough for memory to fill in the story, to fix the date, to bring buried feelings back to the surface.

If you wanted to tell today's gospel story, would you tell it as a movie or in still photographs? Perhaps you'll say, "Neither" because you never liked Bible movies and it is dangerous to choose photographs that "look like Jesus." Let me ask the question another way: When you heard this gospel story read, were you most aware of moving or standing still? Do you remember *walking* on the road or *sitting* at the table? Are you arguing with me now — telling me the story isn't one or the other but both? (I wish we could be talking face to face, you and I!) You have every right to argue for both movement and stillness. Most of the story takes place on the road while three people are walking—it is a *movie*. But perhaps the most memorable scene takes place at the table, at that moment when the disciples' eyes were opened—it is a *photograph* of wounded hands breaking bread.

I'm not speaking only of artistic sensibilities here. This is a matter of faith and of revelation. How does Jesus Christ come to us? What does it mean for Jesus to stay with us? Was Jesus only for one moment, or is Jesus with us now on the journey? Such questions are of pressing importance for Luke, the author of this gospel. Today's story stands between the resurrection of Jesus and the mission of the church described in Luke's second book called Acts. This story comes between Easter and Pentecost. Which is where we are now, you and I. Does revelation come most powerfully in still photographs like the moment when Jesus broke the bread? Or does revelation depend on what happens in the walking and talking on the road?

The story has to begin as a movie. The text calls for it: "two of them were going"—walking, talking, discussing what had happened to them in recent days. Jesus (disguised somehow) came near and went with them. There has to be movement here—going, walking, talking, encountering the stranger who interrupts them with a question: "What are you discussing with each other while you walk along?" His words point to their movement.

Then suddenly everything stops. "They stood still, looking sad." It is no longer a movie, but a still photograph. Focus on their faces. Let their sadness sink into you. Take your time.

Cleopas speaks. The movie continues. They must have started walking again—for they will reach Emmaus (seven miles off) by the time the story ends. But we still hold the sad photo in our memories as they speak. In their sadness they tell the story of Jesus of Nazareth, a prophet mighty in word and deed who had been condemned to death. "But we had hoped that he was the one to redeem Israel."

Once more, the movement slows, perhaps to a full stop. "We had hoped…" How do you capture that hopelessness in a photograph? There is no future. Nothing ahead, everything behind. No dreams, only memories made bitter by too much loss. This must be a still picture. "But we had hoped…" You can see the photo, can't you? What would it look like in your own life? What have you hoped for? When did those hopes die? This photograph doesn't ever really go away.

Even as they move on, the hopelessness weighs heavy upon them: They had expectations that Jesus did not meet. Jesus of Nazareth failed them. So the next part of the story doesn't seem to make any difference to them: Some women from their group had gone to the tomb and found it empty. But that hadn't changed anything for these two—they left Jerusalem. (If you had heard that the tomb was empty, wouldn't you have gone to see it? Wouldn't you have stayed in the city to see if Jesus was alive?) Their hopelessness had no room for any good news. "Some of those who

were with us went to the tomb and found it just as the women had said;
but they did not see him."

"But they did not see him." Slow down now until we have come to
a complete stop. We know the stranger is Jesus (the narrator has let us in
on the secret). We know the two disciples are walking and talking with
Jesus. They have been telling Jesus about his life and death. "We had hoped
he was the one." They have made their decision: Jesus did not meet their
expectations. Now we must be absolutely still. Some women, then others,
found the tomb empty, "But they did not see him." Could a photograph
ever hold such irony? Two disciples stand looking at Jesus and say, "But
they did not see him." *They* did not see him. They couldn't: They had
already decided he could not be the one.

Who can say how long that moment lasted? "Then he said to them,
"Oh, how foolish you are, and how slow of heart to believe all that the
prophets have declared!" He, the stranger, the one they did not see, began
to teach. To interpret the scriptures, beginning with Moses and all the
prophets. They are walking again. How long, we cannot tell. (How long
would it take to interpret the scriptures?) If we were making a movie,
perhaps we would move behind the three of them now—watching the
two disciples as they turn, as they stay close to catch everything the stranger
says (though we can't overhear the actual words). Then, we see the stranger
is moving on ahead of them as though he means to keep going. But
something has happened to these disciples. Something has overtaken their
hopelessness. They cannot let him go (whoever he is). Now the narrator
slows the pace, repeating words and phrases:

"*Stay with us,*" they urged him strongly.

"So he went in to *stay with them.*"

"When he was at the table *with them,* he took bread, blessed
and broke it, and *gave it to them.*"

"And their eyes were opened and they recognized him; and he vanished from their sight." How can this moment be remembered? And which
moment should we remember most clearly? Was it when the stranger
broke and blessed the bread? Would that be the picture—wounded hands
breaking a loaf? Just the hands, no face (for Jesus' face they did not see).
Or does the important picture come later—when their eyes were opened
and he vanished? "Were not our hearts burning within us while he was
talking to us on the road, while he was opening the scriptures to us?"

Their eyes were opened. When? Is there one picture that will give the
answer? Was it when they sat at the table receiving broken bread? Or was
it when he was with them on the road opening the scriptures? You must
know by now, this is not really about movies or still photographs. It is a

story of faith and revelation, a story of remembrance and recognition. While we may long for a special moment of revelation, a datable time of being saved, a heightened experience of God's presence, this story from the first Easter day reminds us that faith is not so neatly captured in isolated moments. Would the disciples have recognized Jesus at the table if they hadn't heard him open the scriptures? Didn't revelation begin on the road, in the slow-walking journey?

These questions are not all past tense. Is something slowly happening to you in the prayer you stammer each morning on the way to work? in the weekly Bible study at your church that doesn't ever seem to bring great revelations?

Perhaps you know, too, that this is not just a story about two disciples on the road to Emmaus almost two thousand years ago. It is a story about two disciples: one was named Cleopas. And the other? The other is you. Or me. Luke left a blank space for us to fill in our name. All our hopelessness is there on the road, every broken dream, every doubt we've ever had or still have. "We had hoped he was the one." Are you waiting for a clearer revelation, for deeper assurance of Jesus' presence in your life? I would like that, too, and some days that assurance is as close as my own breathing. But not always. I know what Kathleen Norris means in her book *Dakota: A Spiritual Geography*, when she says, "Conversion means starting with who we are, not who we wish we were.... Conversion doesn't offer a form of knowledge that can be bought and sold, quantified, or neatly packaged. It is best learned slowly and in community."[2]

The journey of faith moves along frame by frame, most of the segments utterly ordinary. A few still photographs hold particular moments we might dare call revelation. Along the way we are sustained as they were: by hearing once again words of scripture we have heard before. Sometimes, it happens that our hearts are opened and we hear as though for the first time. Then, at a table or an altar, beside a hospital bed or in a nursing home, someone takes bread, blesses it, and breaks it. The one who takes a piece of bread is named Cleopas. The other? You know. God's peace be with you.

---

[2] Kathleen Norris, *Dakota: A Spiritual Geography* (New York: Ticknor and Fields, 1993), 131–132.

16

Sermon Drawing from the Arts

Preachers have long drawn upon the arts (especially novels, short stories, poems, plays, movies, songs) for illustrations in sermons. In recent years, some preachers have come to recognize that the arts can be more than illustrative. A work of art creates a world, a sphere of imaginative perception, into which a person or a community enters. The world of the work of art affects the human being as a *gestalt*; it touches heart, mind, and behavior. When participating in the work in its medium, the community understands the world from the point of view in the artwork. Consequently, some pastors now develop a sermon by re-creating aspects of a work of art in the pulpit. Indeed, preachers can create sermons that are works of art in the service of interpreting the gospel.

In the sermon below, Charles Rice draws on aspects of a work of art as he juxtaposes a gospel text for Easter Day with the movie *As Good as It Gets*. In the sermon, the retelling of the story of the movie is more than an illustration. Fr. Rice describes the movie so that it becomes a contemporary revelation of the witness of the text. Indeed, Rice describes Udall's experience in a such a way that we recognize it as an experience of resurrection. By participating in story of the movie, we, too, imaginatively experience the promise of the gospel.

Charles Rice has also taught us that a sermon as a whole can comprise the retelling of a novel, short story, play, movie, or poem. The preacher simply tells the story, making only those additional comments that are necessary to provide the congregation with information that they need to understand the art piece. The telling of the story is itself the sermon. The preacher does not explicitly articulate "lessons" or "morals" that the congregation should get from the narration. The sermon communicates its message in the same way that a movie does: by inviting the congregation to participate in its world.

When using such an approach to interpret a passage of scripture, a preacher might tell the story and then state the biblical text without commentary. The congregation can then make connections intuitively and explicitly between the text and the story from the arts. In this sense, the sermon itself as similar to a work of art in that it can be an aesthetic form created for the purposes of expressing and forming insight in the community into the relationship between God and the world.

Most sermons that move in this way draw from the language arts. However, as Joseph R. Jeter, Jr., points out in "Ruth People in an Esther World" (chapter 7), a sermon could be in the medium of dance or in some other form of body movement. In the middle ages, aspects of the Christian faith were sometimes expressed in dramatic form. In today's church, some congregations make use of drama for whole sermons. Occasionally, preachers incorporate dramatic vignettes into a sermon that is otherwise a monologue. In the midst of the sermon actors and actresses step into the chancel and perform a dramatic sketch. Preachers can also create multimedia sermons: messages that make use of slides or video clips, coordinated with music, narration, and occasionally dancers. For a sermon, a preacher once projected a slide of an evocative painting. The sermon consisted of the preacher's interpretation of the various elements of the painting. A preacher could also project several different paintings— calling attention to different nuances of interpretations in the different pieces. Thomas Troeger develops "The Alchemy of Grace" (chapter 22) by centering on a poem by George Herbert.

The layout of the following sermon on the page in a style that was first used by Peter Marshall illustrates a way of preparing a manuscript that helps the eye follow it. For similar layouts, see the sermons by Jana Childers, Thomas Troeger, and Kathy Black, chapters 17, 22, and 27.

CHARLES L. RICE is professor of homiletics at The Theological School, Drew University, Madison, New Jersey. At the time he preached this sermon, he was priest-in-charge at St. John's Episcopal Church, Montclair, New Jersey. His first book, *Interpretation and Imagination: The Preacher and Contemporary Literature*. Preachers' Paperback Library (Philadelphia: Fortress Press, 1970), is the pioneering study of the relationship of preaching and the arts. With Morris Niedenthal and Edmund Steimle, Professor Rice wrote *Preaching the Story* (Philadelphia: Fortress Press, 1980), a textbook that envisions the sermon as having many of the qualities of a story. His recent book, *The Embodied Word: Preaching as Art and Liturgy*, Fortress Resources for Preaching (Minneapolis: Fortress Press, 1991), explores the relationship between art and worship. *Preaching in the Context of Worship*, edited by David Greenhaw and Ronald Allen (St. Louis: Chalice Press, 1999) is a collection of essays honoring Professor Rice.

CHARLES L. RICE

Sermon for Easter Day

Luke 24:1–12

How shall we say it this time, on this particular Easter Day?
You can look around the church this morning and see that the Altar
    Guild has tried to say it with flowers.
The choir has been rehearsing for weeks, to say it worthily.
We began to say it when we woke up, got up, and opened our windows
    and doors to a new day,
got dressed up, out of the house, and on our way to church.
All of that was saying it, before the bell rang, or the choir sang, or the
    Bible was opened, before the Table was prepared, and the candles lit.
In fact, our just being here—like every Sunday morning that we meet
    like this—is telling the amazing news of Easter Day.

There is a movie at the theaters right now that says it.
In *As Good as It Gets*, Jack Nicholson plays Melvin Udall, a gifted,
    reclusive author who is as frightened of getting close to people as
    he is of germs.
When he opens the medicine cabinet in his bathroom, it is filled with
    wrapped bars of soap.
Every time he washes his hands, he uses a new bar.
In the smallest organism, in his neighbors down the hall, he sees danger.
He spends most of this time in a dark apartment at a computer key-
    board creating imaginary life on paper.
When he goes out to the one restaurant he trusts, he takes his own
    sterile cutlery,

and when he comes home, he bolts the front door with five locks.

Our first word for him would probably be eccentric.

But behind the barred door and under the protective wealth and
    barbed words

is someone waiting for what we celebrate here on Easter.

It *is*, on many days, a scary world out there.

And we are not so unlike Melvin, at least no more strangers to fear than
    those early Christians.

Those stories of the days leading up to Easter, and even of the morning
    itself, are filled with scared and perplexed people.

Luke even uses the word "terrified."

But then, something happens: Fear and perplexity give way to amaze-
    ment and, finally, to confidence and courage.

So they begin to tell this story of the stone rolled away, the angels' good
    news, and the empty tomb.

That is the story we tell today, of a door that, against all odds, opened,

and of One who has come to meet us in the closed, shut-down places
    of our lives,

bringing us into the light and into freedom.

We see ourselves in those women coming to the tomb in the light of
    early dawn prepared to anoint the dead,

leaving the tomb as glad witnesses of the news we echo this Easter
    morning.

This is, however, not the kind of news that we get at dinner time from
    Dan Rather.

In the way he tells the story, Luke makes it clear that we get this first-
    hand news for ourselves.

"They found the stone rolled back from the tomb....they went
    in....they did not find the body."

Bowing to the ground, they receive the gospel from the radiant
    messengers:

"Why do you look for the living among the dead?

He is not here, but has risen.

Remember how he told you while he was still in Galilee that the Son
    of Man must be handed over to sinners, be crucified, and on the
    third day, rise again."

This story has about it all the signs of a living witness, of someone who
    has come to know for herself the truth that Jesus, crucified, is alive.

The evangelist who is telling us this story is looking back already from
    the perspective of a community that has come to believe,
to stake everything on what it has experienced,
that Jesus crucified lives,
and that he is the source of freedom and peace to all who have faith in
    him.
At the end of Luke's story, Peter has to see for himself.
No mere report will do.
When the women tell the disciples about the empty tomb and the
    angels' news,
"These words seemed to them an idle tale, and they did not believe them."
But Peter got up and ran to the tomb; stooping and looking in,
he saw the linen cloths by themselves.
Then he went home, amazed at what had happened.

You and I have not looked into the vacated tomb, and most of us have
    had no angels' voices.
But we have, in one way or another, in the most unlikely places and
    from the most unlikely people, come to know for ourselves the
    truth of this day.
Amos Wilder, the great biblical scholar at Harvard, has called the
    miracle stories in the Gospels "mini-dramas of the resurrection."[1]
Wherever we see people being healed, reconciled, set free, we catch a
    glimpse of that morning at the tomb
among the women with the spices of death in their hands,
with the stone rolled back,
all turned toward life, and hope, and freedom.
We know the truth of this day by sick beds,
at a meeting of AA,
in the presence of a person whose loss is too keen even to mention yet,
but who keeps going.
We hear Easter in the laughter on the day of the funeral,
in the babble of a child,
every asking and giving of forgiveness.

The truth that this day celebrates may hit us when we least expect.
The women in Luke's story are prepared to anoint his body and say
    good-bye forever,

---

[1] Amos Wilder, *Early Christian Rhetoric: The Language of the Gospel* (Cambridge, Massachusetts:
Harvard University Press, 1971), 60–66.

only to find all changed one fine morning.

I have probably never known more profoundly—or believed more
 deeply—the truth of Easter more than when holding in my hands a
 small cardboard box,

heavy as a stone,

the mortal remains of my tall and happy friend from Texas,

dead at age forty from AIDS.

Most of us here, if we stopped to think about it, could recall such a
 time and place

when there at the tomb itself we came to know what we are celebrating this morning:

Jesus the Crucified has risen

to set us free from sin and fear and every form of bondage.

At the earlier service today, I told the children about a summer day
 last year.

I was driving to church, quite early, when I saw a small animal moving
 erratically along the side of the highway.

By the time I stopped the car, the animal had disappeared in the bushes.

Not quite sure what kind of animal it was, I tried, "Kitty, kitty."

Surprisingly, out of the bushes came a little creature with a small blue
 potato chip bag—

one of those made of thin polystyrene—pulled tightly over its head.

Fortunately, just at that moment, a man in a large jeep-like vehicle
 came along.

He stopped, put on his flashers, and sheltered this little unfolding
 drama.

"Kitty, kitty," I said, moving toward the animal.

Cocking its head, the creature stood still just long enough for me to
 pop off the bag.

Dazzled by the light, shaking its body from nose to tail as if getting rid
 of a very bad memory,

a wide-eyed baby fox looked up at me.

The fellow in the jeep went wild, honking and yelling like a ten-year old.

Then, the little fox moved slowly into the bushes, no doubt in search of
 a drink.

That morning on the road—a picture of eyes opened and freedom
 regained, of surprise and joy—has become for me one more story
 of what we celebrate this Easter morning,

and at every Eucharist where we give thanks to the One who has "brought us out of error into truth, out of sin into righteousness, out of death into life."[2]

But one of the best mini-dramas of the resurrection is in the movie.
It happens in a way we could hardly imagine.
The opening scene shows Melvin chasing the neighbor's dog.
Melvin is no more fond of his gay neighbor than of the dog that makes a mess in the hall.
When he catches the dog, Melvin dumps him down the laundry chute.
But as things turn out, when a group of thugs put the neighbor in the hospital,
Melvin is forced to take the dog into his apartment.
This simple act changes his life.
Reluctantly taking the dog in, learning to care for the animal, then feeling as accepted and safe as a dog can make you feel—something in Melvin opens up.
When his neighbor comes home from the hospital and has lost his apartment,
Melvin, who himself can hardly believe it—has a room ready.
And then the most amazing thing happens: One day, as he is leaving his apartment,
Melvin discovers that he has forgotten to lock the door.
In the middle of taking care of a dog and the fellow next door, something very large moves in Melvin.
And he is—for the first time—free.
The door, like his life, is open.

And that is it, is it not—having life, having something someone needs, and the freedom to give it—as good as it gets?
It must be, seeing how far we go to celebrate this,
that the One who gave his all
is not dead,
but among all who live and love in his name.

---

[2] *The Book of Common Prayer and Administration of the Sacraments and other Rites and Ceremonies of the Church* (New York: Church Hymnal Corporation, 1979), 368.

17

Sermon Developed as an Author Develops a Novel

Several models of preaching in this collection manifest distinct move-ments, e.g., the Puritan Plain Style. Some approaches to preaching are distinguished by distinctive approaches to the subject or particular pur-poses (e.g., preaching on a personal issue). Others show the relationship between a theological viewpoint and the perspective of a sermon. When speaking of a sermon developed as an author develops a novel, however, we identify a way of preparing a sermon more than a pattern of move-ment in the sermon itself, or a distinctive focus on the subject, or a theo-logical conviction. This chapter is included in the book because a fair number of preachers take this approach. Many of these preachers benefit from naming their custom of preparation and reflecting critically on it.

An author typically begins a novel with ideas and feelings about set-ting, characters, ethos, and plot. The author may sketch a plot. The author knows the general direction of the novel, several of the main themes, perhaps even some of the major episodes. But as the author begins to write the novel, a strange thing happens. In a sense, the novel begins to write itself. The characters take on personalities. The plot begins to take on a life of its own. The setting deepens. Unexpected characters write themselves into the book. Unplanned episodes appear. The plot takes unexpected turns. A novel may turn out very differently from the one the author planned. The process of creativity can bring forth things the author did not—could not—envision as the process started. Many artists in other media find that their works develop similarly.

These processes do not excuse the artist from careful preparation. The new insights must be honed and incorporated aesthetically into the developing work. Artistic creation requires discipline and critical reflection.

Many preachers develop sermons in this fashion. They have a biblical text or topic. They have a purpose in mind. They have exegetical discovery, theological illumination, and a good story or two. As the sermon develops, it takes on a life of its own. This process can be immensely creative. It can call forth some of a preacher's deepest insights into the relationship of the gospel with life. It can generate incredible intensity and energy.

However, at some point, the preacher needs to step back and reflect critically on the emerging sermon to make sure that it witnesses to God's unconditional love and call for justice and to think clearly about the purpose of the developing sermon in the community. The preacher also needs to see that the creativity emerging in the sermon does not call attention to itself in such a way that the people will so focus on the preacher-artist's creativity that they bypass the message embodied in the sermon.

Jana Childers' pattern of sermon preparation is to begin each day by "writing off the page."[1] The preacher writes down thoughts, images, questions, and feelings in response to the subject of the sermon. This exercise, taking twenty-five minutes, follows three rules. (1) Write with a pen or pencil. (2) Write without stopping. (3) Fill at least three pages. It sometimes results in nuggets, or seed-ideas, or whole sermons. Sometimes, she says, "It clears the mental and spiritual decks" for other aspects of sermon preparation.

This sermon was prepared for a congregation of leaders in youth ministry. On the first two days, Professor Childers—who is approaching mid-life—wrote about her loss of youth. The preacher pictured the congregation and meditated on their youthfulness, Samuel's youthfulness, and the youthfulness of the youth who were the subject of the conference. The process of creative writing led her to the question, "What would it take for a young person to be able to respond to God's call today?"

The preacher felt a sermon coming. She had material that she had gathered on the "Whatever Generation." She ruminated on Samuel's

---

[1] See, e.g., Julia Cameron, *The Artist's Way: A Spiritual Path to Higher Creativity* (Los Angeles: J.P. Tarcher, 1992); Natalie Goldberg, *Writing Down the Bones: Freeing the Writer Within* (East Lansing, Michigan: Shambhala, 1986).

aridness in contrast to the ennui, even listlessness, of many contemporary youth. She made notes on intergenerational tensions. She felt a sermon in these materials, but it wouldn't come to expression.

The moment of insight in sermon preparation came in conversation with her spouse (an event to which she refers in the sermon). He is a college teacher. He said that his students need an Eli. That observation became the catalyst that caused the sermon to take on its own life.

JANA CHILDERS is associate professor of preaching at San Francisco Theological Seminary, where she served as interim dean. She is the author of *Performing the Word: Preaching as Theater* (Nashville: Abingdon Press, 1998). With Lucy Atkinson Rose, she edited the *Abandon Women's Preaching Annual: Series 1* (Nashville: Abingdon Press, Year B—1996, Year C—1997, Year A—1998).

JANA CHILDERS

With Both Ears Tingling

1 Samuel 3:1–11

Like a guy in a pornographic t-shirt carrying a boom box through a crowded street. Like a young woman, in what used to be called polite society, using language that used to be called shocking. Like the king of trash-talk radio emitting bodily-function-sounds into his microphone and broadcasting them at 50,000 watts. I guess it would make your ears tingle.

If the word of the Lord came to you and said, "I am firing good ol' what's his name...Mr. Dithers, Prof. Whitehead, Rev. Trueblood. He's weak and fat and he can't keep his own kids' hands out of the offering plates. This is it for him. Out with the old. In with you." I guess it would make your ears tingle.

If the word of the Lord, having been scant and scarce for all of the years that you knew anything about, suddenly said, "I need someone to speak for me, here in this crack, here in this gap, here in this transition, I need someone to help my people turn this corner. I need someone. And you're it," I guess it would make your ears tingle.

I guess it would make me do more than tingle and twitch. I don't know about you but I guess I'd be at the bookstore fortifying myself with textual commentaries. I'd be closing my study door and hunkering down in the small pool of light at my desk—searching out jots and tittles, reading between the lines and behind the text. Looking for something to clear my ears and calm my feet. Looking, in short, for an out.

Not that there aren't worse things than receiving a word from the Lord in the wee morning hours. Not that there aren't worse things than what happened to the young boy Samuel in this story.

Actually, I've come to realize in recent weeks that someone who has officially crossed that ugly black line in the sand called "forty" cannot just go on indefinitely reading this text and identifying with the twelve-year-old fledgling prophet. Interestingly enough, I noticed this year for the first time—out of the many times I have consulted this commentary—that forty actually is the dividing line for those of us reading this text.

Na'ar, the word used to describe Samuel here, is the Hebrew word for a male of any age between infancy and forty. So even though we don't know that Samuel was twelve years old that morning when the voice of Yahweh woke him up just before dawn (that's Josephus' idea) we do know that he was younger than I am. Younger than many of us. We know that he was the student in this story and Eli was the preaching professor.

Once you get used to the idea, you have to admit that the role of Eli is an easier fit for a lot of us—regardless of our role in this community. Identifying with Eli is easier than identifying with Samuel. It is just not the case for most of us as it was for the young favored prophet that "God has never let one of our words fall to the ground."

We are more like Eli than Samuel, more like poor, old, well-intentioned Eli, whose worst fault was not being able to control his "greedy-eyed" children. Eli cared about the temple and the ark and died grieving for the captured ark, but was too "overweight"—as the NRSV actually comes right out and says—to do much to defend it.

Well, both Eli's and Samuel's stories probably occur in most every generation—maybe even in the hearts of most seminarians. But I'm interested in what we can learn from the original models whose story is told in today's text. I am interested in what can we learn that might help the next generation of the church avoid living out this old, old story, that might help them avoid the kind of spiritual drought that plagued Eli's generation.

I wonder if the next generation, the one that follows the boomers and the busters and challengers and the calculators, the Gen Xers and the so-called slackers, might be a Samuel generation. A "Speak Lord for thy servant heareth generation." A "be it unto me according to thy word" generation. A "Lord speak to me that I may speak" generation that has the ability to hear and pronounce God's word of wholeness to the fragmented world we are leaving them in our wills. It is possible. It could be. Lord knows we could hardly have done a better job setting the stage. "The word of the Lord was rare at the close of the twentieth century. There was no frequent vision."

I have heard it said that the two millennia that followed Abraham belonged to God. The two millennia that followed Christ belonged to him. And the next two millennia might well belong to the Holy Spirit, to the One who speaks God's word and spreads abroad God's visions. So maybe. The next generation could indeed be a generation tuned to the voice of the Holy Spirit, a generation of Samuels. You have to hope so. If there is anything in you of the fond old heart of the indulgent teacher Eli, you have to hope so.

Not that it's easy to picture. A number of essayists and pundits seem to be conspiring to tag this era of American life with the less than flattering name the "Whatever Generation." Some even call the nineties the "Whatever Decade." You hear it on radio talk shows, sports shows, in college classrooms, and on Saturday Night Live. Complex conceptual thought, whole philosophies, and passionately held positions laid out before an audience to be dismissed in three syllables. "Whatever," *Time* magazine's Richard Rosenblatt calls it the word of the decade.[2] "Whatever."

What would it take for the Whatever era to become a "Speak Lord, for thy servant heareth" era? What would it take to turn the generation known for their shoulder shrugs to a generation who bows their heads in wait for God's word? What would it take to turn those known for their vituperative language—for what is called in my husband's college classroom, "running the numbers"—to a generation that preaches the word?

What helps people learn to hear the word of God? What helped Samuel?

When the word of God came to the next generation in today's text—when the word of God came to the *na 'ar*, to Samuel, it is interesting that it did not go straight into his ear, enlighten his mind, purify his heart, and come straight out his mouth. It did not send him into spiritual ecstasy. It did not send him to seminary. It sent him back to sleep.

Maybe there's an encouraging word here for us who are called to preach to this particular, peculiar era of the church's life. When the word of God came to Samuel, it had to come repeatedly, and it had to be interpreted by a weak and fat old teacher.

Now let me ask you the question I posed lightly a few minutes ago. What if we are not Samuel in this story anymore? What if we are Eli? What if we have crossed that line?

---

[2] Richard Rosenblatt, "To Be or Not to Be...Whatever," *Time* magazine (December 30, 1996): 105–108.

I asked a friend who teaches public speaking to nineteen and twenty year-olds (and who happens not to be weak or fat) what he thought was peculiar and particular about this generation, about what they seemed to need. This person who has given the last twenty years of his life, including more than half of the weekends, to coaching the young to find their voices and their feet paused a long time before he answered.

"The problem with the kids I teach," he said, "is they've been beaten down instead of lifted up. But what they need is not so much praise, not so much 'self-esteem building.' They need someone to sit down and say to them 'This is what I see in you.'"

This is what I see in you. Here's a place to start. Here's a place to stand. This is what I see in you. It's essential. It's unique. It's precious. This is what I see in you—and it's not a whatever thing. Maybe the thing that this flailing generation needs is the very thing that was surely said to Samuel every day of his life from the day he was born, "This is what I see in you."

Here is what I see in you, Laura…a sharp mind and a quick tongue, a gift for analysis. Here is what I see in you, Linda…a wide and deep heart—the gift of humility and an ability to draw people to you. Here is what I see in you, Steve…a gift for comforting, leading, and making your own fun…and God wants to use it.

I hope you have had one of those moments. I hope it is part of what got you this far. But whether you did or not, the possibility that I am posing to you is that it is time now to turn around and offer this kind of a moment to the young people in your life.

Barbara Brown Taylor says in her story of coming to faith, that she was not a child raised in the church. "At twelve," she says, "I took to organized religion like a pig to mud—which makes me wonder if puberty does not unlock some doors of the soul along with those of the body."[3] She credits her epiphany, though, to a young pastor who "became a regular guest at our dinner table…vital and funny and could catch an airborne fly with one hand. He listened to me when I talked and let me lead him on tours of my projects around the house. He seemed able, when he looked at me, to see a person and not only a child, and I loved him for it."[4] This is what I see in you, Barbara.

I knew a college professor once who every June would sit in a circle with the graduating seniors he had mentored. There were rituals, remarks, and good-byes, and the circle ended with the old Eli looking briefly into

---

[3] Barbara Brown Taylor, *The Preaching Life* (Boston: Cowley, 1993), 16.
[4] Ibid, 14.

the eyes of each student and leaving them with one word. "This is what I see in you, Debra. You are ebullient. This is what I see in you, Mark. You are focused. This is what I see in you, Jana...."

In his new book, *The Soul's Code,* the eminent psychologist James Hillman makes a case for what he calls the "Acorn Theory" of human development. Each person embodies something essential, an acorn, from which our lives grow. At a signal moment something calls us to a particular path. Something like an annunciation takes place, and we begin to put together the pieces of our life into a coherent picture, to find the basic plot.[5]

The basic idea is not original to Hillman, of course. Plato has each soul choosing its lot in life from heaven and then passing through the plain of Lethe (oblivion, forgetfulness), so that the destinies they had chosen for themselves would be forgotten by the time they arrive on earth. Luckily, in this version each soul is accompanied by a daimon whose job it is to remember and goad the soul toward its path.

Maybe you don't particularly care to think of yourself as a daimon in the lives of the young men and women of your church family. If not, there is another version of this myth. It's a story that is more congenial with 1 Samuel's sensibilities—a Jewish legend that claims that the evidence for the soul's prenatal forgetting is pressed right into your upper lip. According to this version of the legend, the crevice below your nose is where the angel pressed its forefinger to seal your lips. That little indentation is the only thing left to remind you of your preexistent life and its mission. So, the legend claims, when we conjure up insight or a lost thought, our fingers go up to that significant dent.

People are not born knowing. They need to learn. The next generation of God's people stands before us—ears ringing, shoulders shrugging, fingering their upper lip. Let us not leave them wondering. Let us tell them every chance we get what we know is true about their soul's predestination: that they are made by God, for God, and that they may expect to be awakened at any hour by God's voice. Let us tell them that they can expect a call that will put a vision of the future in their mind, a word in their mouths, and set both ears tingling. Let us remember that we believe it ourselves.

---

[5] James Hillman, *The Soul's Code* (New York: Random House, 1996).

18

Sermon as Portrayal of a Biblical Character

A sermon can sometimes take the form of an extended narrative that tells the story of a biblical character. The narrative can be a third-person retelling. It can also take the form of a more conventional sermon in which the preacher studies the Bible's presentation of a character for its help for today's congregation.[1] In the sermon below, Ella Pearson Mitchell demonstrates another approach: a monologue in which the preacher tells the story from the point of view of the character. Preachers sometimes dress in costume from the biblical era and leave the pulpit in order to speak the sermon as a soliloquy.

Through this approach, a congregation can enter the world of the Bible, and, hence, can increase its biblical literacy and its empathy for people and situations in biblical times. When the characters are developed with real-life complexity, they can deepen a congregation's experience of the gospel. Such sermons can hold a congregation's attention. However, this approach comes with several warnings. The preacher can dwell on the world of the Bible in such a way as never to make contact with the contemporary world. Some preachers project contemporary thoughts, feelings, and cultural assumptions onto biblical characters without taking

---

[1] Henry Mitchell refers to this approach to preaching as a character sketch. See his *Celebration and Experience in Preaching*, 101–108.

account of how these matters might have been understood in antiquity. Through the sermon the biblical figure can become little more than a mirror of contemporary individualism and psychological concern. The sermon is then only an authentication of the congregation's existing view of the world; the gospel's potential transformation is lost. Some sermons lack depth, thereby trivializing the Bible and the gospel. Furthermore, some preachers develop these sermons in ways that can only be described as hokey.

Most sermons in this genre sketch characters from the Bible. A similar approach could narrate the lives of characters from church history. For instance, a preacher could develop a character sketch of Julian of Norwich.

In the sermon that follows, Ella Pearson Mitchell spends most of the sermon telling the story of Joanna. Professor Mitchell's description of customs and situations in Bible times is obviously informed by careful work with Bible dictionaries and other interpretive helps. In the last fourth of the sermon, the preacher effortlessly and unobtrusively moves from the biblical story to the contemporary story, so that the community finds itself addressed directly. This sermon also shows how the retelling of a biblical narrative can help the preacher and the congregation interact with a large segment of biblical material. The sermon was preached on Palm Sunday at Tabernacle Baptist Church, Detroit, Michigan, and was the first of a series of seven sermons during a Holy Week preaching mission.

ELLA PEARSON MITCHELL has been preaching for over sixty years. She is the editor of four important anthologies: *Those Preaching Women* (Valley Forge: Judson Press, 1996), volume 3; *Women: To Preach or Not to Preach* (Valley Forge: Judson Press, 1991), *Those Preaching Women* (Valley Forge: Judson Press, 1988), volume 2; *Those Preachin' Women* (Valley Forge: Judson Press, 1985). She served as Dean of the Chapel at Spelman College, Atlanta, Georgia, and is now Visiting Professor of Preaching with Henry H. Mitchell (her spouse) at the Interdenominational Theological Center, also in Atlanta, Georgia.

ELLA PEARSON MITCHELL

Were You There?

Matthew 21:6–11 & 27:19–26

Good morning. My name is Joanna. When you ask the question, "Were you there?" I was one of those faithful women who were there with Jesus. Of course, as you well know, women were not supposed to go anywhere in public without their husbands in those days. But, like the other women in our little group, I was deeply attached to Jesus. I wanted to be where he was as often as I could. You see, he was the one who healed me after all other efforts had failed.

This morning, I want to tell you what happened on that first Palm Sunday and then later that week. Nobody seems to realize what all that cheering and hoopla and hosannas was about. Jesus knew exactly what would happen, of course. But believe me, we didn't have the faintest notion what was going down after that demonstration. All we knew was that we really enjoyed the whole thing: the palms, the shouts, and the enthusiasm for our Lord.

Well, I suppose it was all about what always happens with crowds— any crowds. That day, it got started when Jesus sent a couple of the disciples into town to get a colt for him to ride on. We began to get the feeling that he was about to go public—to stop being so low key.

We women had long been convinced it was high time he let the whole world know who he was. So we got really excited. We joined the very first cries of the disciples: "Hosanna! Blessed is he that cometh in the name of the Lord!" Soon we were joined by many more people. They seemed to come from everywhere.

I tell you, it was amazing how fast the crowd gathered and how large the crowd got. One would join, and three would follow. Then more would join, and more would follow. People a block away would hear the shouting and come running to see what was going on. They would join right in and start chanting, too. It seemed that many of the folks had heard about Jesus, and, like us, they were just waiting for him to do something like this—to take advantage of his popularity. Of course, I couldn't help suspecting also that some of them didn't have the slightest idea what it was all about, but they were shouting and chanting and waving their arms anyway, just following the crowd.

And they didn't just join in the shouting; they tore off palm branches and waved them or laid them down in the road. There were mothers carrying their babies, toddlers, teens, old folks leaning on sticks, and all the ages in between. Some could hardly walk, and some ran and leaped as they were shouting Hosanna!

This gathering crowd wore every color in the rainbow. Some bright and new and some faded and ragged. Some solid colors and some striped. It was a dazzling collection of colors. Precious as their clothing must have been to them, some even took off their cloaks and threw them down in front of Jesus for his colt to walk on along that dusty road.

The excitement was high, and the crowd was so large that we just knew it would be only a short while before this bunch would convince our humble Lord to accept a crown.

Jesus led this procession through this cloud of dust, and we followed all the way into Jerusalem. By that time the host of people was blocks long, and the crowd was almost in a frenzy. The whole city was all stirred up; "Who is this?" some asked. The crowd replied, "This is Jesus, the prophet of Nazareth."

When Jesus entered the temple courtyard and cast out the money changers, his popularity went even higher. Even children were shouting at the tops of their voices. We had never seen anybody who had the nerve to challenge the rackets of those money-hungry, power-drunk priests.

The chief priests saw right there and then that they would have to do away with our Master. These pompous priests were really peeved. I could see it plainly on their faces, but of course I had no notion they'd go as far as they did. They set their plans to catch him when he didn't have so many people around to defend him. That's why, when they did arrest Jesus, they did it at that odd hour of the night. It took them from Sunday to Thursday night to put their murderous plan into action.

One of the ladies in our little group of women got word that our Lord had been arrested, so some of us went down to Pilate's court. We just had to see what would happen at the trial. We wanted to see what kind of bold lies and trumped up evidence they would charge Jesus with. And sure enough, it was as ridiculous as we thought it would be.

The Roman governor passed the buck to Herod, because he didn't want the burden of guilt for this legal lynching. And then old Herod passed the buck right back to Pilate. It was not hard for us to figure out how these old scoundrels, the king and the governor who hated each other, could now be so very polite. Each was willing to honor the other with responsibility for getting rid of Jesus. Neither wanted Jesus' blood on his hands.

Finally, Pilate tried to appease Herod and get off the hook with everybody. He was willing to let the people decide what to do with Jesus. You see, even Pilate's wife had gotten in the act and warned him about Jesus, and old Pilate wanted out.

The courts had a custom of releasing one prisoner at Passover. To Pilate, that meant that the crowd could be blamed for going against the plot of the priests. So Pilate decided to let this crowd we were in make the choice. He offered us Jesus or Barabbas, that bloodthirsty anti-Roman radical.

My heart leaped for joy. I just knew this crowd would choose Jesus, and this arrest business would be all over with. After all, many of the same folks who had been in the Hosanna crowd and screamed so loudly on Sunday were there with us.

But then I heard a low buzz all over the place. The priests were whispering—almost hissing—"We want Barabbas. Give us Barabbas."

When the crowd finally spoke, they asked for Barabbas. Then Pilate asked, "What then shall I do with Jesus?" Would you believe those idiots followed the priests again, and this time they shouted, "Crucify him! Crucify him! Let him be crucified!" Pilate was still aghast, and he asked, "Why do you say that? What evil has he done?" They shouted all the more, "Crucify him! Crucify him!" Pilate was, as we say, really "shook." He didn't know what to do, with his wife warning him on the one hand, and the rabble and the priests screaming on the other.

When Pilate saw he couldn't do a thing with that lynch mob, he finally made it plain that he didn't intend to have Jesus' blood on his hands. Exasperated, Pilate took a basin of water and washed his hands right there and then before the mob. "I am innocent of the blood of this just person. Go on and see about this bloody crucifixion business yourselves!"

You know, I thought that would scare them a bit, but it did not. They were so caught up in their diabolical lynch-mob spirit that they cried out, "His blood be on us, and on our children!" I gasped. I couldn't believe my ears. How could anybody put such a load or such a blemish on their descendants, on unborn generations? How little did they dream that some bigots would one day try to take that crazy, hasty judgement seriously.

Well, they released Barabbas and publicly beat and scourged our Lord, and then sent him off to be crucified. I cried and cried and cried. I went with the sisters to the crucifixion, but I could not bear to watch it. They took my Lord's bleeding body down off the cross and carried him to a tomb they had borrowed from Joseph. We followed as closely as we could. This Joseph of Arimathea was a nice man, but nobody had made preparations for a proper embalming. It was too late to go and buy the supplies. Sabbath began minutes after they laid Jesus' body in the tomb. We made up our minds to be there with our preparations the minute the sun came up after the Sabbath was over. It was hardly daybreak when the six of us got to the tomb.

We hadn't bothered to figure out how we could roll back the great big stone. But just when we were thinking about going over and giving it a try, we noticed that it had been moved already. No signs of who or how it was moved. Just gone! Our jaws dropped.

We were so startled we didn't rush right over to the entrance, but when we did we almost fainted. Can you imagine how surprised we were when we found our Lord wasn't even there! There was this angel sitting there on the stone couch, legs crossed, and in a long white robe. He told us Jesus was risen, just like he said. He invited us, "Come and see the place where the Lord lay." Then he told us to go quickly and tell the disciples, "Jesus has risen from the dead. And he is going before you to Galilee to meet you there." Oh, you should have seen us getting away from there then, hurrying to find the disciples and tell them what had happened. At first the disciples didn't want to believe us women. But it was up to us to spread the news.

But it still bothers me what that crowd did to Jesus. How could they turn so, especially on a man they knew was pouring out his life in kindness? He had healed the sick and given sight to the blind, and the people had seemed very grateful. But I shouldn't have been so surprised. You see, I've known now for a long time that only a few people think for themselves.

[PAUSE]

Joanna, you're so right! And I do thank you from the bottom of my heart. What you said is still true. All too many people simply follow the herd—the crowd, the fads, the popular trends in clothing, in recreation, and in the way they act.

They don't have any thoughts of their own.

If I ever had to teach a lesson or preach a sermon on what I learned from you and these crowds, I'd do it from the words of a man named Paul, whom you may have met up yonder. He never actually saw Jesus, but he taught a great deal about our Lord.

He was dead on it when he said to the church at Rome: "And be not conformed to this world: but be ye transformed by the renewing of your mind, that ye may prove what is that good and acceptable and perfect will of God" (Romans 12:1, KJV). In other words, don't let the world pour you into its mold. Whatever you do, do it because you know it's right.

Somebody said, "The crowd is a lie." And everything you do with a herd could turn out to be false. When you shop for clothes, buy the styles that are appropriate for your character: your face, your age, your figure, your vocation, and your witness. Choose your hairdo to match your face and your head. Don't even try to be like anyone else. God threw the pattern away when God made you, and you're not supposed to match anybody else.

And, above all, live your life the way you know God wants it. There may be safety in numbers where thieves are concerned, but there is no safety in the most popular patterns and principles of life. In fact, quite the opposite is true. Look at our modern, everyday experience. A classical case of how dangerous it is to follow popular religion can be seen in the celebration of Mardi Gras that leads into the solemn and serious season of Lent. Millions of people, young and old, rich and poor, engage in orgies of expensive sport. They don't even blame it any more on getting ready for Lent. "What does the cruel suffering of our Lord mean to these fun seekers?" At the moment, it means nothing.

Faith only gets this popular when it has already lost its salt. It has always been a fact that large numbers are drawn to Christ only after the faith is watered down. When it comes to numbers, beware of any very popular religious movement or crowd.

As for me, I don't want to be judged among the best dressed one hundred women of anywhere or any time. I don't want to be numbered among the most popular women of high society—the blue book or any other book. I can't think of any number that my soul cries out to be in. I guess I've always been uncomfortable with popularity. I found that you can always get popularity for a price, but the price is always too high. The only numbers I crave to be in are the small number of the folks faithful to our Lord. I want to be in the same number with Mary and Martha, Simon the Cyrenian, and John the beloved disciple, with Joanna and those other women, and with that top sergeant—that centurion who broke down and cried, "Surely, surely, this was the Son of God."

Oh yes, and there's a number I want to be in even more than those. It's the number that John saw—the number he talked about in the book of Revelation. That number that no one can number, the one our ancestors sang about so beautifully:

> O when the saints go marching in,
> When the saints go marching in,
> O Lord, I want to be in that number,
> When the saints go marching in.
> O when they crown Him King of Kings;
> O when they crown Him King of Kings,
> Lord I want to be in that number,
> When they crown Him King of Kings.

19

Sermon as Jigsaw Puzzle

Some sermons are like putting together jigsaw puzzles. The sermon is cut into several small parts. The parts are scattered on the table of the congregation's mind. The pieces are related to one another, but the community cannot see the whole picture until near the end of the sermon when the last pieces are snapped into place.

This pattern of discovery is associative. Through a process of experimentation, trial and error, the preacher and the congregation try to associate the various pieces of the puzzle with one another. A preacher might take a biblical text that contains several pieces and discuss it in this fashion. For instance, the preacher could discuss each element of an apocalyptic vision from the book of Daniel, finally offering an interpretation of the whole vision from the standpoint of what preacher and congregation have discovered about the various pieces. A preacher could take this approach with a text or topic that contains different characters who have different viewpoints. How does a miracle story sound from the viewpoint of the healed person? the crowd? the disciples? the reader of the gospel? Jesus? A jigsaw puzzle format could help a preacher and community consider multiple pieces of a doctrine, a practice, or a situation. In the sermon that follows, Joseph Jeter considers different possibilities for resolving a difficult problem.

This approach can be helpful when a text, doctrine, practice, or situation contains multiple and confusing elements or when the subject of the sermon is open to multiple and confusing interpretations. The particular danger of this model is that the sermon might leave the congregation even more puzzled than before—if the preacher discusses the pieces but does not help the community determine their relationship.

Joseph R. Jeter, Jr., preached this sermon at baccalaureate at the University of Texas. The sermon introduces a problem then considers different ways of resolving the problem. The different resolutions do not appear to fit together until, near the end of the sermon, Jeter looks at the pieces of the puzzle from a fresh perspective. The sermon has both deductive and inductive qualities. At the beginning, the preacher describes the problem and explains that the sermon will explore solutions to the problem. However, the resolution does not appear until the end. Shortly before the preaching of the sermon, the Coca-Cola Company announced that it was retiring the traditional formula for Coca-Cola and introducing a new version of that product. Jeter refers to this historically conditioned detail in the sermon. He also refers to an event that took place during the conflict in Vietnam when a group of United States troops destroyed the village of Mai Lai. The village was friendly to the Republic of South Vietnam and to the United States, but the U.S. military commander in the field ordered the village destroyed in order to "save it" from potential use by the Viet Cong, the enemies of the South Vietnamese at that time.

JOSEPH R. JETER, JR., is Granville and Erline Walker Associate Professor of Homiletics at Brite Divinity School, Texas Christian University, Fort Worth, Texas. He is the author of *Crisis Preaching* (Nashville: Abingdon Press, 1998) and *Re/Membering: Meditations and Sermons for the Table of Jesus Christ* (St. Louis: Chalice Press, 1995). With Cornish R. Rogers, he edited *Preaching Through the Apocalypse: Sermons from Revelation* (St. Louis: Chalice Press, 1992). He has also written *Alexander Proctor: The Sage of Independence* (Claremont, CA: Disciples Seminary Foundation, 1983). He preaches in congregations and conferences throughout the U.S.

JOSEPH R. JETER, JR.

How to Divide a Popsicle Three Ways

2 Timothy 1:8–14, 2:14–15

When my sister and I were growing up, we got along amazingly well for siblings. My little friend from down the street put that relationship into perspective, however, when he said to me one day, "You are lucky. You just have one sister. I have two." "But your sisters are nice," I said. "Yes," he replied, "but have you ever tried to divide a popsicle three ways?"

I saw his point, although it was much later before I realized that my friend had posed one of the foundational questions of human civilization. How *do* you divide a popsicle three ways? How do you feed three children from two bowls of rice? How do job, career, family, religious and civic responsibilities, and personal time all fit into one day's living? How do we balance what seem to be unlimited wants with what are limited resources? And what does any of this have to do with graduating from college?

Just this. What you've learned to do here is not nearly so important as what you've learned to do when what you've learned to do here doesn't work. Education is about solving problems when the obvious solution fails. Education is about perseverance and courage in the face of all the obstacles the world will throw your way.

This is what the biblical texts read for you are all about: the encouragement to be strong, to take your share of suffering, to avoid extraneous entanglements, to play by the rules, to work hard, and, above all, to do your best. It's Timothy's graduation and he is being sent out to do difficult work. His baccalaureate sermon, preached in the name of Paul the apostle, calls upon him to see his way through to the end, to stay with the tough problems, and to handle with care the precious truth which has been entrusted to him.

I was at an event last night much like this one, at a high school in a town that shall remain nameless. The address, given by a noted Texas humorist, consisted of twenty-five minutes of slightly off-color jokes followed by two platitudes. Is that all there is? Is that all we have to say? In the letters to Timothy there is much instruction. But why all the hortatory material—hang in there, keep the faith, you can do it? Because the work to which Timothy has been called will require his best efforts. He is going to have to stand against the powers of darkness even when he does not understand clearly how to do that.

The symbol I've chosen this evening for the tough problems we face is the three children huddled about a two-stick popsicle. The problem is obvious. A popsicle is naturally meant to be divided two ways. To divide it three ways is unnatural, a "crime against nature." But it is also one of those crimes we must commit, one of those tough decisions we are going to have to make if we are going to have society. Oh, sure, there are easy solutions, but they are unacceptable to most of us. Hitler's solution: three children, one popsicle, shoot one child. The U.S. politician's solution: promise everybody a popsicle, whether you can produce it or not. Easy solutions, but not very good. The best solutions are harder. I have four that I want to share with you after having read this text. And I plan to hang around after this service is over; so, if you have some better ideas, I want to hear them.

(First Piece) First, take the popsicle melt it down and start over. Re-mold it to shape your need. Sometimes when we cannot solve a problem, we need to reformulate the problem. This is the way of critical inquiry. By breaking the problem down, we can see it in its essence, we can see the real monster that we are up against, and if we can name that monster—the Rumpelstiltskin effect, psychologists call it—we have a handle on solving it. Our friends in mathematics and the sciences have led the way in this approach, and we are indebted to them. Sometimes the problem turns out to be not what we think it is.

When I was a little boy, my family went to Carlsbad Caverns. I wanted to be carried on the long walk. My parents got tired of that. I had to walk. I kept telling them that my feet hurt. I got fussier and fussier. They got more and more frustrated, until the day disintegrated into disaster. I am sure that they thought the problem was that I was a rotten kid, which I may have been, but the more immediate problem that day was that they had put my shoes on the wrong feet. The disciples cried to Jesus, "The problem is this storm. Our boat shall be lost." And Jesus said, "No, the problem is that you have no faith." I seem to remember Harry Emerson Fosdick, a famous preacher in a previous generation, once saying that when we find ourselves in storms, bent and tossed like trees, we naturally think the problem is the wind, when actually the problem is our rootage. Sometimes we need to break the problem down and reformulate it.

This methodology does have one limitation and that is losing the sight of the whole. What did the commander say in Vietnam? "We had to destroy the village to save it." We in universities tend to forget sometimes that the shoot of the sporophyte of a higher plant modified for reproduction and consisting of a shortened axis bearing modified leaves is still a flower—delicate, beautiful, and ultimately mysterious. Remember that.

(Second Piece) Second, take the popsicle and divide it the best way you can. This is the way of philosophers and children. Both of them realize that in dividing a popsicle three ways, the natural order is being violated, but they also realize that the situation is given and they must work with it. They neither melt the popsicle down nor do they avoid popsicles because of the dilemmas they bring about. They hassle and fret and stew and wonder and struggle and pray and work and cry and argue and divide that popsicle. On a given day, the division is never equal. One will always get a little more or a little less. But in a sibling situation, the clumsy, unequal division somehow works. If we organize ourselves and agree upon some basic rules, such as, one person divides and the other two

choose their portions first, then three things can happen: (a) We all get popsicle, (b) if we play fairly we all get the same amount of popsicle over the long run, and (c) we can still live together in this troubled world.

This is a very practical solution, but like the first, it has a problem: Everyone involved must agree that fairness is important. We have not learned that lesson very well. We are sometimes quite good at taking much more than our share of the world's goods and much less than our share of its suffering. God, help us to learn before it is too late.

(Third Piece) Third, we could say to our two sisters, "Here, you take the popsicle today and divide it between yourselves. I really don't mind. I'd like for you to have it." If the first solution is the way of critical inquiry and the second is the way of justice and fairness, then this is the way of self-giving love. The prophets did not ask for their fair share of things. Neither did Jesus. Instead, they gave all they had. They gave of themselves, asking nothing for themselves in return.

(Fourth Piece) The fourth possibility I will just mention and leave with you. Three children, one popsicle. We could hope for a miracle. Strange things happen in this world. History is full of occurrences when what could not happen did. Hope, in spite of everything, is a genuine response to this world. God told the prophet, "Your old people will see visions and your young people will dream dreams." Fiddler, in the television version of *Roots*, says, "There's gonna come another day." Before he died, Martin Luther King, Jr., said, "I've been to the mountaintop and I've looked out and I've seen the promised land."[1]

My wife and I were driving in the Texas hill country last summer and we came to a little village named Utopia. We stopped at a little roadside cafe, and I could not help but think, "I haven't been to the mountaintop. I haven't seen the promised land. But I've had a doughnut in Utopia." And I realized that the first step in building a new and better world is to dream a world worth building. To paraphrase a song, "We've got to have dreams, in order for our dreams to come true." So do not give up hope. Remember only that this fourth solution generally happens to those who practice the other three.

I trust that by now you have realized that dividing a popsicle three ways is a symbol for what is waiting for you on the other side of those doors. The easy problems have already been solved. We need you for the

---

[1] Martin Luther King, Jr., "I See the Promised Land," in *A Testament of Hope: The Essential Writings of Martin Luther King, Jr.,* ed. by James M. Washington (San Francisco: Harper and Row, 1986), 286.

tough ones. I heard on the news the other day after my topic for this evening had already been printed in the program that a popsicle company is going to stop making two-stick popsicles, so the problems of dividing them three ways, like the problem of smallpox, may no longer be with us. My first reaction was to wish their new product the same hearty reception given new Coke. My second reaction was to realize that other problems beckon. The tough problems you're going to face are still being manufactured, triple-shift, twenty-four hours a day. One tool, one weapon against the problems we will face will be inadequate. That is why you have come to the university, to fill your quiver with a variety of arrows: the way of critical inquiry, the way of justice and fairness, the way of love, the way of hope and faith in God's own future and ours.

And all these individual methods not only lend themselves to meeting the challenges before us, but when fitted together in a creative approach to problem solving, they produce something greater than the sum of the parts: a call, a vocation, a reason for living and living well. The author of the second letter to Timothy gave his young charge not only the methods with which to do his work but the encouragement to do his work well. "Do your best," he said. Do your best. That is all anyone can ask.

I have a little boy. The first two years of his life were very tough and he was sick most of the time. He could not go out and play with the other children. So he used to sit in his chair by the picture window and watch the other children play. His greatest joy, however, was the neighbor's dog. How he loved to watch that dog run and jump and bark, and he used to call me to come to the window and see the "bow-wow."

The day finally came when we bundled him up and took him to the park for the first time. It was the first time he had stood on grass. He stood there a little uncertainly, eyes big as saucers, as he watched all the children run and jump and swing and slide and shout. I thought for a moment he might cry, but he did not. Finally he drew himself up to his full little height and began to shout "Bow-wow, bow-wow, bow-wow."

I was taken back. I looked around and there were no dogs anywhere. Then it hit me, and I scooped him up and hugged him. You see, "bow-wow" was his best word, his very best word. He went out into that new and very frightening world and he gave it the best he had.

Do not give up on the future. It is rich with possibilities and problems. Face them with courage, and do your best. I salute you for all that you have done and all that you will do. I congratulate you on your splendid achievement and I leave you with an affectionate farewell and a hearty bow-wow.

PART 3

Patterns for Subjects

20

Wedding Homily

The purpose of a wedding homily is to help the community interpret marriage and its relationship with the larger community from the standpoint of the gospel. The preacher's calling is to help the congregation to name and experience the gospel in the context of two people coming together in the covenant of marriage. The wedding homily focuses on the gospel and its promise and demand for the couple and for the communities with which they are in relationship.

The wedding homily is not a private message to the bride and the groom. Premarital counseling is the venue for intimate, personal messages from the pastor to the couple. The homily is addressed to the gathered community of which the couple is a part. Of course, a marriage—like a death—is not generic. Two particular people are conjoining their lives. The homily should take account of the particular context of the couple whose lives are coming together. But the homily should always be more than effervescence over the love of the two people for one another.

A preacher can usually a select one or more biblical passages or some aspect of Christian doctrine or practice as a lens through which to interpret the significance of the gospel for the marriage that is taking place. The preacher can identify ways in which God's unconditional love and call for justice can help the couple and the larger community. How do God's love and call for justice help the man and the woman to relate to one another? How does the gospel help the couple relate to the wider church and world? How does God's love and call for justice help the church relate to the couple?

The preacher may be able to draw on the personal and familial histories of the couple, on their social worlds, on incidents from their lives individually, together, and in connection with others in the congregation. However, such material should make its way into the homily only when it helps refract the gospel to the couple and the community.

Few marriages are unending joy. Unresolved questions, tensions, and other problems are often a part of the fabric of the wedding. For instance, prior marriages may have ended in divorce. Children from previously different households will be blended. The members of the wedding party may be passing through vocational, financial, or health crises. The preacher often helps brings an air of realism to the occasion and helps the wider community by naming such tensions in a gentle way and by acknowledging the difficulty of dealing with them. The preacher can help the congregation remember that even in the midst of difficulty, God is present, and working to help their relationships conform to the divine purposes. If some of these matters are too painful to mention directly, the preacher might allude to them.

In most European American congregations, a wedding homily is 5–10 minutes. In the African American community and in some other churches, a wedding homily may be as long as the usual Sunday morning message.

In the sermon that follows, Lisa Leber places the marriage relationship in the context of the wider Christian community. Marriage is a particular arena through which the couple can know God's love and through which they can witness to that love. The preacher emphasizes the interrelationship of all in the community. The homily was prepared for the wedding of two persons who were in their retirement years, Barbara Kolumban and Samuel Schmitthenner. Both had lost their previous spouses to death. The couple chose the gospel text because of the imagery of vine and branches suggested the intertwining of their lives in Christ over many years. Sam, a retired pastor in the Lutheran Church, was a missionary in India for many years. Barbara had been a missionary spouse in India for part of that time. While the preacher does not directly talk about the couple's personal lives, the preacher evokes aspects of their previous experience and brings those aspects into the presence of the gospel.

LISA LEBER is a pastor of St. James Lutheran Church, Gettysburg, Pennsylvania. She is a graduate of The Lutheran Theological Seminary at Gettysburg.

LISA M. LEBER

God's Love and Our Love

Colossians 3:12–17, Philippians 4:4–8, John 15:7–17

I'm afraid that time has made a liar out of me. About a year-and-a-half ago, I got up and preached a sermon in which I said that I rarely break down and cry. Ha! In the months since, I've discovered that weddings do it to me every time. I can run around, make sure the bride is dressed, the ushers are passing out the bulletins, the candles are lit, and everyone is ready to go. Then the moment hits, and the bride and groom are standing in front of me gazing at each other, and I start to blubber.

I try to keep it on the inside, since it's not always helpful to have the minister up front going like this [wiping tears away].

As we've been preparing for this weekend, this special opportunity Barb and Sam have given us to celebrate marriage and community, I've thought again about what it is that "gets us." I know I'm not the only one who turns to blubber at weddings. I think it is this. Whether we're really conscious of it or not, what we see at a wedding is a glimpse of the holy. That's what we see when a man and a woman promise lifelong faithfulness to one another. We hear and see something sacred.

It is awesome. A man and a woman led by God to make a commitment to one another, to take the huge risk of promising to face years together, to experience life's joys and life's sorrows as one.

Even more than that is involved. God has created human beings to enjoy the gift of relationship, the gift of community. God's desire for us is that we experience life together. From the beginning of time, when God created us male and female and then built up families and communities and tribes and nations, life together has been a mark of God's people. God gave the commandments to help us live in relationship with one another and with God. God knows that life is too hard for us to make our way through it alone. Human beings cannot live in isolation, cannot be all that we are created to be without nurture and support, without touch, and love, and forgiveness, without security and safe places to draw strength to live in a broken and harsh world.

So, in love, God gives us the yearning to be with one another, to live in relationships that are holy, sacred. A marriage is one of those relationships—one in which two people draw uniquely together. At its best, a marriage is a community of trust, intimacy, a community in which man and woman know one another in ways that no one else does, in which they learn to sacrifice and compromise, forgive and love, with all their beings.

But—and this is a big "but"—a marriage is not just about two people. That's the myth we've perpetuated, some romantic notion that it's just "you and me against the world." Marriages have much to do with the larger community, with the whole body of Christ, the whole people of God.

Marriage is one of those peculiar relationships in which we are empowered to live out our baptisms, in which we are nurtured for mission to be disciples of Christ. Before we are husbands and wives, before we are parents or children, brothers or sisters, friends or co-workers, we are baptized children of God. Before anything else, we are chosen by God to be God's very own. Being chosen by God, we abide in the divine love with one another.

I read a beautiful book called *Whisper from the Woods.*[1] The author uses the story and pictures of the life cycle of a forest to talk about life and death. Acorns must fall from trees, seedlings root in the forest floor, trees grow, storms ravage the woods. I think the most beautiful picture in the book is a picture of the forest in which you can see the tree roots underneath the soil. In the earth, you see the roots all painted as if they have hands growing at the ends of them. The roots are woven together in the dirt, intertwined, reaching out to one another, hand grasping hand.

The narration of the picture speaks of the interconnectedness of the roots of the trees, which enables each tree to stand firmly and grow, blossoming and bearing fruit.

That's how it is for us in the body of Christ. In our community of the children of God, we are all connected. Our lives are woven together by God, intertwined in the soil of Christ's love, and we reach out in that love to grasp one another so that we can grow together and bear fruit together.

Each of us is essential to this community. We need each other, need the love that comes from outside ourselves, the love of God. So often that loves comes to us from people around us.

Some of us are given to one another in very special ways. Some hands reach out to each other as husband and wife. As we celebrate today with Barb and Sam, God is with them in the particular relationship of marriage. Some hands reach out to each other in deep friendship, or as parent and children, or as brother and sister.

But our particular relationships are lived in larger community. And we all have important things to offer this incredible network of

---

[1] Victoria Wirth, *Whisper from the Woods* (New York: Simon and Schuster Children's Books, 1991).

intertwined lives. Single people pray for the marriages of their friends, while they enrich the lives of other singles. Married and single persons support others going through divorce. Couples care for other couples, as they nurture those who are single, and empathize with those experiencing the pain of a broken relationship. All of us cherish the children. Those celebrating long, successful marriages and widows and widowers share the lessons they've learned about marriage with couples just starting out on their journey. Parents help other parents figure out what in the world is going on with their teenagers. The amazing energy and joy and hope of children helps people deal with the deaths of spouses of fifty years.

We support those who have much in common with us and those whose lives are very different. Our hands reach out to one another, and in our grasp of love, we give each other strength, and courage, and faith, and hope.

This community, this linking of one to another, is a gift of God to us. We abide together in the love of Christ. As we draw on the nourishment of that love as roots draw on the nourishment of the soil, we are able to bear the fruit of discipleship. We are able to confess our sins, to forgive, to proclaim the gospel, to show mercy and compassion. We are able to love one another as Christ has first loved us.

Our lives intertwined, our hands grasped, are to the world a glimpse of the holy. Through our community is revealed something of the sacred. God gives us the gift of interconnectedness, the gift of life together rooted in the rich soil of Christ's love. May we always abide in that love. And as we celebrate this morning with Barb and Sam, as we watch these two grasp hands in marriage, may we all rejoice in the holy and sacred gift of one another.

21

Funeral Homily

The purpose of a funeral homily is to help the congregation interpret the life and death of the deceased and the situation of the continuing community from the standpoint of the gospel. The preacher's responsibility is to help the congregation name and experience the gospel in the presence of death. The funeral sermon is not primarily a recitation of the fine qualities of the deceased (a speech that is sometimes called a eulogy). However, because death is very particular, the preacher should interpret the life of the decedent through the gospel. A generic funeral homily limits the power of the sermon to help the congregation name their specific circumstances in a gospel way.

A preacher can usually select a biblical passage, a Christian doctrine, or practice as a lens through which to interpret the death that has occurred, as well as the situation of the survivors. The preacher can identify ways in which God's unconditional love and God's call for justice make sense of the life of the deceased.

An important pastoral dimension of many funeral homilies is to help the community name, as honestly as possible, its feelings. Depending upon the circumstances of death, these feelings can range from bone-deep sorrow, through shock and dismay, to anger and even relief. The homily needs, further, to help the congregation accept its feelings, offer them to God, and assure the community of God's unconditional love and acceptance.

At the heart of the funeral sermon, the preacher can often identify qualities in the life of the decedent that show how God's love and will for

justice were manifest in that life, or how the gospel made a positive different in that person's existence. Telling and hearing stories is often a very
therapeutic aspect of the funeral homily.

The preacher can assure family and friends that the future life of the
deceased is in the hands of a trustworthy God. The preacher can offer
the same assurance to the continuing community. Despite the fact that
the death has forever reshaped their world, they leave the grave site in the
perpetual company of a God who does everything that God can do to
help them rebuild a world that has meaning and hope.

When the life of the deceased has been problematic for the survivors,
the preacher may need to help the community gently acknowledge that
problematic character (without dragging the community's dirty laundry
into public view) and suggest how the gospel can help them resolve lin-
gering feelings of unsettledness, even hostility, and make their way into
the future.

The funeral homily is an occasion to articulate the preacher's understanding of the Christian hope. What does God ultimately promise to the
deceased? to the community? to the world?

Death brings many of life's deepest and most aching questions to the
surface. The preacher needs to acknowledge these questions. However,
the emotions of the community are usually too torrid in the immediate
presence of death for the community to stay with the preacher during a
sustained, complicated theological discussion of such matters. Instead, the
homily can offer strong pastoral assurance in the face of these uncertain-
ties. The preacher can promise to return to the larger theological issues in
a more detailed way when the community is better able to concentrate
on the questions and the resources necessary for responding to them.

In the European American churches, a funeral homily is typically 5–
10 minutes in length. In the African American community and in some
other communities a funeral homily is usually as long as a typical Sunday
morning sermon.

In the sermon below, Mary Alice Mulligan interprets the life and
death of her brother-in-law, Louis R. Pondy, through gospel perspective,
by using images from the book of Revelation. Dr. Pondy, a college professor, suffered greatly from cancer for several months prior to his death. The
sermon honestly faces the difficulties of the illness for the decedent, family, and friends, and it also articulates a strong affirmation of the gospel in
the face of such suffering. Dawn was his spouse.

MARY ALICE MULLIGAN is senior pastor of Central Christian Church
(Disciples of Christ) in downtown Indianapolis, Indiana. In addition, she is

developing a homiletic for the believer's church, based on a believer's church ecclesiology, for a Ph.D. dissertation at Vanderbilt University. She contributes to *Word and Witness* and to other resources for sermon preparation.

MARY ALICE MULLIGAN

The First Member of This Generation in the Family Triumphant

Revelation 3:7–13; 21:1–8

Several weeks ago, Lou had such a bad afternoon that he thought he was going to die. Then, he thought he was dead. Even though he thought he was dead, he picked up a pad and paper and wrote a letter to Dawn, full of love for her and gratitude for the many people who had touched his life. I have read the letter. It takes one on a whirlwind tour through Lou's life and reminds Dawn of some final tasks to be completed. Make sure you call the people at Wharton. Make sure your mom and dad know that I love them and appreciate their visits, especially the prayers your father always says.

When that crisis was over and Lou found that he was not dead, he talked about how it had not seemed strange that he could write a letter to Dawn when he thought he was dead. Death, he assumed, would be like life. He would just cross over into it.

Now, Lou really is dead. The five-month struggle with cancer is done. I heard a close friend at the visitation discussing his illness and dying. Finally, she fell silent then whispered, "God, he did it so well." Those of us who sat by his bed watching him grow thinner and thinner and more and more tired, know that she said it exactly. He did it so well.

Lou Pondy did many things well. He was an excellent professor much loved by students. An author whose publications are respected by colleagues throughout the country and just recently offered a named chair in the school of business administration at Wharton. Lou was also comfortable out of the classroom—singing in the choir at Emmanuel Church, or pulling on that ratty sweatshirt and heading for the garden, or climbing on the roof to fix the gutters, or heading downstairs to figure out some new computer program. I'll especially miss Lou's sense of humor at our family gatherings—the twinkle in his eye when he caught me in a word joke, how delighted he was by windup Christmas toys, and how he loved a funny birthday card. So many things Lou did so well. Even his struggle against cancer, he did so well.

This is not to say Lou didn't hate it. He did. He struggled with the question of "Why me?" He shook his fist at God, at some of us, at himself. But he died victoriously. Fighting cancer is no easy battle. Victory is not easily won. The opponent is so powerful. This was a fight to the death. But Lou won it.

You and I have been left with a remarkable example of what it means to be victorious. We, too, have our big questions of "Why?" Why did my brother-in-law have to die? Why did cancer take hold at the pinnacle of Lou's life, when the position at Wharton—the one about which he had always dreamed—was offered to him? Why, God, why take Lou now?

If you had asked Lou, he probably would have told you, "God isn't doing this to me. But God is seeing me through it."

For many people who learn that they are dying and have a few months to prepare for it, the twenty-first chapter of the book of Revelation becomes a great comfort, a great promise. John's vision of the new heaven and the new earth gives them comfort and hope. In the vision, we are told that the dwelling of God is with us. We shall be God's people, and the one sitting on the throne declares, "Behold, I make all things new." The one who conquers is promised a place in the new world as a child of God. This passage meant a lot to Lou. It helped him conquer.

Earlier in the book of Revelation, we are told that the one who conquers becomes a pillar in God's new temple (Revelation 3:12). Christ writes the name of God on the pillar and the name of the new Jerusalem. Lou knew that he was conquering. Those who watched him handle his sickness knew it, too. He became a pillar in God's temple, and we could read God's name on Lou's life.

We wish it had been different. We wish Lou had never gotten sick; but you and I know that he did get sick, and in that sickness, he kept his faith even to death. You could see the name of God imprinted on Lou when he attempted to understand and explain his faith in the face of death. The name was imprinted when he sent his three-piece wool suits and camel hair jacket to share with some of you, with his sister-in-law's seminary friends, with people he had never met. He was the one who sponsored a tie party. The name of God was imprinted when he took delight in giving away his books. The name was imprinted in the way Lou was able to grieve for himself and to trust God to comfort him. Those who knew him could read God's name clearly upon Lou's life.

Gathered here are family and friends who love Lou Pondy. In our grief and fatigue, we can have the confidence that we may collapse into God's love and presence. God will uphold us. Together we, too, may be conquerors.

Lou has left us a witness. We are sad over the seeming victory that cancer should have won. But we are filled with gratitude for the witness we received from Lou. John wrote that the conqueror becomes a pillar in the temple of God. Lou was a pillar in his trust of God and his faith. In his time of illness when he was physically at his weakest, he became a pillar of support for the worshiping community. As he grew more dependent on the assurance of God's love and presence, Lou grew more confident of the love and support of the church family. Someone told me that in these last weeks when Lou was no longer physically able to attend the corporate service of worship, the community always felt his presence. The community was with him, and his support was with the community.

In the days of sadness ahead, you and I may trust God's support and love to uphold us through this congregation. This is a part of the witness Lou has been for us.

When a friend of mine heard that Lou had died, she responded, "That makes him the first member from this generation in the Mulligan Family Triumphant." I like that. I think Lou would like it, too.

22

Topical Preaching

As noted in the Introduction, topical sermons are typically sparked by a Christian doctrine, a Christian practice, a personal situation, or a social situation. In a topical sermon, the preacher helps the congregation interpret a topic from the perspective of the gospel. The preacher may draw upon the Bible, as well as on materials from Christian history and theology, from philosophy, from the human and physical sciences, from the arts, from general life experience, from intuition and feeling. However, topical preaching does not center on the exposition of the Bible in the same way as the expository sermon. In a sense, the gospel is the "text" on which the sermon is based. The preacher examines the topic from the perspective of the gospel.

Topical preaching can serve occasions when the Bible is silent on a subject that needs to be addressed, or when the Bible offers imprecise analogies. A topical sermon often helps the preacher when the topic is larger than any single biblical passage, or when the preacher is tempted to use a biblical text as nothing more than a springboard to a topic. A preacher might take a topical approach when a crisis has erupted in a community, and the preacher has little time to engage the Bible in a serious way. A topical sermon might help the preacher talk with the congregation about a subject on which the Christian community has not come to a conclusion.

The great danger of topical preaching is theological amnesia. A minister may become so mesmerized by psychology, sociology, political analysis, the arts, or something else, that the preacher forgets to consider the topic from the perspective of the gospel. However when powered by a clear theological energy cell, topical preaching can help a community interpret its situation in a Christian frame of reference.

Thomas H. Troeger now offers a topical sermon that helps the community interpret the relationship between Christian faith and the arts. The sermon was prepared as a part of a series of sermons at the Chautauqua Institute in New York. The theme of the series, identified by the committee that invited Troeger, was "The Arts and Social Change." In this sermon, Troeger draws upon material from the Bible and from church history to indicate the intimate relationship between the arts and religious life. In the heart of the sermon, the preacher uses a poem by George Herbert, "Rise Heart," as the basis for a sermon that notes that if the arts are to serve social change, they must take account of "the irrepressible religious yearnings of the human heart." Likewise, religion must take account of the capacity of the arts to express visions that shape the human heart.

Each sermon in the series drew from poems by Herbert set to music by Ralph Vaughn Williams in the latter's "Five Mystical Songs." As a part of the service of worship, the choir sang the song that interprets "Rise Heart."

The sermon manifests integrity between form and subject matter in that the sermon is itself aesthetic in character. The preacher does not simply talk about the relationship between faith and art, but creates a sermon that is itself a form of art.

While we usually associate preaching verse by verse with preaching from the Bible, Troeger takes a similar approach to the poem by George Herbert. In serial fashion, the preacher explains each element of the poem and its relationship to the larger poetic work, as well as its contribution to the sermon. A pastor could take a similar approach with almost any kind of text, e.g., an affirmation of faith, a document written by the church, a passage from a figure in church history, a writing in contemporary theology, a passage from a contemporary novel, a movie.

By writing the sermon in free verse, the sermon manuscript itself suggests an aesthetic quality. The sermon manuscript represents visually something of the way the preacher hopes the sermon will sound. And a manuscript prepared in this fashion often helps the preacher maintain eye contact with the congregation. The varying lengths of the sentences and other variations in the written text make it easy for the preacher's eyes to follow the sermon. The preacher does not have to search through the manuscript to find her or his place. For similar approaches to the layout of the sermon, see chapters 16, 17, and 27.

THOMAS H. TROEGER is Ralph E. and Norma E. Peck Professor of Preaching and Communications at Iliff School of Theology, Denver, Colorado. Among his influential books are *Ten Strategies for Preaching in a Multi-Media Culture* (Nashville: Abingdon Press, 1996); *The Parable of Ten Preachers* (Nashville: Abingdon Press, 1992); *Imagining a Sermon* (Nashville: Abingdon Press, 1990). Troeger is an accomplished flutist who frequently integrates the flute and other aspects of the arts into his many lectures and seminars on preaching. He is also a noted hymn writer, e.g., *Borrowed Light: Hymn Texts, Prayers, and Poems* (New York: Oxford University Press, 1994); with Carol Doran, *New Hymns for the Lectionary: To Glorify the Maker's Name* (New York: Oxford University Press, 1986).

THOMAS H. TROEGER

The Alchemy of Grace

I was alone
in a strange city
where I had completed
a sad visit.
It would be several hours
before my plane left,
so I went into a restaurant,
attracted less by the menu in the window
than the simplicity of the furniture
and the pastel color of the walls.
I wanted peace
more than I wanted a meal.
I ordered just enough
to buy myself the right to sit at a table.

While I waited for the food to come,
a harpist appeared
on a small raised platform
at the far end of the restaurant
and started playing
arrangements of various pieces
by J. S. Bach.

There were not yet many people
in the restaurant,

and the room was resonant enough
for the harp sound
to fill the space.

I sat back in my chair
and as Bach's melodic lines
intertwined with the hummings of my soul,
I was like Saul
listening to David on the harp:

"And whenever the evil spirit from God
came upon Saul,
David took the lyre and played it with his hand,
and Saul would be relieved
and feel better,
and the evil spirit would depart from him" (1 Samuel 16:23).

David's musical art
was in the service of healing,
a ministry
of restoring human personality to wholeness.

The great church reformer
Martin Luther
had a special affection
for musical powers.
Luther considered music
to be one of God's greatest gifts.

Once when a woman
was suffering depression,
Luther instructed members of the church
to meet regularly with her
and to sing a particular sequence
of psalm tones and hymns.

It was a form of musical therapy,
and the historical record
indicates that it worked.

The woman,
like me in the restaurant,
experienced
the truth of the biblical verse:

"And whenever the evil spirit from God
came upon Saul,
David took the lyre and played it with his hand,
and Saul would be relieved
and feel better,
and the evil spirit would depart from him."

David's art,
Martin Luther's art
were in the service of healing,
of restoring wholeness to the human personality.

And so was George Herbert's.

Or to be more accurate,
George Herbert's poetry is a witness
to the One
who is the source
of healing and restoration:

Rise heart: thy Lord is risen. Sing his praise
Without delays,
Who takes thee by the hand, that thou likewise
With him may'st rise:
That, as his death calcined thee to dust,
His life may make thee gold, and much more just.[1]
Calcine is a technical term
from alchemy,
the medieval philosophy of chemistry
that had two goals:

1. transforming
base metals into gold

---

[1] George Herbert, "Rise Heart, Thy Lord is Risen," in *The Works of George Herbert*, ed. by F. E. Hutchinson (Oxford Clarendon, 1941), 41–42.

and
2. preparing
the elixir of longevity.

Wealth
and
youth!

All you have to do
is watch television
to know that we human beings
still practice
alchemy,
still ache and yearn for
a magic formula for
wealth
and youth.

In medieval alchemy
the first step was
to calcine the base metal,
to purify it in the fire,
burning away all its
volatile
and impermanent constituents.

The first stanza of the poem
suggests there is an alchemy
of grace,
a spiritual process
that follows the same basic order:

His death calcined thee to dust.

By the death of Jesus
we are calcined to dust:
we realize
that suffering and death
are part of the destiny of all mortal flesh.

By the death of Jesus
we are calcined to dust:
we realize
the capacity for evil
that lies in our hearts.

By the death of Jesus
we are calcined to dust:
we see the futility
of our alchemy,
of our frantic, magical pursuit
of wealth
and youth.

By the death of Jesus
we are calcined to dust,
but it is only
the first step.
For the risen Lord takes our hand
so that

His life may make thee gold, and much more just.

Gold!
Wealthy at last.
But not wealthy
in the way of the world.
Wealthy in love.
Wealthy in hope and faith.

Wealth that disappears
the minute we hoard it.
Wealth that grows
the minute we give it away.
Wealth that makes us
much more than wealthy:
wealth that makes us *much more just.*

To be just
is to do justice,

it is to be a citizen of the world
who is committed to seeing
that every single person
is treated with integrity
and fairness.

This is the true alchemy,
the alchemy of grace,
the alchemy of transformed
values
that makes social change possible.

It is an alchemy
that needs to happen
in the soul of the individual,
in the soul of our churches,
in the soul of our culture.

It is an alchemy
we often sense in the presence of art.

We stand in front of a great painting
and we shudder
at what we see of our own life.
We are *calcined* to dust.

We hear a great piece of music
and our hearts rise,
and for a moment
we are made
gold, and much more just.

George Herbert knew
that art
could participate
in the alchemy of grace.
In the second stanza,
following the pattern of Psalm 57,
he parallels the rising of the heart
with the awaking of his lute,

the awaking of music,
that stands as well
for the awaking of his poetic art:

Awake, my lute, and struggle for thy part
with all thy art.

The *struggle for thy part*
is a struggle that every artist knows.

For years I studied
to be a professional flutist.
I practiced scales
and arpeggios
for hours and hours,
and then spent hours and hours
more to get to technical perfection
in playing sonatas
and chamber music parts
and concerti.

And if you are a dancer
or a potter or graphics designer
or a preacher
or any other kind of artist,
you know the truth of Herbert's command

struggle for thy part
with all thy art.

There is a technical perfection
that demands

all thy art.

And yet
the most accomplished technique
is no guarantee
that the work of art
will participate

in the alchemy of grace,
the alchemy of transforming the soul.

We have attended
the polished concert
that was dead.

We have seen
the well crafted painting
that did not reach the heart.

Herbert insists
that his lute, his art
must be in tune
with the greatest realities
of human existence.

For him as a Christian,
this means
his art must be tuned
to the redemptive music
that flows from Christ's
death and resurrection.

In an extravagant and daring metaphor,
Herbert pictures Christ on the cross
as a divine harp
whose music gives the key
to all other music.

The cross taught all wood to resound his name
Who bore the same.
His stretched sinews taught all strings, what key
Is best to celebrate this most high day.

For Herbert
this is the profoundest struggle of art:
to reflect the height and depth
of the struggle of God
to redeem us.

When art does this,
then it is in the same key
that was sounded by Christ's
stretched sinews.

But what key is that?
What key does the cross teach us
Is best to celebrate this most high day?

Is it a minor key
suggesting
lament, sorrow, sadness?
The sadness of what was done to Jesus.
The sadness of what we continue
to do to the innocent and defenseless.

Yes, a minor key
but not only a minor key.

The music from the cross
also sounds in a major key,
to trumpet forth
the joy of love poured out,
the joy of death transfigured by the resurrection.

The music of the cross
sounds in both
a minor key
and a major key.

It is a complex key,
surpassing the usual tonalities of music,
exceeding the harmonies of our usual thought.

How are we to master this key signature?
How are we to blend in our lives,
utter realism
about the depths of human evil
with the irrepressible hope
in our hearts?

Herbert's final stanza points the way:

Consort both heart and lute, and twist a song
Pleasant and long:

To consort is to blend in harmony.
To consort is to act
as partners in love,
partners committed to a common purpose.

Heart and lute,
religion and art,
theology and creative imagination,
belief and aesthetics
are to work as partners
in love.

Let faith illumine art.
Let art illumine faith.
Let them together
twist a song
Pleasant and long.

George Herbert's poetic wisdom
brings theological depth
to our understanding of the ministry
of church music.

Our goal,
like Herbert's,
is to maintain
a mutual openness
between faith and art,
between theology
and the creative imagination,
between belief and aesthetics.

Let the music of the heart
give resonance
to the music of the lute.
Let the music of the lute

give resonance
to the music of the heart.

One of the great wounds
in western culture
has been the increasing
split between many serious artists
and the church.

This tragic split
has too often
kept artists
and religious people
from drawing upon
the riches
and possibilities
that each holds for the other.

And this split
has fed the so-called
"culture wars,"
making it more and more
difficult for communication
across the boundaries
of theology and secularity.

But if the arts
are going to be a power
for social change,
then they will have
to attend to the irrepressible
religious yearnings
of the human heart,
and religion will have
to attend to the visionary
capacities of artists.

Consort both heart and lute, and twist a song
Pleasant and long:
Or since all music is but three parts vied,
And multiplied:

O let thy blessed Spirit bear a part,
And make up our defects with his sweet art.

The last two lines
are a prayer
for the assistance of the Spirit.

At the end of today's anthem,
Vaughan Williams
offers a purely musical amen
to George Herbert's prayer.
After the last phrase of the poem,
the instrumental accompaniment continues
with an ascending sequence of
mystical sounds,
as if the poet falls silent,
and the Spirit carries us
to a haunting resolution
beyond language.

For a brief moment
heart and lute,
religion and art,
theology and creative imagination,
belief and aesthetics
consort in perfect harmony
and we experience the truth
of the apostle Paul's words:

"We do not know
how to pray
as we ought,
but that very Spirit
intercedes with sighs
too deep for words" (Romans 8:26).

23

Preaching on a Biblical Theme

Most expository preaching focuses on the interpretation of one biblical passage. The preacher may look elsewhere in the Bible for other passages, words, or details, but these excursions are typically in the service of making sense of the text that is the basis for the sermon. However, a preacher can also develop a sermon on a theme from the Bible. The term "theme" is not a standard category of biblical scholarship. In this book, it refers to a motif, e.g., an idea, an image, a feeling, a prescription—that is found in several biblical texts and whose meaning is not completely encapsulated in any one occurrence. A preacher needs to be careful not to reduce a theme to a word study.

A theme may be found in a single biblical book, or in a biblical author, or it may run across several books and authors. For example, the motif of the clean and the unclean is a theme in the priestly writings. The notion of the righteousness of God is a theme in the writings of Paul. Covenant is a theme that is manifest in differing portrayals of covenant—with Noah, with Abraham and Sarah, at Sinai, with David, through Jesus Christ.

A minister often considers how a larger theme helps a congregation understand a single passage. On occasion, however, the community needs to encounter the theme as a theme. In this case, the "text" of the sermon is not an isolated passage, but is the theme itself. The preacher offers an exegesis and hermeneutical appropriation of the theme.

Such preaching helps strengthen biblical literacy by helping the congregation gain an overview of an aspect of the Bible, thus providing a framework within which to interpret specific passages. Biblical writers often use a particular word or phrase in the knowledge that the particular expression will evoke a wide range of associations from across the world of the Bible. A single word can trigger a complex set of thoughts and emotions. Thematic preaching can help today's community discover these wide-ranging associations and develop empathetic identification with them. Such sermons can also help the congregation recognize different voices that speak through the Bible. The preacher can often help the congregation think critically about which manifestations of the theme are most appropriate to the gospel and to their situation, and which manifestations are theologically or morally troubling, or do not correlate so well with their setting. This helps the congregation realize the importance of placing individual texts in their larger contexts. Thematic preaching can help the preacher avoid the trap of considering a biblical text atomistically.

When preparing a sermon on a theme from the Bible the preacher needs to identify key passages in which the theme is found and note how the different occurrences add to the community's understanding of the theme. The preacher traces how the theme develops across a book, an author, or the Bible itself. While some themes are associated with particular words, a theme is typically woven more widely into the biblical fabric. The thematic preacher needs to take account of the range of words, ideas, and passages that are associated with a theme. A concordance and Bible dictionary can help the preacher prepare a thematic sermon, but the preacher needs to locate the theme in its wider world of associations.

The sermon below relates the theme of joy to the question of how Jesus and we can persevere in witness in the face of difficult circumstances. The preacher draws on pertinent passages in both testaments and on an overarching theological understanding of joy. The sermon below was preached as a part of a Lenten series at a small United Methodist Church in a midsized Ohio city. The congregation was comprised mainly of older adults.

DIANE TURNER-SHARAZZ is instructor in homiletics at the Methodist Theological School, in Delaware, Ohio. She is completing the Ph.D. in preaching at Vanderbilt University. She is an elder in the United Methodist Church. In addition to her ministry at the seminary, she preaches in many congregations and in meetings of the broader church.

DIANE TURNER-SHARAZZ

When All You Can See Is the Cross, What's Joy Got to Do With It?

I've had a strange experience as I have been preparing for this sermon. I kept feeling as though I wanted to preach on the subject, "When All You Can See Is the Cross." I wanted to deal with the issue of being in the midst of crisis, suffering, and severe distress and only being able to see crisis, suffering, and severe distress. And so I started out looking at Jesus' experience in the Garden of Gethsemane, in which he struggled with the inevitability of his crucifixion and asked God to take "that cup" away. And he ended up, "not my will, but thy will be done." But I had the sense that passage wasn't going to be enough.

As I continued to go through scriptures, two passages stood out. In John 16, Jesus is talking with his disciples as he prepares them for his leaving them, and he says to them, "Very truly, I tell you, you will weep and mourn, but the world will rejoice; you will have pain, but your pain will turn into joy…When a woman is in labor, she has pain, because her hour has come. But when her child is born, she no longer remembers the anguish because of the joy of having brought a human being into the world. So you have pain now; but I will see you again, and your hearts will rejoice, and no one will take your joy from you."

Hebrews 12 states, "Let us run with perseverance the race that is set before us, looking to Jesus the pioneer and perfector of our faith, who for the sake of the joy that was set before him endured the cross…."

There it is again—joy having a prominent place in relationship to Jesus and the cross.

Most of us have found ourselves facing difficult times. We struggle with trials and tribulations—times in which circumstances seem so unbearable and unbeatable that we aren't sure how we're going to make it through. We feel overwhelmed with the enormity of what we face. All we can see is our problems.

At such times, we relate to Jesus in the Garden of Gethsemane. We understand his prayer to God, "…if you are willing, remove this cup from me." Jesus was facing the most difficult time of his life. If he were going to fulfill the purpose that he understood God had for his life, it meant that he would have to voluntarily face suffering and death. There was no avoiding this unless he chose to not go along with God's will. "Lord, would you please just take this problem away. Won't you, Lord, get me out of this?" But then, Jesus added a few more words, "Yet, not my will, but thy will be done." Jesus was able to recognize his own feelings in the matter, but then deferred his feelings to the purposes and will of God.

Certainly there are times in which our trials and tribulations are not related to God's will. But there are other times in which we know that we have been faithful to God's will and purposes. And because we have vowed to walk the path of faith and chosen the Lord's way, we now recognize that we are walking into a time of trial. Martin Luther King, Jr., believed all persons are of value and worth in God's sight and that God, according to the scriptures, desires justice and equality for all persons. He found that standing up, sitting down, or marching for his beliefs often landed him in jail, or facing police dogs or fire hoses, or having his home bombed. It led to his death. But he chose, again and again, to witness to God's will.

Jesus saw the inevitability of his suffering and ultimate death. He struggled with it, but he moved forward. How do you deliberately walk into suffering? Not easily. Jesus, in his human nature that was just like ours, struggled. How do we know this? "...if you are willing, remove this cup from me; yet, not my will but yours be done." Then an angel from heaven appeared to him and gave him strength. But even after the angel had strengthened him, Jesus still struggled. "In his anguish, he prayed more earnestly, and his sweat became like great drops of blood falling down on the ground." Jesus could have become immobilized. How many of us would easily face suffering and death and decide to walk toward it? But after his tremendous struggle in the garden, Jesus got up, gathered up his disciples, and went to face his destiny.

If Christ struggled as he faced tribulations, surely our own anguish and struggle is understandable. But the bigger question for us today is, How can we move forward when all we can see are the trials and tribulations in our way? Our scripture from Hebrews tells us that we are to continue to look to Jesus who is the pioneer and the perfector of our faith who, for the sake of the joy that was set before him, endured the cross.

What is it about joy that can enable one to endure the cross? What is joy? The dictionary defines joy as "a very glad feeling; happiness; delight."[1] That definition doesn't tell us enough for our purposes. We need to understand joy in relationship to who we are as the people of God.

Both the Old and New Testaments talk about joy as an integral part of religious experience. It encompasses rejoicing, gladness and mirth, loud cry,

---

[1] *Webster's New World Compact School and Office Dictionary* (New York: Webster's New World, 1982), 249.

proclamation and singing, shouts, grace, and thankfulness. One understanding of joy indicates eternal expression—spontaneous emotion of unsustained, yet extreme happiness that has been prompted by an external stimulus and is expressed in some visible form. We hear this usage in 1 Samuel 18:6, "As they were coming home, when David returned from slaying the Philistine, the women came out of all the cities of Israel, singing and dancing, to meet King Saul, with timbrels, with songs of joy, and with instruments of music." In the Hebrew tradition, the experience and expression of joy are very close.

Joy comes from being faithful to God's law and God's purposes. "And the ransomed of the Lord shall return, and come from Zion with singing; everlasting joy shall be upon their heads; they shall obtain joy and gladness, and sorrow and sighing shall flee away" (Isaiah 51:11).

God is also the giver of joy. God gives all holy joy. But times come when people are not joyful. They come to God in prayer for restoration. "Restore to me the joy of thy salvation, and uphold me with a willing spirit" (Psalm 51:12).

God is also the ground and object of the believer's joy. "The godly are to be glad in the Lord, and rejoice...and shout for joy" (Psalm 32:11).

God can be the subject of the joy. God is the one who rejoices and is jubilant. "The Glory of the Lord shall endure for ever: the Lord shall rejoice.... " (Psalm 104:31).

Luke tells the story (15:1–7) about a shepherd who has a hundred sheep, but loses one, leaves the ninety-nine to go after the one, and brings the lost one home. Then the story says "there will be more joy in heaven over one sinner who repents than over ninety-nine righteous persons who need no repentance." The parable of the woman who has ten silver coins and who loses one is the same (Luke 15:8–10). When she finds the one, she has a party, and we're told that there is joy in the presence of the angels of God over one sinner who repents. The angels share in the joy of God. I used to think it was just the angels who rejoiced, but today I understand that the divine joy is present, and the angels are present in that joy. The story of the prodigal exemplifies that joy as the prodigal repents and comes home. The father rejoices and then calls together everybody to come and rejoice with him for his lost son has returned home. This is the joy of God. And God invites us into that joy.

Joy in the biblical sense, I believe, is a deep and abiding state that is felt and poured out when God's people acknowledge God, turn back to their Creator, and who seek to do God's will. Joy comes from knowing that God is with us come what may.

Think about it, at church we have the opportunity to participate in the joy of the Lord that is always present. Just like we learn when we fly in airplanes that the sun is always shining above the stormy clouds, so we learn that God's joy is always present whether or not we participate in it. We have the opportunity to be glad about what God is glad about. When we think about what God is glad about, we remember that God is the one who already knows the end of our story. God has seen around the corner of our lives, the Lord has seen the entire picture and knows how our circumstances will turn out. And knowing all of that, God still has joy and is glad, because he knows that regardless of how the circumstance appears, it is possible for us to survive and for good to come through in the end if we allow God to help us through.

Let me not suggest, however, that the presence of God's joy and gladness means that God belittles our pains and struggles. Nothing is further from the truth. How many times in scripture do we hear of God hearing the cries of God's people, and God sending someone or coming down Godself to respond to the cries? Certainly God knows, aches with us, and cares for us in all of our circumstances. God promises to be with us through it all. We can hang on, persevere, and endure with God who will bring us through. We can participate in the assurance of God's ending, rather than succumbing to the seeming defeat of the present.

We do not rejoice because we have trials and tribulations. But in their midst we can have joy. Paul was in prison when he wrote, "Rejoice in the Lord *always*; again I will say, Rejoice!" (Philippians 4:4). In James we read, "Count it all joy, my brothers and sisters, when you meet various trials, for you know that the testing of your faith produces steadfastness. And let steadfastness have its full effect, that you may be perfect, and complete, lacking in nothing" (James 1:1–2). Jesus, in the words in the fourth Gospel that I spoke early in the sermon, makes the relationship between joy and suffering more complete than any other source when it compares the tension of suffering and joy with the labor pain of childbirth. "When a woman is in travail she has sorrow, because her hour has come; but when she is delivered of the child, she no longer remembers the anguish, for joy that a child is born into the world. So you have sorrow now, but I will see you again, and your hearts will rejoice, and no one will take your joy from you" (John 16:21–22). No wonder Nehemiah affirms, "The joy of the Lord is our strength" (Nehemiah 8:10b).

The joy of the Lord that will come fully at the end enables us to get through the now. We have the opportunity to participate today in the joy of the Lord, to receive glimpses of that joy. And we have the present assurance that God will strengthen us to help us endure.

Recently, I was reminded of what it means to live in God's endings and how they can change our perception of the present. Last November,

I was invited to preach at a worship service that would take place in South Carolina in mid-March. The person who asked me promised to send me information—the theme, my travel, and hotel. I began to pray about what I should preach. Well, in mid-February I still had not received any information. I needed to make travel and hotel arrangements. So I called the person who had originally contacted me. She checked her computer and discovered that although she had written a letter, she had not mailed it to me.

I made my airline and hotel reservations. Well, about five days before I was to leave, I had not received my airline ticket. So I called the travel agency. They told me they had the reservation, but for some reason they had not ticketed me. They would get the ticket to me. By this time, I was beginning to wonder whether I was really supposed to be preaching at this event. But I remembered that God had given me something to talk about.

On Friday, I received a call from the person who had invited me to preach. "When are you planning to arrive?" "The next day." She told me that she was already in the hotel and had asked them when I was arriving, but they had no information as to my arrival or departure dates. But now that she knew, she would tell them. After my phone call, I again asked, "Lord, am I supposed to be there?" But I remembered that God had given me something to say.

I went to the airport to fly to Charleston, South Carolina, changing in Charlotte, North Carolina. My flight was over four hours late leaving, because the plane on which I was to travel had maintenance problems. The folks reticketed me for a later flight out of Charlotte, but I missed that flight, too. So I stayed in Charlotte overnight. "Lord, am I really supposed to preach at this meeting?" I was reminded that I had already been given the word.

The next morning, I made it to Charleston and went to the hotel. Though I had already written a rough draft of my sermon, I wanted to type it. I had brought my typewriter for that purpose. I knew that I would have all day Sunday to type and prepare the sermon for Monday after-noon. As soon as I put my fingers on the keyboard, I realized that the letters I was typing were not the letters that were coming out on the paper. I tried typing my name over and over again. Sometimes it would type the same letters twice and at other times it would type something entirely different. And so, I rewrote the sermon by hand. By the time I wrote, ate, and slept, I finished rewriting the sermon a half-hour before I had to preach. I knew that God had given me something to say, and I had to constantly hold on to that. I had to constantly remind myself that the ending had already been promised, and therefore the intermittent circumstances were not the whole picture. It was only in remembering the promised ending that I was able to get through the present situation.

After I preached the sermon, I was able to say with great joy, "Thank you Lord, for getting me through." I experienced the fulfillment of the joy of the Lord and the victory that had been given to me in glimpses all along the way.

Well, my experience is not the same as real difficulties and suffering. It is certainly not the same kind of experience that Jesus had when he was about to face the suffering and death of the cross. But the principle is similar. The circumstances of our present situation may be difficult, discouraging, and distressing, even devastating, but God promises to be with us not only in the by-and-by, but to be with us always, including now.

The joy of the Lord that we know will come fully at the end is that which helps us get through now. We can participate in the joy of the Lord, and we can have the present assurance that God will strengthen us to help us endure to that final joy.

When Jesus was in the Garden of Gethsemane, he was facing the suffering and death of the cross. He opened himself up in prayer to his heavenly Parent so that he could participate in God's will; and God sent him an angel who gave him strength for the joy that would be his in the end. It was for the sake of that joy, God's purpose and fulfillment, that was set before him that he endured the cross, and now he has taken his seat at the right hand of the throne of God. The psalmist says, "I keep the Lord always before me; because [the Lord] is at my right hand, I shall not be moved. Therefore my heart is glad, and my soul rejoices, my body dwells secure...Thou dost show me the path of life; in thy presence there is fullness of joy" (Psalm 16:11).

We know the end of the story. Jesus faced his suffering, endured the cross, and died on Calvary's hill. But God raised him from the dead and exalted this Christ to a seat at the right hand of God forevermore. And because of his death and resurrection, we all have the possibility of life.

We may be in the hardest times of our lives, but God is with us and will enable us to get through to the end. The joy of the Lord is our strength. The cross is before us. Good Friday is at hand. But, thank God, Easter is coming.

24

Preaching on a Doctrine

By Christian doctrine, I mean the systematic, coherent, comprehensive statement of what a Christian community believes (or ought to believe) concerning essential elements of Christian faith and life, e.g., God, Christ, the Holy Spirit, the church, baptism, the Lord's supper, specific acts of Christian witness. Doctrine typically develops in much the same way that a seed matures into a plant. It typically begins with affirmations that are in the Bible. Over the course of history, the church reflects on these affirmations—clarifying, enlarging, deepening, and correcting. Doctrine evolves. Doctrine emerges formally when the church makes a statement that sums up the heart of its belief about an aspect of its faith and practice. Doctrine can also come to informal expression in thought and practice. Doctrine is typically more than any single statement found in any single biblical text. The various elements of doctrine articulated from the pulpit should be logically consistent with one another. They should help the congregation make coherent sense of life from transcendent perspective, so that the community can believe and witness with integrity.

Theologically alert preachers regularly connect the exposition of biblical passages to the larger world of Christian doctrine. Beyond that, preachers need to develop occasional sermons whose purpose is to give an interpretation of an aspect of Christian doctrine as such. For example, a preacher might develop a sermon whose text is a statement in the Nicean formulation of Christian faith. The sermon is controlled by the exposition of the doctrine. In the sermon, the preacher would likely draw on the Bible, on Christian tradition, on the congregation's experience, and on reason. But the preacher would aim to help the congregation grasp the overarching theological claim of the doctrine.

Such preaching directly helps a congregation become more theologically literate. The preacher can help the congregation grasp the core Christian content of the doctrine and how the particular doctrine relates to other things that the Christian community believes and does. The sermon can draw out the implications of the doctrine for the life and witness of the contemporary Christian community and for the wider culture. The sermon with a stress on doctrine often creates an imaginative experience of the doctrine.

In the sermon below, Barbara Shires Blaisdell offers a doctrinal sermon on repentance. The sermon considers repentance in biblical, historical, and theological perspectives. The preacher hopes that the sermon will encourage the members of the congregation to repent.

BARBARA SHIRES BLAISDELL is senior minister of First Christian Church (Disciples of Christ), Concord, California. She has published several articles. She contributed to the *Abingdon Women's Preaching Annual* and to other resources for preaching. With Scott Black Johnston and Ronald J. Allen, she is co-author of *Theology for Preaching: Authority, Truth, and Knowledge of God in a Postmodern Ethos* (Nashville: Abingdon Press, 1997). She preaches extensively at assemblies of the church.

BARBARA SHIRES BLAISDELL

Repent, for God's Sake, and for Yours

Today, we begin the season of Lent—forty days of preparation for Easter. We prepare to remember the death of Jesus and to celebrate the resurrection. Ever since the church first set aside Lent as a season, repentance has been a major aspect of Lenten preparation.

Repent. What does that mean? Members of our denomination aren't much used to the language of repentance. What does it mean? What *difference* does *repentance* make in our world, in our church, in our personal lives?

By way of answering these questions, let me meander a bit, with a little personal biography. Lyndon B. Johnson was the first president whose term of office I really remember. Yet, I didn't take much interest in him until I lived in Texas. Suddenly I was surrounded by Texas lore and an LBJ that, like all Texas lore, was bigger than life. I began by reading a biography of LBJ serialized in *Texas Monthly*. I went on to read others.

I was fascinated by this man LBJ: author of both the war on poverty and the war in Vietnam. I remember reading something Johnson said after he had left office—as he reflected back on his presidency, reflected back on his handling of the Vietnam crisis. "I never felt I had the luxury of reexamining my basic assumptions. Once the decision to commit military force was made, all our energies were turned to vindicating that choice and finding a way, somehow, to make it work."

"I never felt I had the luxury of reexamination."

This is an old and pervasive notion—that reexamining one's basic assumptions is a luxury that busy, active people (people like you and me) cannot afford. And there is truth in it. One can deliberate only so long. Then one must act one way or another. One must "fish or cut bait."

However, instead of regarding the reexamination of previous basic assumptions as a luxury, the Jewish community—especially the prophets—saw it as an absolute necessity. Indeed, the tradition claims, reexamination of assumptions is *the* way God intends for us to grow to our fulfillment as a world, as a church, as individuals.

Repentance: in the Hebrew language, the word literally means "to turn," to return, to relook at old positions, old decisions, old promises, old assumptions. Reassessing, reexamining old assumptions is a positive, not a negative thing.

As I say, repentance is a staple, a central part of Jewish life from the beginning of their history. Life is a journey with God that requires constant monitoring to make sure we are keeping on the path. When we wander from the path, we need to turn to adjust course. We turn away from the danger toward which we are heading. We turn toward God's ways.[1]

Judaism developed regular liturgies for repenting. The people would examine their lives, confess the places they had abandoned God, and seek God's help in doing better. These liturgies often contained symbolic acts—tearing their clothing, spreading ashes, wearing rough garments. These acts were signs of penitence. We mark our foreheads with ashes on Ash Wednesday as a sign that we acknowledge our transgressions, and that we resolve to turn from them.

God offers the community the act of repentance as a means of grace. When the community repents, we are renewed. When we need to repent, but do not, we suffer.

In the days of the prophet Amos, for instance, the people strayed from God's justice. The middle class and the wealthy exploited the poor. They

---

[1] Joseph P. Healey, "Repentance," in *The Anchor Bible Dictionary*, ed. by David Noel Freedman, et al. (Garden City: Doubleday Anchor Press, 1992), vol. 5, 671.

worshiped idols. The priests passed the hand of blessing over these activities. The people had the chance to repent, to correct their behavior and their faith, but they did not. The community began to decay. "Yet," even in the midst of decay, God says, "You did not return to me" (Amos 4:6). As a consequence of failing to repent, the community collapsed. It was overrun, its leaders carried into exile.

Circumstances were similar in the days of Jeremiah. God pleads with the people.

> Return, faithless Israel, says the LORD
> I will not look on you in anger,
> For I am merciful, says the LORD;
> I will not be angry forever.
> Only acknowledge your guilt,
> That you have rebelled against the LORD your God,
> And scattered your favors among strangers under every green tree,
> And have not obeyed my voice, says the Lord.
> Return, O faithless children, says the Lord,
> For I am your master;
> I will take you, one from a city and two from a family,
> And I will bring you to Zion (Jeremiah 3:12–14).

Later, Jeremiah says that repentance makes it possible for God to create a new heart in the people (Jeremiah 24:7). Ezekiel takes the motif of the new heart even further. God says, "I will remove from your body the heart of stone and give you a heart of flesh" (Ezekiel 36:26).

Jesus begins his ministry with this very theme. After being immersed by John in the River Jordan and after facing off Satan in the temptation in the desert, Jesus comes to Galilee and proclaims, "The time is fulfilled, and the reign of God is at hand: *repent, all of you*, and trust in the good news" (Mark 1:15).[2] The first words of Jesus' public ministry are an invitation to do exactly what LBJ felt he could not do regarding his policy in Vietnam.

What is repentance actually, if not the power to go back and re-examine old assumptions and whenever needed, wherever needed, to *undo* and *redo* and *set forth in a new direction*?

Now such an interpretation of repentance—to think again about old ideas and old promises—comes as quite a shock to the human psyche. For we tend to associate repentance with condemnation and reprisal. "Repentance"—the word calls forth images of a pulpit-pounding preacher describing an angry God looking down with a glare and a pointing

---

[2] The translation is the preacher's.

finger, demanding that we "come clean" and come out from hiding so as to receive the punishment we so richly deserve.

No wonder we have held on to the notion that we cannot afford to reexamine old decisions! Some defensiveness buried deep within us would rather spend all our energy justifying old positions rather than discovering we may have been wrong from the beginning. But one way of understanding the gift of the gospel given to us by Jesus Christ lies in seeing what he did with this concept of repentance. From the very first day of his ministry, Jesus linked repentance with *trust*, trust in the gospel, trust in the good news that God loves us. Rather than fear it, Jesus claimed repentance is a gift bequeathed to us by the God of love.

On what did Jesus base this fantastic claim: that reexamining our lives, reexamining old decisions is something to be trusted and not feared? He based it on his insight regarding who *we* are and upon who God is; who we are as *creatures* and what kind of *Creator* God is.

Who are we? God did not create us whole, complete. "First the seed, then the blade, and then the flower came to be." Process is the law that characterizes all of nature. We begin as sperm and egg, a bit of ancient genetic tissue, and we and God bring ourselves forward by stages of growth. Incremental growth, step by step, is the usual way we come to fulfillment. God is the *author* of that process. God is the one who, through Jeremiah, pleads, "Come to me."

Such growth, such blooming growth in human beings, brings God delight—just as a first step, a first word, a first smile brings delight to a parent. Growth, step by step, is not something God merely tolerates. It is what God expects and blesses and encourages in us.

In practical terms this means that God does not expect or delight in our achieving perfection or wholeness at the beginning or even in the middle of our lives. The rightful place for wholeness is at the end of this process we call life. And it is reached by trial and error; by falling down and getting up again; by "falling forward" as someone has described the process of letting our mistakes teach us something.

Remember that point in childhood when you could observe far better than you could interpret? The three-year-old fear that you would be sucked down the bathtub drain along with the water; the teenage observation that your parents failed to practice all that they preached; observations which have different interpretations at this point in our lives. We have reprinted, rethought our earlier judgments of bathtubs and parents, and have a kinder, gentler view of both.

Our tradition teaches us to *repent* and to *trust* that God will work with us. Our tradition recognizes the kind of creatures we are and how we come to our truth. Because God is our Creator, God understands, encourages, and even blesses our growth by trial and error. It is in this sense that repentance can be thought of as a *gift, a joy,* a privilege. We need not live in fearful defensiveness of our past. God does not take what has been as seriously as we seem to. God sees our past, the good, the bad, and the ugly of it as a part and by no means the only part of life. God also sees that we have a present and the future, dynamic and alive. And so, you and I can learn things today that shed a whole new light on yesterday's conclusions.

We can indeed repent, turn and look again, and risk having been wrong because we *trust* that God loves us. God is more interested in our growth and in how much we have learned from our mistakes than in how many mistakes we make.

God does not preside over life as if it were a spelling bee—one mistake and you're out. A demon fear within us threatens that. God presides over life as a tender, gentle wise parent (a parent far wiser than we) who celebrates growth without begrudging the price paid for it.

That is the good news this morning. Repent, reexamine your past, your old assumptions, ancient prejudices, and treasured assurances. Think again about your present. And know that, as you look back even at your glaring mistakes, God loves you and goes with you into a future that is filled with possibilities for a better world, a better church, a better you.

That is the good news I want to proclaim to the dropout who didn't learn to read, to the young woman in the battered women's shelter who wonders if she must go back to the abusive husband she promised to love always, to the tired, old bigot who has guarded and treasured his prejudices all his life! Repent, reexamine your life in the light of your wisdom today and trust that God loves you. That is the good news I want to shout to all the world's leaders who are considering war: repent, reconsider, think again, and trust in the gospel, the good news that God loves you and *all* God's creatures. Repent! For God's sake.

I recall that Carlyle Marney, somewhere, speaks of mistakes and growth in life and puts it this way: "It's too late to worry about innocence. That was never a possibility or ever the issue, anyway. Becoming a responsible steward of our mistakes and growing from them, that is the challenge."

I do not know the past mistakes that haunt you. But this is the gospel I proclaim to you today: Repent, reexamine your past, your old assumptions and ancient prejudices and treasured assurances. Be willing to find your mistakes because you can trust in the gospel, the good news that God loves you, and all God's creatures. Repent, for God's sake—and for yours.

25

Preaching on a Christian Practice

Only a few years ago, the term "practice" in the Christian community typically referred to things that people did in order to achieve an immediate and utilitarian end. Often, theory and practice were regarded as opposite poles on a spectrum. Theory was abstract. Practice was the actual doing of the theory in the everyday life of the church. One of the goals of the church—especially of ministry—was to integrate theory and practice. Theological education sometimes contributed to this dichotomization by segregating the "practice of ministry" into courses in which ministers learned how to perform certain ministerial tasks, e.g., preparing a sermon, planning a campaign to raise the church budget, even running a photocopy machine.

A renewed understanding of practice is emerging in the Christian world. Many Christians today think of practice as something that we do that shapes who we are. Who we are, then, shapes what we do. Practices are specific activities that take place in the community in which people embody the community's deepest values. These values are informed by tradition. They are accompanied by norms that allow the community to gauge the degree to which a practice is being carried out in such a way as to have its optimum effect in community or the degree to which the conduct of the practice needs to be revised in order for it to manifest the highest standards of the community. By doing certain things, we not only learn how to do them, but they become a part of the ways in which we understand the world and the ways in which we relate to one another and to nature. We develop identity in accordance with what we do. New-comers become a living part of the community by joining its practices. Over time, especially as they learn the history and meaning of the prac-tices, they come to understand what it means to be a part of the commu-nity, and their practice becomes more profound.

In the deepest sense, the Christian community practices the gospel. That is, we do things that help us experience, understand, and witness to God's unconditional love for us and for all, and God's call for justice for us and for all. Craig Dykstra identifies thirteen specific practices that, working together, create the church as a community of the gospel. These are: worship, telling the Christian story to one another, interpreting the Bible and the history of the Christian tradition, prayer, and confession of sin to one another, tolerating and encouraging one another, carrying out acts of service and witness, suffering with and for one another, providing hospitality and care, listening attentively to one another, struggling to become conscious of our context, criticizing the principalities and powers, and working together to maintain social structures that sustain life as God intends. Engaging in these practices both forms and expresses Christian identity.[1]

One of the callings of the minister is to help these practices take place in the congregation. Through the sermon, the preacher can alert the com-munity to the importance of the practices, to their history and meaning, and can encourage people to partake in them. In the next sermon, Sally Brown helps the community name how corporate singing contributes to the Christian practice of worship. While common singing expresses what is on the minds and hearts of the community, it also contributes to the formation of what Christians think, feel, and do. Such singing is not an ornament, but glorifies God, involves the whole of the community's be-ing. The physical act of singing initiates resonance that permeates the self; members of the community embody their connection with one another. Through singing, the church can understand more deeply its corporate nature, and how the gifts of each member are caught up in the larger witness of the community.

The sermon was prepared for a service lifting up music as a part of the practice of worship and beginning the season of Lent at First Presby-terian Church, Bethlehem, Pennsylvania. Professor Brown served as a pastor in the congregation at that time. Brown interprets this practice through

---

[1] *Growing in the Life of Christian Faith* (Louisville: Presbyterian Church [U.S.A.], 1989), 27–28. Dykstra is identified as the author of *Growing in the Christian Life* in *Practicing our Faith*, ed. by Dorothy C. Bass (San Francisco: Jossey-Bass, 1997), 205.

the lens of Psalm 98, thus demonstrating the interrelatedness of the practices. The chant-like cadence of the opening paragraph anticipates, rhetorically, the sermon's themes. The practice of interpreting the Bible helps interpret the practice of corporate. A pastor could preach directly from a practice. For instance, a preacher could develop a topical sermon on the notion that we are to confess our sin to one another. The practice itself can become the "text" of the sermon.

> **SALLY A. BROWN** is assistant professor of Preaching at Lancaster Theological Seminary, Lancaster, Pennsylvania. She is preparing the chapters on worship and preaching as practical theology for an introductory text on practical theology co-authored with Richard Osmer and John Stewart.

SALLY A. BROWN

Singing the Overture

Psalm 98

The burden of the scriptures, from beginning to end, is primarily this: to bear witness to the great acts of God.

In the beginning, God broods. God speaks, God creates.

God calls, God wrestles, God rescues.

God builds, God shatters, God weeps.

God pursues. God saves.

The scriptures reveal that human beings respond in a great variety of ways to encounter with the living God. But two responses seem more characteristic—more fundamental and universal than the rest. These most fundamental human responses to the activity of God are utter silence and the lifting of the human voice in song.

Sometimes, when the sheer holiness of God bears all its weight upon our awareness, we are stripped of words and struck silent. But the God we meet in the Bible is not only the God whose weighty holiness at times fills the horizon of our consciousness. The God we learn to know through the scriptures is a God whose initiatives impact our lives, whose deeds shape our common histories and break open new fissures of liberating grace. God does not observe creation coolly at a distance, but acts ceaselessly in its midst. Among the most characteristic impulses of human beings in response to this unresting divine work seems to be not mere speech but music.

Did you hear the music of Psalm 98? Imagine that under the great arch of the sky stands one lone figure. A single voice, pure, unaccompanied rises into the vault of heaven: "Sing to the Lord a new song, sing to the Lord, O wide earth." It is a summons. Far in the distance, a swell of sound begins. A fuguing melody weaves above and below the original voice—first rising from the lyre and harp, then trumpet and horn. Now the music builds in waves of sound, voices upon voices upon voices. Finally, the very ground begins to tremble beneath our feet. The rhythm is jubilant and deep as time: "Let the *sea roar* / let the *floods clap* / let the *hills sing.*" Do you hear it? "Let the *sea roar* / let the *floods clap* / let the *hills sing.*" We who had taken the rocks and trees for granted have been taught by the psalmist to listen with expectant ears to the universe: It is a great antiphonal organ, waiting to echo the praises of the people of God.

From ancient Israel to the present-day church, people who worship the God revealed in the scriptures have never stopped singing. From Miriam chanting God's victory above the rumble of foundering Egyptian chariots, to Paul and Silas singing at the midnight hour in Philippi, God's people have raised voices of praise to the One who saves.

We have just begun the season of Lent. Traditionally in the Christian church, Lent is a time when Christians recommit themselves to the basic disciplines of the Christian life. By disciplines we don't mean, as some seem to think, arbitrary deprivations or artificial procedures designed to chasten our egos and underscore our sins. Christian disciplines are deliberate habits of life that render us more responsive to the creative work of God's Spirit in us, through us, and in the world.

In Lent's forty days, we Christians down the centuries have given ourselves to scripture reading and to prayer. We follow hard on the footsteps of Jesus from Galilee to Jersualem, and discover to our amazement that Jesus' journey leads us straight into the broken places of our own communities. There, one of us serves a meal to a hungry woman and her children. Another listens to the pain of an angry man out of a job. And almost unaware, we are caught in the surge of God's struggle on behalf of the whole beloved world. Such are the disciplines of Lent.

In Lent, the church witnesses in word and deed, and the church also sings. We sing our wonder and our longing. We sing our anguish and our hope. We sing our convictions, and we sing our prayers. Singing sacred music is among the most basic disciplines of the spirit, one of the central disciplines not only of Lent, but of the whole Christian life.

Paul writes to the early church, "Speak to one another in psalms, hymns, and spiritual songs, making melody in your hearts to God," and this comes not so much in the tone of suggestion as command. Singing to the glory of God, say believers from the beginning until the present, is an *indispensable* practice of this community called church.

Singing, no less than prayer or the study of scripture or acts of compassion, is a spiritual discipline. Singing claims the singer, body and soul. Sacred singing is full-bodied prayer, an act of worship that demands head and heart and sinew, a metaphor of discipleship itself. I watched a documentary not long ago about a famed baritone. With his accompanist he rehearsed a passage from a Bach mass. He sang it once, then shook his head in disgust. "No, again," he said. "This time I will be in it." All of ourselves, in all of the notes, for the glory of God. As you cannot sing a challenging piece of music giving anything less than all of yourself so with the life of discipleship. It is glorious and liberating, and it can be painful, too, and costly. Live to the glory of God, and no part of you will be spared its joy or pain. Singing sacred music is a living metaphor of discipleship itself.

And singing sacred music is a discipline of the whole community. We sing together and learn something we could not have told one another about the communal nature of the Christian life.

One of the humbling realities of the singer's experience is that, except for a few rare, oddly gifted individuals, it takes at least two to create harmony. When we sing together we proclaim something musically about the multidimensional work of God that we cannot say or sing alone. The work of God is about difference woven together with harmony. The work of God is about unison dissolving into difference and dissonance, about dissonance resolving again into harmony. When we sing with one another, we learn how important it is to embrace our own gifts, our own calling, instead of envying the gifts, or calling, or notes of others. I learned this early in my musical experience as an alto. Altos sometimes have unenviable notes. (Why, I ask you, nothing but D-flat for seventeen measures?) I learned as an instrumentalist that cello players are not much better off. When our notes are seldom noticed by the audience, we are tempted to abandon our notes for more glamorous ones. Making music with others teaches us, in music and in life, to play our own notes and live our own gifts, and not to envy the notes or resent the opportunities of others.

Corporate praise further teaches us to listen and, for the good of the company, to blend. A chorus of voices becomes a harmonious tapestry of sound thanks to the disciplined, mutual listening of the singers. The total performance, in music and in life, is for the glory of God, and not to flatter anyone's personal vanity. In fact, the voice that pierces the fabric of the music in a self-congratulatory bid for distinction ruins the performance, plain and simple. Singing corporately is a discipline of trust. We learn to trust that by serving the greater good of the ensemble we will be blessed and served in return. Our own sound is enhanced, God is honored. The church is edified. Singing sacred music together teaches us that community is indispensable for discipleship.

Finally, making music is a practice that reminds us how important it is to return from time to time to those basic themes with which we began. A musical work can be highly complex as it progresses through multiple variations and inversions of its basic motives. Yet the winding paths of musical structure traverse, again and again, the original themes of the work. A musical work draws its coherence and balance from this pattern of return to a few basic notes.

In the Christian life as in Christian praise, we must return from time to time to those basic themes with which we began: The cleansing confession that we are sinners saved by grace, no more and certainly no less; the central truth that God in Jesus Christ has been revealed above all as love, so that whoever loves is born of God and knows God; the ancient acclamation that Christ has died, Christ is risen, Christ is coming again, so that sin and evil and tragedy will finally not have the last word in this world.

Our spiritual lives are most enriched, not by a questing after esoteric subtleties of spiritual insight, but by plowing ever more deeply the rich soil of the most basic confessions of the Christian church. In the spiritual life as in music, we must return when all has been said and sung, to the basic themes with which we began.

Church musicians have a particular calling in the body of Christ. Their particular calling is to lead the whole church in its discipline of praise, its music-making and singing to the glory of God. Sometimes our singing is corporate prayer, sometimes lament, and other times rejoicing. Sometimes our singing is proclamation. No less than the sermon, hymns and anthems can broadcast the gospel story.

But above all, when we make music to the glory of God, we are singing the overture of a work of praise that no one has ever yet heard in its entirety. According to the vision of the apostle John, there will come a day when God's redeeming work is finished. Then, says John, saints and angels and the whole redeemed creation will erupt in music. Our songs are the opening bars of the music of that transformed world.

When you sing, if you listen carefully between the notes, you may just hear creation itself—the sea and the rocky shores, the deep forests and the high mountains—drawing in one long, slow, great breath. All creation is readying itself for the time when God's work is finished. On that day, a voice will cry, "Sing to the Lord a new song; sing, all the earth!" And then every saint will chant, "Holy, holy, holy," and every pebble and star, every cedar and cataract will burst into sound, one great antiphon of praise, beautiful beyond all the beauties yet sung or imagined.

26

Teaching Sermon

From time to time, preachers feel the need to speak in a teaching mode. Of course, all sermons teach in the sense that all sermons communicate to the congregation ideas, images, feelings, and behaviors that are appropriate to the community and those that are not. Preachers need to become cognizant and critical of what we teach (and do not teach) through our sermons so that all of our preaching teaches the gospel.

Some occasions call for sermons that are explicitly designed to teach. Teaching helps the congregation name its world (its thoughts, feelings, and behaviors) in the terms of the gospel. The preacher identifies an aspect of the congregation's life that needs interpretation or reinterpretation. The preacher helps the community accumulate the resources needed to interpret its situation more adequately. The sermon leads the community in thinking critically about its life and in envisioning how it might need to adjust its life in order to take account of the fresh (or reinforced) insights that emerge from the process of critical reflection. The teaching minister helps the congregation have an imaginative experience of the subject matter that is being taught, so that the congregation thinks and feels its way into the direction of the sermon.

Teaching sermons can have different goals. Some sermons help the congregation gather and make use of information that it does not have and that it needs in order to function optimally as a Christian community. Some teaching sermons seek to help a congregation feel something of the gospel that it has not felt before. Other teaching sermons help a community enlarge or reframe an existing practice, viewpoint, or network of feelings or behaviors. Other teaching sermons seek to help the congregation recognize that some aspect of its life is fundamentally mistaken and needs to be corrected by the plumb line of the gospel. Still other teaching sermons have other goals.

The methods of teaching through the sermon can be as varied as subject matters of the sermons and the preachers. A teaching sermon can be similar to a lecture, with major subdivisions and minor subdivisions clearly enumerated. Another teaching sermon might begin with a provocative image on which the pastor and people subsequently reflect. A preacher might teach by making the sermon an extended parable. The teaching sermon is not distinguished as a single method, but by its purpose.

In the sermon that follows, William B. McClain teaches a local Christian community about the doctrine of the communion of saints. The occasion is the anniversary of Community United Methodist Church in Washington, D.C. The annual anniversary is a major event at Community UMC, as it is in many African American churches. The event is given an even more special quality by the celebration of the Lord's supper. The preacher helps the congregation understand the notion of the communion of saints in the Bible and as it is understood in the United Methodist church. McClain helps the congregation recognize the practical help that the doctrine of the communion of saints offers the congregation on a day-to-day basis. The preacher beautifully ties together the doctrine of the communion of saints with the communion that takes place through the Lord's supper.

WILLIAM B. McCLAIN is professor of preaching and worship at Wesley Theological Seminary, Washington, D.C. A noted preacher and lecturer, he is the author of one of the most thorough and extensively used commentaries on worship and preaching in the African American church, *Come Sunday: The Liturgy of Zion* (Nashville: Abandon Press, 1990). His *Black People in the Methodist Church: Whither Thou Goest* (Cambridge: Schenkman Publishing Co., 1984) opens a searching, sensitive conversation on the future of African American people in the United Methodist church. That conversation is broadened in a book that he edited with Grant Shockley and Karen Collier, *Heritage and Hope: The African American Presence in United Methodism* (Nashville: Abingdon Press, 1991). He has also written *Traveling Light: Christian Perspectives on Pilgrimage and Pluralism* (New York: Friendship Press, 1981).

WILLIAM B. McCLAIN

I Believe in the Communion of Saints

2 Corinthians 13:13; Hebrews 11:32—12:2

My friend and colleague at Wesley Seminary, an ordained elder of the United Methodist Church, Laurence Hull Stookey, never tires of reminding us United Methodists that All Saints' Day was one on which John Wesley, founder of Methodism, was very fond of preaching. Wesley's journals are filled with references to his sermons on All Saints.

In one of his many journal entries, he remarks, "November 1st was a day of triumphant joy, as All Saints' Day generally is. How superstitious are they who scruple giving God solemn thanks for the lives and deaths of his saints."[1]

This church anniversary can be seen as a time of communion with those of the past, the present, and the future. For it is a service of remembrance so that we can render thanks to God for the lives and deaths of those who have labored here as colleagues and family in the church on earth, reminding us of our connection with the church triumphant in God's love. This is a service of triumphant joy as we remember and celebrate those "of whom the world was not worthy" and "who surround us as a great cloud of witnesses."

In a sense, they are invisible onlookers as we continue the noble tradition that they have bequeathed to us. We who are gathered here in this place are here because they have gone before us, and believed, preached, taught, and lived the gospel. *We who are gathered here today have faith because those who have gone before us were faithful.* We who are gathered here today to recall and reclaim and celebrate the past are here because they gathered together across the years—and perhaps some of them tough years of hardships, low salaries, sacrifices, self-denial. Some of those years were years when jobs were scarce, segregation and discrimination were the order of the day. The harvest was often scant, the assessments were hard to meet, and the budget meager. Some of those whom we remember today and whose lives and deaths we render thanks to God for, lived through the depression and the lean years of soup and bread lines. Some of them lived through the years of a broken and splintered church, a church who struggled and continues to struggle with the compelling and critically important

---

[1] John Wesley, "The Journal: November 1, 1756," *The Works of John Wesley* (Salem, Ohio: Schmul Publishers, n.d.), vol. 2, 388.

issues of race, ethnicity, gender, and justice. Some of them lived through and survived a period of a hostile and divided nation, and yet they kept faith and labored toward the day when their faith would be sight, not even receiving what was promised. Yet, they "obtained a good report through faith" and remained faithful even over little things. They came faithfully and stood, and joyfully and thankfully joined others at the beginning of the year, singing:

> And are we yet alive
> And see each other's face?
> Glory and thanks to Jesus give,
> For his almighty grace.
>
> What troubles have we seen,
> What mighty conflicts past,
> Fighting without and fears within,
> Since we assembled last!
>
> Yet out of all the Lord,
> Hath brought us by his love;
> And still he doth his help afford,
> and hides our life above.[2]

We are here today with faith because they were faithful. By the record of their lives, they reassure us that endurance is possible. Because of their faithfulness and their devotion to the spread of the gospel, and their belief in the power of a triune God who draws straight with crooked lines, and their utter resolve that Calvary's Hill is higher than Capitol Hill, we are here as stewards of this "divine mystery." By their perseverance and their sustaining trust, we can have confidence that "sorrow may endure for a night, but joy cometh in the morning," when we will understand it better.

The saints show us "from afar" how to run with perseverance the race that is set before us by looking to Jesus, the pioneer and the perfector of their faith. We can fulfill their faith, or we can cast aside, bargain away, ideologize away, fragment away, corrupt, and bankrupt the priceless heritage, the rich and abiding tradition, and the irrepressible hope they accumulated with blood, sweat, and tears, traveling over a stony road and

---

[2] Charles Wesley, "And Are We Yet Alive," *The United Methodist Hymnal* (Nashville: The United Methodist Publishing House, 1989), 553.

sometimes bearing the pains of a bitter, chastening rod and treading a path through the blood of the slaughtered.

The apostle Paul developed the habit of writing letters to his churches: at Corinth, at Galatia, at Thessalonica, at Rome, at Philippi. And often Paul would remind those saints who were receiving letters that they were not the whole church, that there is a wider church, a larger fellowship, a universal church, by adding the salutation, "All the saints greet you," or as the old King James Version translates it, "All the saints salute you."

Probably the groups that gathered to hear the letter from their spiritual leader, Paul, were small and motley. Probably a few dozen people gathered in someone's living room. Among them were slaves, servants, and working people. A tiny group who felt insignificant in these huge, cosmopolitan, commercial cities of the Roman Empire. As Christians, they felt disconnected, isolated, a *minority* for certain, until they hear the words, "All the saints salute you." Ah, there's the *connection* for them and for us. "All the saints salute you."

And that's the word for the followers of Jesus gathered here today on this beautiful fall Sunday morning in the same place that so many who have gone before gathered. "All the saints salute you." For out of every century and from all over the globe and from the mysterious region beyond grace come the voices of our comrades in Christ who have finished their course in faith, and who now rest from their labors. Can you hear them, saying, "All the saints salute you"? Paul and Philemon and Phillip; Augustine, Athanasius, and Agnes; Luther and Calvin and Melancthon; Charles and John and Susanah; Asbury, Allbright, and Otterbein; Abraham, Martin, John and Mary McCleod; Charles Albert Tindley, and the ordinary saints who served this congregation faithfully, and the pastors who have labored, and who now rest from their labors. "All the saints salute you."

For although they are dead and rest from their labors, they still live and move within us and fight at our sides as comrades of Christ against Pilate and the Good Friday forces that would try to delay Easter and defeat the cause of Christ. They fight with us and at our sides as we fight for justice and liberation and equality, as we struggle to build a world in which there is pace with equality; to build a church and community that will be truly the church where the gospel is preached, where forgiveness is offered, where love abides, and where two or three gather in his name: to build a world in which people can have bread with dignity; freedom with liberation; love with power and justice; and in which a society is in fact, and not merely in empty promises: a kinder, gentler, nation, a nation that cares about its children, youth, and elderly.

Those who have gone before us are part of the tie that binds, a part of the fellowship of kindred minds. They are one with our hopes, our aims, our fears, our cares. Though they be dead, they still live and move within us.

But, without us, their aims are thwarted. Their dreams go unrealized, their ambitions unfulfilled, their sacrifices become futile and of no account. Unless we are faithful to the gospel that propelled them, their faith is bartered away to the whims of the world and right-wing political ideologies.

But these bygone generations are the makeup of the clouds of witnesses. *They are the invisible onlookers.* They are the ones who died in the faith still hoping for the promise. We dare not fail them by losing faith and allowing our zeal to flag. We dare not fail them by giving up the fight and shrinking from the struggle and tossing in the towel. We dare not compromise the imperatives of the gospel that accompany grace. We dare not sell or buy "cheap grace," and neglect the cost of a suffering God on Calvary and make our God's gracious and costly act look ridiculous.

And so we fight on—faithful, true, bold. We are energized by the salutes from all the saints. We are encouraged and enabled by the grace of God, the love of Jesus Christ, and the blessings and fellowship of the Holy Spirit.

And so we fight on with all of the courage we can muster—knowing that the race is not given to the swift or to the strong, but to those who endure to the end.

And so we fight on—laying aside the weights of sin that so easily cling. But we run with perseverance the race that is set before us looking to Jesus, the author and the perfector of our faith.

We run this race with the spirit expressed in a song of our forebears.

> I don't feel no ways tired;
> I' come too far from where I started from.
> Nobody told me the road would be easy,
> I don't believe He brought me this far to leave me.[3]

No wonder we are bold to stand and proclaim the words of the ancient Affirmation of Faith, "I believe in God…I believe in the *communion* of the saints."

Think of the saints in your life, and in your balcony, and in your attic. And the saints in my life. My Aunt Minnie, serving for forty-five years as one of the communion stewards, preparing the elements for the Lord's

---

[3] Curtis Burrell, "I Don't Feel No Ways Tired," *Songs of Zion*. Supplemental Resources 12 (Nashville: Abingdon Press, 1981), 175.

supper with grapes from her arbor and unleavened bread baked on her stove, attending and waiting the tables in the Sweet Home United Methodist Church in Gadsden, Alabama, and shouting the joy she felt when we sang, "The blood done signed my name." And my Cousin Kathleen, faithfully playing the organ and the piano, superintending and teaching Sunday school and organizing vacation Bible schools for more than fifty years across the old central jurisdiction of the Methodist church. And your Uncle John and your Cousin Peter and your saints who led you to find God in your most anxious hour and in your moments of deepest need. The saints in your life who have given you meaning and purpose and given you the ability to believe in yourself and to believe in God. Yes, I believe in the communion of saints who gather with us as we celebrate this church anniversary today.

And what is more, Jesus makes a promise to us. "Where two or three are gathered in my name, I will be among them." What blest communion! What fellowship divine! Name your saints as you come to the Lord's table this morning—those who have died in the faith—and be in communion with them. Render to God thanksgiving for their lives and their death, and may we all be joined together as one and one with the Holy Spirit, as we join together in this fellowship table with those below and beyond.

27

Preaching on a Personal Issue

Preachers are sometimes called to help individuals interpret aspects of their personal lives from the perspective of the gospel. A personal issue is one in which individuals need to make sense of some aspect of their immediate world from the perspective of the gospel. When preaching on a personal issue, a preacher typically needs to help the community clarify the issue and how the members of the community experience it, recognize ways in which the issue is understood in the Bible, in Christian history, theology, and practice, in the sciences (social and natural), and in other arenas of life. The preacher helps the congregation evaluate the different understandings of the issue and identify those that are more or less consistent with the gospel.

A personal issue may arise in connection with individual intellectual life. A person may need to clarify what she or he thinks about an aspect of the Bible, doctrine, practice, or some other aspect of life. In the sermon below, Kathy Black wrestles with how individuals can theologically interpret bad things that happen to them in personal ways. We experience tragedy personally. The preacher helps members of the listening community identify a primal question that many people articulate in the midst of personal loss: Why did this happen to me? Professor Black leads the congregation in naming and reflecting on the adequacy of several ways the Bible and Christian tradition have interpreted this concern. She offers a vivid and positive vision that is powered by the gospel itself.

A personal issue may come to consciousness in connection with what an individual feels. The preacher may help the community describe a

190

certain feeling, name it, interpret it in gospel perspective, and ponder how to deal with it. For instance, in today's world, many people need to learn how to deal with anger—how to name it, how to process it, how to express it in ways that build up the community.

A personal issue may be sparked by choices of behavior. How should I act in certain situations in my personal circle of relationships and choices? Many personal issues, of course, intertwine dimensions of thought, feeling, and action. The preacher helps the congregation consider the question, How can I think, feel, and act so as to be consistent with the gospel?

While useful for purposes of discussion, the categories of personal issue and social issue (chapter 28) are arbitrary. Personal and social dimensions of issues are typically quite interrelated. Social situations often have effects that people experience quite personally. Racism, for instance, is a systemic problem, but African Americans experience the results of racism very personally. Some European Americans demonstrate racism very personally. Of course, individuals can affect social systems. A person is never an isolated individual. A person is always a member of a community and is always affected in mind, heart, and behavior by aspects of the social world of the community. A person contemplating a divorce, for instance, is making an immensely personal decision. However, the high rate of divorce in the United States is affected by powerful social forces that work against conditions that are optimum for making and maintaining long-term covenantal relationships. Of course, an individual can transcend the community's worldview.

In "Why Me?" Kathy Black takes a topical approach. She draws on the Bible, as well as on Christian history and theology, in order to help the congregation sort through possibilities of interpretation. However, the preacher's doctrine of God is the basis for responding to the question of the sermon. That understanding includes many biblical perspectives, but overarches any one of them. The sermon has a highly existential quality as Professor Black draws extensively on her own personal experience with disability. The sermon was prepared for a medium-sized congregation with a diversity of people from all ages. The congregation is biblically literate, mission oriented, and theologically conservative, while being open to new ideas when those ideas are carefully considered.

The sermon is printed in the form of an oral manuscript. In a manner similar to free verse, the preacher writes the sermon in phrases that she will speak. The manuscript itself creates something of a picture of the way the sermon will sound. For similar layouts, see sermons 16 and 22.

KATHY BLACK is Gerald H. Kennedy Professor of Preaching and Worship at Claremont School of Theology, Claremont, California. She is the author of *Worship Across Cultures: A Handbook of United Methodist Worship Practices* (Nashville: Abingdon Press, 1998) and *A Healing Homiletic* (Nashville: Abingdon Press, 1997). She is a pioneer in preaching in the deaf community.

KATHY BLACK

Why Me?

It was a wonderful dance.
   A celebration to end four years of high school.
      He was with his girlfriend
      and they were double dating with his football buddy.
         Life was really good. Graduation was just around the corner.
            After the prom, they were going to the beach...
            but it started to rain.
They were in the car on the freeway deciding what to do
   when someone cut in front of them and
      forced them off the side of the road.
         The car hit the cement barrier, spun around, and flipped over.
The young couple in the back seat dressed in their prom finery were killed.
   The couple in the front seat were rushed to the hospital in critical condition.
      The parents of the driver arrived.
         Later their minister arrived...
            and his father wanted to know...
               "Why did God do this to my son?"

A divorced mother with three children
   who has struggled to provide for her children
      is diagnosed with breast cancer
         and she wants to know...
            "How much more testing
               is God going to require of me?"

Her twenty-first birthday was supposed to be a major milestone
and celebration in her life.
   Instead, she buried her favorite brother
   —a talented actor—who died of HIV/AIDS.
      And shortly thereafter, she was diagnosed
      with schizophrenia.

She has a deep and active faith
and she wants to know...
    "Will my faith be enough to cure me?"

Girl Scout troops and Brownie troops from all over the town
    gathered every summer for camp at this lake.
        We took swimming lessons and got our swimming badges.
        The older scouts got their lifesaving certificates.
            Little did we know that the lake we swam in
            collected the runoff
                from a toxic...waste...dump.
Years later, the former Girl Scouts develop cancers, brain tumors, infertility,
    and other strange disorders that cannot be officially diagnosed:
        "damage to the autonomic nervous system due to toxic exposure."
        That was my final diagnosis after two decades of tests
            at some of the best research hospitals in the country.
And the people of the town where the Girl Scout Camp was
    —a town that was begun as a Methodist Camp Meeting—
    want to know...
        "Why did God allow this to happen to our town?"

My own disability that was a result of this toxic exposure
    manifests itself in what I call "spells."
        For me, a "spell" means I lose all muscle tone
        and basically become paralyzed.
            I can hear and feel but I can't move, open my eyes, or speak.

Recently I had a "spell" in a grocery store.
    A half gallon of milk had fallen
    out of the front section of the grocery cart
        and was pouring out all over the floor.
            I bent down to set it aright
            and the bending over caused me to get dizzy...
                and I slumped to the floor.
    There I was...sitting in a puddle of milk...
        leaning up against the celery in the produce department
            ...unable to move...
                and fearful that I would fall over
                    and hit my head on the floor...
    and I heard two women talking.
        One said to the other,
            "There but for the grace of God go I."

I'm sure you have your own stories about persons you know

who have been diagnosed with serious diseases or
　　who have been born with a disability
　　　　or who developed a disability later in life
　　　　　　because of an accident or illness.
You've heard the well-intended comments:
　　"I know you have the tenacity to pass this test God has given you…or…
　　"I'm sure God will heal you—you have such a deep faith." Or…
　　Maybe you've heard the not so well-intended comments like:
　　"If you just had enough faith you would be cured"…or…
　　"You deserve what's happened to you."

Or maybe you've asked the question for yourself:
　　"Why me?" "Why did God do this to me?"

All of these questions and comments imply certain things about God.
　　That God intentionally caused the accident or illness or disability to happen…
　　That if we just have enough faith, we will be cured…
　　That cure seems to be the only sign that we have "passed God's test"…
　　That we deserve whatever God gives us because we have sinned
　　　　and that persons with good health are blessed by God…
　　　　and persons with poor health or persons with disabilities
　　　　are cursed by God.

Now I realize that all these implications
　　about God's role in relationship to
　　illness and disability can be found in the Bible.
　　　　After all…didn't Jesus say to Bartimaeus:
　　　　　　"Your faith has made you whole"?
　　　　And didn't Jesus say to the man who was paralyzed…
　　　　　　and lowered through the roof of the house:
　　　　　　　　"Your sins are forgiven"?
　　　　And doesn't 1 Corinthians 10:13 say that God tests us…
　　　　　　but that God will not test us beyond our strength?

We have inherited the biblical tradition
passed down to us throughout the ages.
　　And the popular theology we have inherited
　　　　is that God is some great puppeteer in the sky
　　　　　　who is responsible for everything.
　　And if God doesn't intentionally cause
　　bad things to happen to good people…
　　　　God at least sits back and allows them to happen.
　　　　　　We have been taught to believe that somehow…
　　　　　　　　illness and disability are the "will of God."

But what about the other biblical witnesses...
In John 9 when Jesus and his disciples encounter a man born blind...
   Jesus says to the disciples:"Neither this man nor his parents sinned" (v. 3).
And what *about* the man who was paralyzed
   and lowered through the roof of a house...
      Jesus praises the faith of the four *friends* who brought him to Jesus...
        not the faith of the man.
And when Jesus comes down
from the mountain after the transfiguration...
   Jesus chastises the *disciples* for their lack of faith...
      not the faithlessness of the father
      or the boy living with severe convulsions.
And though Jesus did say to the one person with leprosy
   who returned to give thanks
      that his faith made him well...
        the other nine were also cured of their leprosy
         with no mention...
         of their faith...or lack thereof.

And the word faith is not found at all in the stories in which...
   Jesus cured the leper in Matthew 8...or...
      the Syrophoenician woman's daughter...
   or the man who was deaf in Mark 7...
      Faith is not found in the story of the man
        who was blind from Bethsaida in Mark 8...
   or the man named "Legion" who lived in the tombs in Luke 8...
   or the woman who had been bent over for eighteen years in Luke 13...
      or numerous other stories.

And while we have many stories in the Bible
of the people Jesus cured...
   there are thousands more who did not receive a cure.
      And isn't *that* what we struggle with today?
   Not only the question "Why me?" "Why did God do this to me?"
      But also..."Why not me?"
        "Why am I not one of the chosen few
         to receive a miracle...a cure?"

Somewhere along the line, Christians have received a message...
   that if we are faithful...
      we will have health...wealth...and happiness.
      We deserve it as a reward for being a good Christian.
But this message denies the other biblical witness that talks about...

the cost of discipleship...the thorn in the flesh...
the limp we get when we wrestle with God's angel...
the suffering and persecution that we will experience
for the sake of the gospel.

And the truth is *bad things do happen to good people.*
And people who sell drugs, commit murder, or abuse children
are often in excellent health.
So how do we reconcile the biblical witnesses
and what we've been taught about God
with our own experience of health and ill-health?

First, I want to say that I don't believe
God had anything to do with causing my disability.
To believe that...I would have to believe that...
God caused a person to earn a living
by collecting toxic waste...
letting the canisters rust so that the toxins leaked into
two stream beds that flowed into the lake.
Then...God guided the Girl Scout leaders
to choose this lake for their camp.
Then...God urged my parents to send me and my sisters to the camp
and later...
Urged me to become a lifeguard for Brownie camp—
all so that I could get this particular disability.
This is not the kind of God in whom I can believe.
It sounds more like a monster out of a Hollywood horror picture.

Accidents happen...
the factories that make the products we buy pollute our air and water...
Germs and diseases emerge and mutate...
Chemicals in our brain become imbalanced...
Our genes pass on both dominant and recessive traits
that may show up
as diseases or disabilities in future generations
depending on who our offspring marry.
Sometimes we can control things by the choices we make...
and sometimes we have no control over what happens to us.
Given the pollution in our world,
the number of car accidents, airplane accidents,
and sports accidents that happen every year...
maybe the question should be..."Why *not* me?"

Illness, disease, and disability happen.

I do not believe that God is the great puppeteer in the sky
    making decisions about...
        who gets cancer and who becomes blind.
I do believe that God is with us at every moment of our lives...
    loving us...and cradling us...
        as we cope with the many trials we face
            on life's journey.
God is there to give us the strength to channel our
    anger about our condition in positive ways.
God is there to help us move out of feeling sorry for ourselves...
    so that we can get on with our lives.
God is there to change our victim status...to survivor status.

Sure...we learn many lessons...
    and our faith may be strengthened
        because of our illness or disability...or...*in spite of it.*
But that does not mean that God caused someone to be born deaf
    in order to learn these lessons.

But when something does happen...God is there...
    offering us opportunities for healing and transformation
        at every moment of our lives.

One of the confusing things about our biblical heritage
    is this notion of *healing.*
        We tend to equate the word *healing* with *cure.*
        We say "Jesus *healed* Bartimaeus"...
            but what we really mean is...
            "Jesus *cured* Bartimaeus."
But in the English language...there is a difference between *healing* and *cure.*
    Healing has many meanings...
        a healing moment...
            a healing presence...
                a healing relationship...
                a healing touch.

Jesus' ministry was truly about healing—not just cure.
    Jesus touched the man with leprosy...
        Jesus singled out Bartimaeus from the crowd...
            Jesus called the woman with the hemorrhage
                "daughter."

With each touch, Jesus would have been considered "unclean" himself
    according to the Jewish purity codes.

yet Jesus broke the rules
　　in order to bring people back
　　into relationship with other people,
　　to bring individuals back into community.
　　that is what healing is all about:
　　　　being accepted for who you are…
　　　　　　having a sense of belonging to a community…
　　　　　　being in relationship with others.
Too often, however,
　　illness and disability separate people
　　　　from their faith community…
　　　　from important relationships in their lives.

Each of us…those with disabilities and those without…
　　are called to make choices at every moment of our lives
　　　　that will facilitate healing
　　　　　　in the lives of ourselves and others.
　　We may pray for a cure
　　　　for those who live with illnesses that may be curable…
　　We may pray for a cure
　　　　for those who live with permanent disabilities…
　　　　　　There is always hope.

But in the meantime…
　　it is crucial that we focus on *healing* rather than *cure*…
　　　　that we love and accept people for who they are…
　　　　　　and not imply that they are only acceptable
　　　　　　　　and worthy of full participation
　　　　　　　　　　if they are cured.

If we believe God caused the illness or disability,
　　then we feel we are justified to separate out,
　　　　to push aside those we feel God is punishing, or testing,
　　　　　　to turn away those we believe do not have enough faith.
　　They become "unclean" in our day.

But, if we understand that rather than *causing* the illness or disability…
　　God accepts us and is supporting us…
　　nurturing us…
　　bringing healing into our lives at every moment…
　　then Christians can likewise accept…
　　　　support…
　　　　　　and nurture…those who are not cured.
We can be God's agents of healing in our hurting world.

28

Preaching on a Social Issue

Preachers are often called to preach on social issues. A social issue is public. People are aware of it or should be aware of it. The issue affects the community as a community, that is, it creates social consequences. It affects the well-being of the society. Many social issues are systemic. A social issue can be international, national, statewide, regional, citywide, or congregational in size and scope. As general examples of social issues, we might cite sexism, racism, classicism, militarism, the ecological crisis. More specific examples include the national health care debate, reform of welfare and other government services or entitlements, the national or international economy, the drug culture, abortion, life values and visions that appear (or do not appear) in the media, attitudes and laws regarding sexuality.

The preacher is called to help the congregation interpret social issues and Christian response from the perspective of the gospel. The church seeks for every social world to conform to the gospel, that is, to manifest relationships that are loving and just.

Many preachers *mention* social issues, but few preachers give detailed attention to them. When a social issue is mentioned in a typical sermon, it appears only as an illustration, or it is discussed in the oral equivalent of a paragraph.

A pastor's preaching schedule should often include sermons whose major task is to deal seriously with social matters. Such sermons would critically think about the history of the problem, about its various dimensions—sociologically, psychologically, politically, economically, emotionally, its representation in the media and in the arts, how the congregation encounters the phenomenon. The sermon would help the congregation place the subject in theological frame of reference. The preacher wants to help the congregation understand the issue from the perspective of the gospel and determine how best to act in relationship to the issue.

In the sermon that follows, Leonora Tibbs Tisdale considers Christian response to the pressure to remain silent in the face of injustice and exploitation. The preacher focuses particularly on the pressure to remain silent even when one is victimized by sexual harassment or abuse. The preacher explores how selected texts from the Bible and particular themes from Christian tradition and behavior intertwine with social convention to create a culture of complicity and silence that allows harassment and abuse to continue. Tisdale uses two biblical passages to help guide the church to move away from these negative characteristics and to move toward becoming a community with a culture of love and justice. The deeper theological core of the sermon is the doctrinal affirmation that through the cross and resurrection of Jesus Christ God pronounces an "emphatic and definitive 'No!' to anything and everything that would hurt or enslave." The preacher helps the community envision the social consequences of this doctrine. A strength of the sermon is that it helps the congregation envision practical steps that listeners can take to witness to God's will for the church, and wider world, to become a community of openness, encouragement, and support and a community free of exploitation, fear, and abuse.

The sermon was preached at a week-long conference involving clergy and laity, adults and children, at an outdoor conference center in Montreat, North Carolina—a beautiful, forested setting. At the time, many people in North America were familiar with a slogan popularized by Nancy Reagan, married to a former President of the United States. Reagan encouraged people to "Just say no" when confronted by the opportunity to use illegal drugs or to join other illicit behavior. Leonora Tubbs Tisdale plays on this theme. She shows that while this response can help individuals cope with personal encounters with such phenomena, the personal response of saying no does not adequately address the underlying system that fuels the problem. We need to create a community shaped by the values of the rule of God. The preacher emphasizes that saying no to the convention of complicity can result in personal difficulty for those who do so.

LEONORA TUBBS TISDALE is associate professor of preaching and worship at Princeton Theological Seminary, Princeton, New Jersey. She is the author of the groundbreaking *Preaching as Local Theology and Folk*

Art, Fortress Resources for Preaching (Minneapolis: Fortress Press, 1997). She is also editor of the *Abingdon Women's Preaching Annual: Series 2* (Nashville: Abingdon Press: 1999—Year A, 2000—Year B, 2001—Year C). Each year, she lectures on preaching and preaches at clergy conferences, meetings of the church, and in local congregations.

LEONORA TUBBS TISDALE

God's "No" and Ours

Esther 1:1–22; Galatians 5:1

"Just say no." If the '90s were to be characterized by slogans, then "Just say no" would probably rank up there (ironically—with Nike's "Just do it") as one of the most bandied slogans of our decade. "Just say no." The slogan, of course, was coined to communicate a good and needed message in our day—a message of encouragement to children, to youth, to all of us—to resist the temptation to abuse drugs and alcohol. And, from all outward appearances, it is a message that has born some good fruit.

When I see my own children coming home from school, far better educated (through D.A.R.E. and other educational programs) in the facts about drugs and alcohol than I ever was, I am grateful for the fruits of this slogan and the education that accompanies it.

When I read recently in my local newspaper of the efforts of community citizens to provide a safe, attractive, and drug-and-alcohol free evening for high school students in a local hotel ballroom after the senior prom—and of the fact that several hundred high schoolers actually attended that party—I found myself grateful for the fruits of that slogan.

When I overheard some middle school teenagers that I was recently transporting from one place to another speak with great admiration of a small group of high schoolers in our church youth group whom they referred to as being "straight edge" (and, for those of you over thirty who need to have that phrase interpreted, as I did, it means that this group tries to walk a straight line that avoids illegal use of drugs and alcohol, as well as premarital sex), I was grateful for the fruits that slogan is obviously bearing.

As slogans go, this one—though a bit overworked—has been a good one.

But having said all that, there's still something about that slogan that has always bothered me. And it's not the "say no" part. It's the "Just" part. "JUST say no." As if it's JUST that easy. As if a simple forming of the mouth to say no (instead of yes) is all it takes. As if saying no to things that are bad is a simple matter of deciding and doing it. As if saying no doesn't cost us anything, or require an enormous amount of courage.

"Just say no." In our scripture lesson this morning, Queen Vashti said no and it cost her a lot. I suspect that her story is typical.

The scene is a party—not a drug- and alcohol-free party, but its opposite. This party is a drunken orgy that has been going on for seven straight days. The king himself, Ahasuerus of Persia, has thrown it—in order to flaunt his wealth. He has given instructions that this is to be the party to end all parties. The palace gardens have been lavishly redecorated for the occasion, so that guests can lounge on couches of gold and silver, or sip their drinks while walking over floors of marble, mother-of-pearl, and inlaid with jewels. The food is plentiful and the alcohol is even more plentiful. We read that "drinks were served in golden goblets...of different kinds," and that "the royal wine was lavished according to the bounty of the king." And in case we don't get the full picture, the storyteller adds this line. "Drinking was by flagons, without restraint; for the king had given order to all the officials of his palace to do as each desired" (v. 8).

Evidently this is also a men-only party, because we read that elsewhere in the palace Queen Vashti is entertaining the women with a separate banquet.

And on the seventh day of the party, the king decided to bring in a woman—namely his wife—to liven up things. So he, being "merry with wine," called his seven eunuchs—probably the only safe men he could think of for this task—and sent them to fetch his wife, the queen, "in order to show the peoples and the officials her beauty; for she was fair to behold."

But when the eunuchs reached Queen Vashti and told her of the command performance before the king and his drunken guests, Queen Vashti did a very gutsy, very brave thing. She opened her mouth and with great effort, I would imagine, she formed the word no.

Though the scriptures do not tell us Vashti's motives for saying no, the story itself gives us enough details that we can well imagine what those motives might have been. "No, I will not go into a party full of drunken men as a woman alone and risk the dangers of being ogled, or groped, or worse." "No, I will not be put on display as yet one more beautiful ornament of the king's lavish palace." "No, I will not obey my husband, the king, even though I know that the consequences of my refusal may be very serious indeed."

Vashti just said no. But the scriptures tell us that that simple no cost her dearly. The king was not just angry at her refusal; he was enraged, furious. When he consulted with the sages of the kingdom to ask what the law said should be done, one of them said, "Look, King Ahasuerus, you'd better deal with this situation definitively and immediately. This kind of subversion of your authority is intolerable. Do you want word to get out that you aren't even man enough to keep your own wife under control? Think of what might happen then. All the women in the province would quit obeying their husbands, pointing to you as the big weenie that let it happen!"

"If you want to nip this revolt in the bud, there's only one thing to do. Clamp down hard. Send out a letter that decrees that Queen Vashti is never again to come into your presence. Depose her, and find yourself a new queen, and send out a royal decree declaring that every man should be master in his own house."

That is exactly what Ahasuerus did. In chapter 2 we read that he found a new queen, Esther, and the rest of the book is her tale. Vashti is never heard from after chapter 1. We don't know what happened to her. She simply vanishes from the pages of our Bible, vanishes—except for this story here told in her memory.

"Just say no." The truth of the matter is: Sometimes it's very difficult and costly to say no to that which is harmful. Sometimes saying no takes a great deal of courage. But sometimes it is necessary to witness to the world that God wants.

In recent years the issue of sexual harassment in the workplace has been much before us. It is an issue that raises strong emotions as we struggle within the church and in other places of work to fashion guidelines that will both protect victims of sexual harassment from such unwanted activity while also protecting innocent people from being falsely accused. For true justice to prevail, both protections must certainly be instituted.

But I have become increasingly concerned in recent months as I have watched persons who have filed legitimate and well-documented cases of sexual misconduct—cases where several people have even been victims of sexual harassment by the same person—become themselves targets of witch-hunts and verbal lynchings. "How dare she malign his good name?" "How dare they publicly humiliate him?" "If I ever find out who filed these charges, there will be hell to pay." All too frequently, I fear, those who have already suffered the humiliation of sexual harassment in the church or the workplace turn around and suffer the additional humiliation of having their own character and motives unjustly impugned. Saying no to harassment is not always easy.

That is why I find it so tremendously troubling that one contemporary biblical scholar while at first defending Vashti's action in refusing to parade before the king later turns around and engages in a similar attack on her character for doing so. He writes and I quote:

> Although Vashti was perfectly justified in refusing to come [to the King's party], I think she should have thought the situation over in this manner: "I can refuse and I probably ought to refuse. But this is a scandal that will get out and this will hurt my king, my husband. I think, under the circumstances, I'll go." On that basis, she should have gone to the banquet. She should have obeyed.[1]

She should have obeyed, huh? You know, for years that's what the church of Jesus Christ taught women like Vashti. It taught them that no matter what their husbands asked of them, they should obey their husbands. And it taught children and youth that no matter how bad it got at home—even if their parents beat and abused them—they should obey their parents. And it taught slaves that no matter how bad it got—even if they were raped or flogged or robbed of all dignity—they should obey their masters. And it taught employees that no matter how bad it got in the workplace and no matter how humiliated or demeaned or compromised they became, they should obey their bosses. And we are still reaping the consequences of that false teaching.

Last year at one of our denominational youth conferences a thirteen-year-old boy approached one of the leaders and said, "For years my father has been beating up my mom and me. But I'm a Christian. And I've always been taught that I should obey my parents. Isn't that what I'm supposed to do?"

Friends who work in women's shelters tell me that their rooms fill with Christian women who have been taught in their churches that it is a sin to disobey their husbands. Even with bruised and bleeding bodies, these women wonder whether their actions in saying no to their abusive spouses are justified in Jesus' name.

Well, friends, I'm here to tell you that as I read the gospel of Jesus Christ, saying no, for Jesus sake is not only allowed by the gospel; *it is strongly commended to us.* And the reason it is strongly commended is this: In the cross of Jesus Christ, God pronounced an emphatic and definitive NO! to anything and everything that would hurt or enslave us as people of God.

NO to abuse—whether verbal, emotional, or physical.

---

[1] J. Vernon McGee, *Esther: The Romance of Providence* (Nashville: Thomas Nelson, 1982), 33.

NO to winning by intimidation.

NO to coercion of the powerless by the powerful.

NO to the domination of the weaker members of society by the stronger.

NO to the use of our bodies for any but the good purposes for which God intended them.

NO, in fact, to anything and everything that would rob us of the freedom God in Christ Jesus has won for us.

Paul, in Galatians, speaks what I believe to be the very heart of the gospel. "For freedom Christ has set us free. Stand firm, therefore, and do not submit again to a yoke of slavery" (Galatians 5:1).

For our freedom, Christ paid the highest price—offering his own body to abuse and humiliation and flogging and death—so that we, though once slaves to sin and its powers in this world, might be liberated and might no longer live in bondage to anyone or anything that would oppress us. How then can we submit again to a yoke of slavery?

Conferences like this often provide good opportunities for us to sit on a rock in the midst of a mountain stream, or to take a long walk, or to sit and gaze at mountain grandeur—and to take stock of our lives. I encourage you this week as you reflect upon your own life, to ask yourself: Is there anything that is keeping me from being the free person God in Christ Jesus intended for me to be?

Are you perhaps in a relationship (dating, friendship, marriage, or other) in which you find yourself doing things you don't want to do or being things you don't want to be when you're with that person? Then, by God's grace, may you find the courage, the strength to say no to that which is harmful in the relationship and to reclaim the freedom God in Christ Jesus has won for you.

Or—and here I'm especially speaking to you children and youth—are you being hurt in some way by someone who is older or bigger or more powerful than you—someone who scares you and threatens to harm you if you tell others the secret this person is asking you to keep? Then I urge you, find someone whom you know you can really, really trust—a pastor, a counselor, a teacher, a youth advisor, a choir director—and tell them your secret, so that they can help you find a way to stop this person from hurting you.

You know, when I first read the story of Vashti all I could see within it was sadness and pain. For this is a tale of great tragedy. By the world's standards, Queen Vashti lost absolutely everything that mattered to women of her day by her courageous no. She lost her husband, her title, her economic security, her honor within the community, her crown. She was deposed, publicly humiliated, and disgraced by an unjust system.

But you know, it took a woman biblical commentator to help me see the irony, the paradox, at the heart of this tale.[2] For though Vashti lost it all (by the world's standards) she actually gained everything that ultimately mattered when Ahasuerus sent her away from his presence forever: her freedom as a child of God.

For freedom God in Christ Jesus has set all of us free. Therefore, let us stand firm—not only for our own sakes, but also with and on behalf of others in the church who desperately need us to stand firm with them—and let us boldly and courageously open our mouths and say NO! to anything and everything that would require any of God's children to submit again to a yoke of slavery.

---

[2] Sidnie Ann White, "Esther," in *The Women's Bible Commentary*, ed. by Carol A. Newsom and Sharon H. Ringe (Louisville: Westminster/John Knox Press, 1992), 127.

29

Group Study

The category of group study is derived from the work of Professor Henry Mitchell. Mitchell regards a group study as a sermon in which the preacher focuses on a group of people.[1] The group usually appears in a biblical text, in the history of the church, in Christian practice. Groups can appear within biblical texts (e.g., the strangers in the midst of Israel, the Canaanites, the crowds who come to hear John the Baptist, the women who follow Jesus). Or they can be a part of the larger world of the text (e.g., the church at Corinth). The preacher helps the congregation identify the qualities of that group, its characteristic problems, thoughts, feelings, and behaviors. A group study may be prompted by a particular biblical passage, but be supplemented by other passages. For instance, the sermon might begin with the call of the first disciples, but then draw on other passages from a gospel in order to portray the disciples as a group.

The pastor typically encourages the congregation to learn from identification with the group in the Bible, or in church history, or tradition. The congregation can identify either positively or negatively with the group. Does the group provide positive resources for the contemporary community? Does the story of that group mediate the gospel to us? Can we witness in our setting in ways that are analogous to the ways in which they witnessed in their settings? Does the thinking, feeling, and behavior

---

[1] Henry H. Mitchell, *Celebration and Experience in Preaching*, 109–116.

of the biblical group provide a warning for today's church and world? Are groups today in danger of sinning in ways that are similar to the problematic aspects of the life of the group in the world of antiquity?

A preacher develops a group study to move the contemporary congregation as a group. The preacher searches biblical texts, incidents, and themes from Christian tradition and theology and other sources for materials in the sermon that can motivate groups today. For instance, a preacher might use a group in a biblical passage or the life of Harriet Tubman to inspire a group. A preacher could create a group study in order to help a contemporary group interpret its situation from the perspective of the gospel.

In the sermon that follows, Martha Simmons develops a group study on the disciples of Jesus for a nondenominational congregation in Oakland, California. The sermon is not based on a single biblical passage, but on portraits of the disciples in the Gospels and in Acts. The sermon is designed to help the community recognize that Jesus chose people who had made mistakes. By extension, the risen Jesus still calls people who have made mistakes into participation in the church and even into positions of leadership. The congregation is located in an area frequented by drug users, alcoholics, and homeless persons. Indeed, Jesus even calls persons whom the church is not initially willing to accept.

MARTHA J. SIMMONS, a clergywoman and an attorney, is president of Simmons and Associates in San Francisco, California. She edited *Preaching on the Brink: The Future of Homiletics* (Nashville: Abingdon Press, 1996). With Henry H. Mitchell, she is co-author of *A Study Guide to Accompany Celebration and Experience in Preaching*. Professor Mitchell is the author of *Celebration and Experience in Preaching* (Nashville: Abingdon Press, 1990). Reverend Simmons also contributes to resources for sermon preparation.

MARTHA J. SIMMONS

Could Jesus Choose You?

Along the unrosy colored road toward his destiny, Jesus chose a group of disciples. He selected this group carefully, for they were to be his support, his backup, his advocates, and a key part of his legacy on earth. He had much to consider even as we do when we choose church leaders.

We usually look for people of outstanding character. Would we want a tax collector who had ruined our lives by collecting massive taxes due? Would we want people who swear and are prone to violent outbursts?

Would blue-collar workers do? How about do-nothing-but-doubt lead-ers, drinkers, or people from fanatical sects? Or a brother twosome whose meddling mother is their agent? And add one who would sell out the church for a few dollars.

Who would make up this group if Jesus were choosing today? Would some be homeless? Would a few be crack or heroin dealers? a shyster lawyer, a pimping preacher, a corrupt representative of congress? And to round it out, throw in some adulterers and get-rich-at-any-cost business leaders. Would you pick any of these as church leaders?

While you ponder that, let's take a closer look at the group Jesus picked. Neither a first nor a second glance would lead you to describe this group as made up of prominent, distinguished, or promising people. They are more like a dysfunctional crew. Some might call them a too-live crew. But *Jesus* picked, and he never kicked out anyone. He never held a busi-ness meeting and voted anyone out. Everyone who wanted to stay, stayed. This group is the one Jesus chose to walk with him to his death. In the words of a little girl, being told of the disciples Jesus chose, "I hope he had people praying for him."

Yes, this group could elevate your blood pressure and give you gray hair early. Jesus would teach them a lesson, and again and again, they would not get it. Even after three years, many made mindless mistakes. Like thinking that a savior would find little, innocent children a nuisance. Or thinking more of the money that they could have earned by selling a bottle of perfume than of the person who wanted to comfort Jesus be-cause she knew the importance of being in his presence. Can you imag-ine being so close to Jesus for so long and not getting it? Again and again, one reprimand after another. Yet, time after time, they fell flat on their faces. They got so exasperated at one point, they cried out, "Why couldn't we do that?"

One night they sat down to dinner—the last dinner they would have together. As they were passing around a container of water to clean up before they ate, Jesus spoke words that could definitely make people lose their appetites. "One of you fellas is going to betray me." It was as if he said, "One of you has been smiling in my face, but you're a backstabber." After all they had endured—even leaving family and home—one of them was just fronting.

The disciples washing their hands with him, said, "Is it I?" "Is it I?" How could this be? After all of their walking with, and talking with, and working with, and praying with Jesus, how could anyone do that? Even if they only believed that he would institute a new dominion on earth and crush the government, wouldn't that make them loyal? How could they spend three years in the presence of the Savior and still have to ask, "Is it I?"

I know you can't imagine being in their situation. So let me see if I can explain their behavior. When they asked, "Is it I?" it was just like those moments when one says, "I can't believe I said that," or, "My God, how could I have done that?" Or, when we say, "I don't know what came over me. I must not have been in my right mind."

Even after their poor, pitiful showing of loyalty at dinner, things didn't get any better. Jesus said, "Not only is there a backstabber in the group, but all of you are going to let me down tonight." One of the disciples jumped up, and sounding like an addict who has just been caught using again, said, "Not me, Lord, not me. If everyone else leaves, not me. If everyone else refuses to stand up for you, not me. If everyone else loses their nerve, not me. If everyone else sides with society, not me." And Jesus said to him, "You don't know what you're saying. When it comes right down to it, you'll run away, too. When the rubber hits the road, you'll run away, too. When you see what it's going to cost, you'll run away, too." But Peter said again, "Not me, Jesus. I'll die before I let someone else harm you. Even if the head of the government says, 'Deny him,' not me. Even if all of my friends turn away, not me."

All of the others said the same thing. "Jesus, we have momentary lapses, but we do love you. We didn't come this far to leave you. Not us. We've got your back. We're not backstabbers. Not us. No matter what the government says, we won't side with them. No matter what our families say, we're not going halfway. Not us."

Then, Jesus took them with him as he prayed. At one point, he asked three of them to stand as special lookouts. He prayed and then went back to the site of the lookouts, and they were dead asleep. He woke them, and said, "You couldn't even stay awake for an hour. After all of your talk—not even an hour." How could they?

Evil is in a footrace to outrun grace, and they're asleep. Hatred is tilling the soil to uproot love, and they're asleep. Injustice is tipping the scales to unseat justice, and they're asleep. The world is about to be draped with the dragnet of darkness, and they're asleep. Engineers are flipping the switch to derail the train of mercy, and they're asleep. Violence is writing its most memorable dissertation, and they're asleep. The ropes of politics are about to lynch an innocent man, and they're asleep.

Jesus looked at them and said, "The spirit is willing, but the flesh is weak. You really want to do the right thing, but your flesh is weak. You really do want to change the world, but your flesh is weak. You really want to make a difference, but your flesh is weak."

So he gave them another chance to show that they understood his mission. Another chance to stand up and act like disciples. Another chance to show Jesus that his legacy would be in good hands. Another chance to show that they had been listening. Another chance to turn the world upside down. And, guess what, they failed again.

And what did Jesus do then? In his compassion, he gave them still another chance. Another chance to show Jesus that he could count on them. Another chance to show that they knew what was at stake. Another chance to help Jesus shoulder his burden. And, guess what, they failed again.

But, the divine conjunction was at work. This was the group Jesus had chosen. Jesus did not kick out anyone. Jesus knew that when you're weak, you can be strong.

> When you can say, "Lord, I failed to keep promise after promise and messed up time after time," that's when Jesus can introduce you to mercy.

> When you admit that you're so strung out you don't even recognize a point of return, that's when Jesus can clean you up, and turn you around, and place your feet on solid ground.

> When you can confess that your might isn't strong enough and your intelligence has run out of answers, that's when Jesus can introduce you to the strength and wisdom of the ages.

> When you cry out that you've run out of energy and you're falling down from leaning on your own understanding, that's when Jesus can show you why he is the rock of ages.

> When you tell the Lord that your finances are few and your fair-weather friends are fewer, that's when Jesus can be a friend who sticks closer than a brother.

> When you can roll over and tell Jesus that you've reached the end of the ragged rope to which you're clinging, that's when Jesus can lift you to heights that no one can lower.

> When you're weak, that's when you can be strong.[2]

---

[2] This piece of free verse is by the preacher.

So, after Jesus was crucified, he rose. After a few ticks of the stop-watch of eternity, these same disciples—every one of them who chose to stay in the group—showed up again in biblical history. We find them in the book of Acts. They heal a person. They preach with such power that over 5,000 say, "We, too, believe in Jesus." Then, as they are still addressing the crowd, local authorities come and put them in jail for preaching about the resurrection.

The next day they are interrogated. One of the same people who failed as a lookout in the garden, the same one who thought violence was the first resort, the same one who denied knowing Jesus, was asked, "By whose authority are you doing these things?" And, *guess what*? Peter stood boldly and said, "We do these things in the name of Jesus. The one whom you crucified, who is now risen." This time Peter said, "It was Jesus. Not by our might, but in the name of Jesus." This time he said, "We were too weak to do these things on our own, Jesus does it through us. He is the stone whom you rejected, but we know that he is the chief cornerstone."

The authorities warned Peter and the disciples, "You had better stop going around talking about Jesus." But this time things were different. The disciples had gone from zeroes to heroes. This time they said, "We cannot stop talking about what we have seen and heard. We came to Jesus just as we were. We let him down again and again. But he still chose us and kept us. We were cowards and confused, but he chose us and kept us. We kept getting it wrong, but he gave us a second, third, and fourth chance. He chose us. Jesus saw who we would become. Maybe no one else could see it. Sometimes we didn't even see it. But Jesus saw it. Now, we're prepared for the journey."

As they were released and went on their way, I thought I heard some-one begin to sing, "I'm going through. I'm going through. I don't care what the rest of the world decides to do. I made up my mind, and I'm not gone turn around. I'm working for Jesus, and I gotta go through. I'm going through. I'm going through. I don't care what the rest of the world decides to do. I made up my mind, and I'm not gone turn around. I'm working for Jesus, and I gotta go through."[3]

---

[3] Herbert Buffum, "I'm Going Through," *Gospel Pearls* (Nashville: Sunday School Board of the National Baptist Convention, 1921), 76.

PART 4

Patterns for Theology

30

Preaching from the Perspective of Evangelical Theology

The term "evangelical" transliterates the Greek *euaggelion*, meaning "gospel" or "good news." In the broadest and deepest sense, all Christian communities are evangelical in that they derive their origin and identity from the gospel. However, in the contemporary Christian scene, the designation evangelical is often used to refer to a particular way of viewing the relationship among God, the Bible, and our knowledge of God.

In the evangelical sector of the theological spectrum, Christians stress the divine authorship of the Bible, its unity, and its validity in every time and place. According to evangelical theologians, the Bible gives us all that we need to know about God, Christ, the Holy Spirit, the church, and the Christian mission.

However, the evangelical community is not a monolith. The evangelical world contains multiple understandings of the means and extent of divine authorship. Some conservatives believe that God moved the hands of the biblical writers. Most evangelicals allow for a human element and cultural conditioning in the wording of the Bible. For instance, thoughtful conservatives regard the description of the mustard seed as "the smallest of all the seeds on earth" (Mark 4:31) not as scientifically accurate, but as reflecting the era in which the parable was spoken. But in matters of faith and ethics, the Bible is true because God wrote it.

Evangelicals also regard the Bible as making a consistent theological witness from era to era, from author to author, from text to text. As I once heard an eloquent conservative say, "The Bible speaks in one voice." The contents of the Bible are in essential agreement with one another.

Evangelicals regard the Bible as valid in every time and place. If the Bible seems to contradict what the community otherwise believes to be true, the community needs to consider one of two possibilities. (1) The community may need to align its urges or understandings with those of the Bible in order to be in tune with God's will. Or (2) the community may need to reexamine its understanding of the Bible. While the Bible itself is a reliable guide to faith and ethics, its human interpreters can misunderstand it. Fresh exegetical insights can reformulate how the church appropriates the Bible. Evangelicals acknowledge that human beings can make mistakes in interpreting the Bible.

Some evangelicals regard the Bible as largely propositional. Each text, they say, contains a proposition that can be extrapolated, articulated, and applied to the life of a congregation or the world. The purpose of the sermon is to help the congregation identify, state, and apply the propositions of the passage to the congregation. However, many evangelical preachers now believe that the form and content of a biblical text are related such that the form of the text is a part of its content. The form of a passage is part and parcel of the content of the revelation. Extrapolating a proposition from a text that is not propositional in form might alter the church's understanding of the revelation. Consequently, many evangelicals are open to ways in which the form of the biblical text can shape the form of the sermon.

The sermon below is based on a part of an epistle that provides instructions on how the church is to live. Bryan Chapell identifies the lessons that a congregation needs to learn from the text in the sequence in which those lessons appear in the passage. The sermon names these propositions in the sequence in which they are found in the text. In this respect the sermon has the character of both preaching verse by verse (see chapter 4) and one of the ways by which the form of the text shapes the form of the sermon (see chapter 10). The members of the congregation would receive maximum benefit from this sermon by having their Bibles open, and following the written text as the preacher discusses each part of it.

BRYAN CHAPELL is president of Covenant Theological Seminary, St. Louis, Missouri. Chapell preached this sermon in the seminary chapel. He served a local congregation for a decade before joining the seminary faculty. This sermon was preached at the seminary in order to help students struggling to know God's will and as a resource for occasions when the students are asked by parishioners how to determine the divine purposes. His *Christ Centered Preaching: Redeeming the Expository Sermon* is a basic preaching textbook in many seminaries. He is also the author of *Each for the Other: Living Christ's Love for the Love of Your Life* (Grand Rapids: Baker, 1998), *Using Illustrations to Preach with Power* (Grand Rapids: Zondervan, 1993), *In the Grip of Grace: When You Can't Hang On* (Grand Rapids: Baker, 1992), and *Standing Your Ground: A Call to Courage in an Age of Compromise: Messages on Daniel* (Grand Rapids: Baker, 1989).

BRYAN CHAPELL

Between the Fences: Knowing God's Will

1 Thessalonians 4:1–12

About four years ago, my family and I had the wonderful experience of spending a year at a cabin in the woods while I was on a writing sabbatical. We chose a cabin about an hour away from town so we could be far enough away from normal seminary operations for me to write while still close enough for my wife, Kathy, to continue her calling as choir director at our church.

One Wednesday night after choir rehearsal, Kathy called me to say that she and the children were going to try to make it to the cabin despite the fact that it was snowing. The snow had not been falling for long, and she expected that the highways would still be passable. The only potential problem could be the last leg of the trip that included two miles of twisting, hilly, country lanes that led up to the cabin—lanes that got slippery fast and had more than one treacherous turn. We decided that she should come ahead and that I would hike to the main road to meet her.

As soon as I began walking to the main road, I realized we were in trouble. The snow was coming far faster than we had anticipated, and it was rapidly covering those country lanes from edge to edge. By the time Kathy arrived at our meeting point, you could not even tell that there was a road. I got into the van and we began to inch our way forward. Soon, we discovered that despite the obscurity of the road, we could still see the fencelines that ran down the sides of the lane. Even though the road ahead was not clear, we could stay on track by staying between the fences.

In all my years of pastoring—both in the congregation and at Covenant Seminary—one question has been asked of me more frequently than all others combined: "How do I know God's will?" I do not have an exhaustive answer to that question, but a passage to which I repeatedly turn for guidance is 1 Thessalonians 4:1–12. This chapter provides guidelines similar to those that directed my family through those snowy lanes. It does not remove all obscurity regarding what is ahead, but it does tell us what we must do to stay in God's will. We must keep between the fences.

On one side of the road of life, God gives us *the fence of Christian righteousness.*

The first question God gives us to consider when making a decision or considering an option is, "Is it righteous?" If a certain choice will cause us to participate in unrighteousness—either because what we are seeking is wrong or what will be needed to get there is wrong—then that is a wrong path even if the destination is right. Staying within the fenceline of righteousness requires us to honor God's authority and to obey God's standards.

Honoring God's authority. In the opening verses of 1 Thessalonians 4, Paul reminds us of the authority behind the standards he will give. Before you follow the fenceline, you must trust that the fence is correctly laid. "For you know what instructions we gave you *by the authority of the Lord Jesus.*" (v. 2). The apostle makes such a point of authority because he wants to remind us that staying in God's path is not right merely because we have done so in the past nor because there is a practical reason in the present, but because the path has been laid by a higher authority. The biblical path may seem to lead into a valley. It may not *feel* right. We may strike some potholes along the way. Still, the path indicated by God's authority is the proper path.

Obeying God's standards. We must also remember that remaining in God's path requires obeying God's standards. (The preacher reads 1 Thessalonians 4:3–6, 8.)

What do you know without question is God's will for you? Does God want you to go to Timbuktu or to marry Nancy Sue? We cannot speak with total certainty about such issues, but we can know with certainty God's will as stated in scripture. Paul's words in v. 3 tell us, "It is God's will that you should be sanctified." God's will is that you should be more like him in holiness and righteousness. Of this, you should have no doubt. Nor should you doubt how God expects for this increase of the divine likeness to occur in you—by obeying God's standards.

The standards of this passage relate primarily to sexual purity (v. 3–5), but they reveal other values that God wishes us to heed. The call to sexual purity is initially a call to be mindful of one's self (v. 3–4), but then Paul adds that we should be pure out of concern for others (v. 6). Just as sexual purity affects other people—as present or future spouses are robbed of the purity and unity that God intends for marriage—so all aspects of our conduct are to be examined for their community as well as their personal impact.

We do not need to wonder if it is God's will for us to remain sexually pure, deal honestly in our business practices, or love our spouses. Christians who want a sign to confirm that they could be unfaithful to their spouses or take a job with a company known for unethical business dealings are seeking to read God's will in the wrong places. What God has said about these matters is authoritative and does not change.

But what if the word has not already been given? What if I cannot find a verse that says, "Take Job A instead of Job B" or "Go to Church A instead of Church B"? If God has not specifically addressed the issue, do not pretend that God has.

I hear many Christians giving moral status to "life options" rather than "life standards." They say, "I do not know what to do. I have these two options. I can only pick one. I must know God's will because I do not want to be out of that will." In saying as much, they give the status of right or wrong, moral or immoral, to life options. That is dangerous.

Such an assessment can create choice paralysis—doing nothing because something might be wrong. In addition, assigning moral status to life options causes us to add new standards to God's word when we have no authority to do so. If choices were apples in a basket, we would not contend that the selection of one of those apples is good and that the other apples are evil. We would simply delight that God has given us so much bounty from which to choose. In the same way, it is better to rejoice that God gives us options, a blessing of multiple choices, than to condemn an option as evil without the warrant of God's word.

The understanding that more than one option can be righteous, however, leads to another question. If there are two (or more) righteous options, then how do I choose between them? The answer lies in remembering that:

On the other side of the road of life is *the fence of Christian prudence*.

Christian prudence does not allow us to dispense with issues of right and wrong. The fence of righteousness always stays in place for that. Rather, prudence involves using biblical principles and priorities to make wise choices among righteous options.

Paul moves to a different category of instructions in the latter portions of this passage. Whereas the early verses (3–8) are absolute prohibitions against immorality and taking advantage of others, the later verses (9–12) give instructions about matters that involve judgment by weighing priorities in the heart. (The preacher reads 1 Thessalonians 4:9–12.)

Is it loving? The basic question to consider in weighing our actions is, "Is it loving?" We cannot make Christian decisions without Christian priorities in place, chief of which is God's command to love others. This means that concern for self becomes secondary to the needs of others. Paul says those at Thessalonica have been pursuing this kind of selfless concern for the good of others, yet he reminds them that it is also the responsibility of Christians to pursue such love more and more (v. 10).

Perhaps the decision you are considering is not evil in itself, but Christian prudence requires us also to ask, "Is it loving?" Are you willing to consider the good of others and how this decision may have an impact upon them? Are you willing to suffer hardship for the sake of their good and for their knowledge of the gospel?

These are not always easy questions to answer. They may require a deep and lengthy searching of the heart, so Paul gives us further means to evaluate the appropriateness of our actions.

Is it legitimate? We also need to ask, "Is it legitimate?" Is what you are considering a legitimate pursuit for a Christian? Does it honor God? Does it respect others? Does it challenge you? If we are seeking God's will, we will ask if what we are considering honors God rather than whether it brings honor to ourselves. After all, Paul says that it should be our ambition to lead a quiet life (v. 11). Some commentators summarize that our ambition should be to have no ambition. This does not mean that others (including God) may not chose to use our names for divine purposes, but this is not to be our goal. Living to be a no-name is not easy for any of us, but the Christian is living for Christ's glory rather than personal notice.

Is it responsible? How do we determine places of service that are truly consistent with our calling, whether we receive glory or not? By applying the final standard of prudence that the apostle mentions here. "Is it responsible?" Responsible actions come when we consider whether our choices create damage or dependence. Paul says to engage in legitimate work "so that your daily life may win the respect of outsiders" (v. 12). The words remind us that the way we conduct ourselves bears testimony to the gospel. When our actions are ambitions to the extent that we disregard others or take advantage of them for our benefit, then we damage the testimony of the gospel.

I am surprised at times that people do not consider the damage that their choices may do to family, friends, church, or business associates. I do not contend that God never wants us to change our present position or choice, but we are obligated to bear regard for the effects of our choices on others.

Does that mean that we are forever locked into a present position or choice? No, for what else we must consider is evident in the last of Paul's statements. Paul's concern is not merely that we walk so as not to create damage to the gospel, but when we consider a choice, we must also ask whether it creates dependence.

Paul says to engage in legitimate work "so that you will not be dependent on anybody" (v. 12). The most obvious concern here is that the idleness of some of the Thessalonians had made them wards of the church. Paul's obvious caution is that we should use our gifts for the good of the gospel rather than depending on the gifts of others.

As you make decisions, a basic question you must answer is whether you are a giver or a taker. Will you apply your gifts to a greater effort or use others for self? This kind of question requires deep searching of the motives of the heart, as well as thoughtful evaluation of one's gifts, and how they can best be used for God's purposes. In essence, this consideration gives us the final piece of the puzzle of prudence. Does the choice we are considering give us the best opportunity to serve the purposes of the gospel rather than to be served?

To be honest, at times in my life I have pushed for position and self-promotion. Ambition can still raise its head and strike me. But the best and most significant things that happen in my life have come when I have sought to do what is righteous, loving, legitimate, and responsible. What do I hope for you? The same.

I would encourage you not to depend on external signs of which way the birds fly or verses lighting up in neon signs in the sky, in order to determine God's will. Neither should you depend upon subjective feelings of pressure or peace. People can feel peace about a great many unwise or even immoral decisions. Rather, make decisions that are righteous and prudent. Consider first whether the course of action you are considering is within the fence of righteousness then consider it in the light of the needs of God's people, the promotion of the gospel, and the nature of your gifts.

What if, after all this rumination, you still make the wrong decisions? Then return to the first verse of 1 Thessalonians 4. Paul urges us to walk in ways that please God "in the Lord Jesus." These beautiful words should be your best comfort. Remember your position. You are in Christ Jesus not because you walk into his will, nor because you walk into his way. His work—not your own—makes you a child of God. For that reason alone, you are in Jesus' care wherever you walk. Trust him. As you make choices in accord with righteousness and prudence, the God who holds you will direct your path. If the step is a misstep, God will correct it. Do what is right and wise and trust God to take care of the rest.

Imagine again that snowy road that I first mentioned. Picture that road as one that you may need to travel to discern God's will about a particular decision. Now, in your mind's eye, also place that scene in a snow globe, such as they sell in the department stores at Christmastime. When you shake the globe, the snow can get pretty intense, and the way ahead may become obscure. Still, no matter how much snow falls on the road, remember God holds the whole scene in his hands. Walk in righteousness and prudential care for God's priorities in the confidence that you are in God's hands. Do what is right, and God will take care of the rest.

31

Preaching from the Perspective of Liberation Theology

For liberation theologians, God intends to liberate the world from oppression. Oppression is a form of sin in which a person or community exploits other persons or communities (or the realm of nature). Oppression is frequently systemic, that it results from patterns of thought, feeling, and behavior that are transpersonal. The oppressive tendency is so deeply embedded in some social structures that oppressors do not even know that they are complicit in oppression. Among the most common and deeply entrenched systems of oppression are racism, sexism, poverty, classicism, ageism, handicappism, ecological abuse. Religion, too, can be used to oppress.

Liberation preachers believe that God operates through the processes of history to free humankind and nature from oppression. God aims for all people and all elements of the natural world to have their own integrity, secure living conditions, freedom, opportunities to relate with all created entities in love and justice. The best liberation preachers are aware that oppressors are oppressed by their oppressive ideas, feelings, and actions. The liberation preacher alerts oppressed and oppressor to God's present activity in using individuals and groups to move toward a world in which all live together in love, justice, dignity, and shared material resources.

The liberation sermon helps the community identify oppression in specific settings. The sermon tries to name the individuals, communities,

223

and social movements through whom God is seeking to make the world a community of love and justice. The liberation preacher helps the community envision the practical implications of liberation and encourages the people to join God's liberating initiatives. The preacher needs to help some people recognize the possibility of liberation. The preacher needs to help many people make a commitment to participate in the historical struggle for liberation. The sermon encourages oppressors to repent, to turn away from complicity in oppression, and to turn toward God's liberating work in history.

Liberation preachers need to be cautious not to oversimplify the situations of the oppressed and the oppressor. Some preachers think in caricature of a bifurcation between the completely evil oppressor and the completely innocent oppressed. Both oppressed and oppressor are complex mixtures of good and bad, as Carolyn Ann Knight notes in the sermon below. Oppressors need to renounce their participate in oppression and to make reparations to the community. At the same time, the preacher needs to help the oppressed recognize and repent of their own forms of sin. Furthermore, some preachers announce liberation in a way that it is good news for the oppressed, but only bad news for the oppressor. The oppressed are liberated, whereas oppressors are thrown down in condemnation. This motif is sometimes articulated so as to suggest that God abandons the oppressor to torment. Furthermore, it would eventuate in a new oppressed class: Former oppressor becomes the new oppressed, while the formerly oppressed become the new oppressor.

Carolyn Ann Knight preached the sermon below at a conference for pastors and laity on the church in the new millennium. Most of the attendees were under the age of fifty and are in large, growing congregations. Professor Knight emphasizes a theme prominent in liberation theology: Communities need to take an active part with God in their own liberation. The preacher wanted to support the nontraditional, highly liberating approaches to ministry already underway in many of their congregations, and to encourage such approaches in other congregations.

CAROLYN ANN KNIGHT is assistant professor of homiletics at the Interdenominational Theological Center in Atlanta, Georgia. During a highly effective pastorate in New York City, she also taught preaching at Union Theological Seminary, New York. She is at work on a book on preaching on social issues.

CAROLYN ANN KNIGHT

If Thou Be a Great People

Joshua 17:13–18 (King James Version)

A change in the leadership can create a crisis in any people's movement. In the succeeding years since the deaths of Mary McLeod Bethune, Marcus Garvey, Malcolm X, Martin Luther King, Jr., and Adam Clayton Powell, Jr., we in the African American community have been praying and searching for a personality that can galvanize the masses of people in much the same way that they did. In the twenty-first century we need a consistent voice that can capture the attention of the African American community.

Such was not the case with the people of Israel. After the death of Moses, the transfer of leadership was swift, smooth. Joshua was a fitting successor to Moses because Joshua had great courage and vision. Moses sent twelve spies to survey the land of Canaan. While ten saw only giants, Joshua and Caleb saw grapes and milk and honey. Because Joshua was able to see the invisible and believe the impossible, he inherited the role of leader. After the conquest, the children of Israel were ready to cease their wanderings in the wilderness. Joshua had the assignment of dividing the territory among the twelve tribes.

The allotment proceeded without difficulty until Joshua got to Ephraim and Manasseh. Ephraim and Manasseh were children of Joseph and Asenath, the wife that Joseph married while he was in Egypt where these children were born. Jacob adopted them and gave them a share in the inheritance with his other children. Now if I understand my geography, Egypt is in northern Africa, which means that Ephraim and Manasseh were an Afro-Asiatic people: people of color.

Upon receiving their inheritance, Ephraim and Manasseh began to grumble and complain that their share of the allotment was too small. Their assertion was based on the fact that they were a great people. Great in size and great in stature. Because of their history and family lineage coupled with a personal and abiding relationship with God Almighty, they insisted that their share of the land should be more. They said to Joshua, "We are a great people and the Lord has blessed us until now. This share of the land is too small." Joshua replied, "If you are a great people then go to the hill country and make a place for yourselves." They countered that the Perizzites and the Canaanites and giants were in the hill country with weapons of iron and chariots. Again Joshua says, "If thou be a great people go up against the Perizzites and the Canaanites and the giants."

I believe this passage is a word to this New Millennium Pastor's Conference as we prepare to face life in the twenty-first century. "If thou be a great people go up into the hill country and clear a place for yourself there!" At this uncertain point of our perilous pilgrimage upon this planet, we must recognize who we are as a people and appropriate our rightful inheritance in God and in this world. If thou be a great people...a great preacher/pastor, a great community, a great family, a great sister, a great brother...the challenge of the hill country awaits you.

Mind you, we are not here talking about great as a perception that is based on race or gender or class alone. I am talking about greatness as a way of harnessing and husbanding the best of our spiritual, intellectual, financial, educational, and political resources and empowering our communities and enriching this society. I am not talking about greatness as a way of exalting everything that is African and trashing everything that is European. I am talking about the greatness that the Bible says is in all of us who claim to be the people of God.

The first thing Ephraim and Manasseh had going for them was a healthy self-identity. They said of themselves, "We *are* a great people!" They practiced the art of self-definition. They refused to be defined by circumstances, or environment, or culture, or class, or race. We know who *we* are. We have a unique sense of somebodyness. We have a good memory. We know our oral tradition. We are well aware of our ancestors. Our father Joseph was Jacob's favorite son. Jacob, our grandfather, was a schemer, but one night by the ford of Jabbok, he wrestled with God and prevailed. Isaac, our great-grandfather was the only son of our great-great grandfather Abraham, a friend of God who received the promise by faith. Oh yeah, we come from good stock.

Not only that, we have this covenant thing. God promised through Abraham and Sarah never to forsake us. That our family would be as numerous as the stars in the heavens and the sand on the seashore. Throughout history the blessing of God has been upon us. Joshua's response to all of this was, "I know that you are indeed a great people. But, if thou be a great people, you go up to the hill country and make a place for yourselves." Great people are trailblazers. Great people are visionary. Great people know how to chart a course, build a bridge, expect a miracle. Great people refuse to be victims to circumstance, color, class, or culture. Great people are not condemned by the conditions of their birth, or locked into Euro-centric thought patterns. You have enough imagination, ingenuity, intelligence, and integrity to make a place for yourselves. Do not linger on the low plains of life crying and complaining, fretting and fuming, moaning and groaning about what you cannot do or what you do not have. Be creative. Accept the challenge of the hill country.

When I think about our African American people, I know we are a great people. I submit that what we are experiencing right now—ethnic cleansing in Bosnia and Mississippi and Arkansas, bombings in New York and Oklahoma, Birmingham and Atlanta; high unemployment, no health care, poor child care, insecure social security, babies dangling from bridges, babies with bullets, children with guns, runaway teenage pregnancy, children with no hope, mothers who can't cope, fathers on dope; more black men in jail than in college; women forgotten too soon; men gone too soon; children dying too soon; sisters waiting to exhale; brothers trying to get paid; heroes becoming zeroes; many of us kept out, kicked out, knocked out, locked out, pushed out, put out, pulled out, phased out; the hopelessness and despair that pervades our communities—what we are experiencing right now is an aberration. We are wandering in a wilderness called the United States. This is not who we really are.

We are a great people. We have a great history. But you have to travel farther than the slave ship, segregation, and second-class citizenship to know who we are. We are an African American people. But more importantly, we are an African people. Many of us struggle with low self-esteem because we are more familiar with the American side of who we are than the African side. We need to get in touch with the African side of our identity. Then we will know that we come from a great family structure; where men are kings, where women are queens, where children affirm every aspect of their identity. We need to remember the great ancient cities that we built; the many contributions that we made to science and medicine, literature, the arts, religion, business. We need to get in touch with the African side to know that we are a great people.

We are a great people with a great history. We must stop reciting the failure studies that have been done on our communities. We must never forget that God has always done great things through Africans. We are formed out of adversity. From it we have fashioned our unique perspective on humanity and divinity. They gave us straw. We gave them bricks. They gave us seeds. We gave them cotton. They gave us sorrow. We wrote songs. They gave us pain. We wrote poems. They gave us trouble. We turned it into testimony. They gave us the blues. We made music. They gave us segregation. We gave them Spelman. They gave us misery. We gave them Morehouse. They gave us terror. We gave them Tuskegee. They called us failures. We gave them Fisk. They gave us burdens. We gave them Bishop. They gave us hell. We gave them Howard.

When God created beauty, God came through Cleopatra. When God created science, God came through George Washington Carver, Daniel Hale Williams, and Garrett Morgan. When God wanted music, God came through Beethoven, Duke Ellington, Marian Anderson, Paul Robeson, and Jessye Norman. When God wanted business people, God came through Madame C. J. Walker, A. G. Gaston, Earl Graves, and Reginald Lewis. When God wants athletes, God comes through Jackie Robinson, Althea Gibson, Muhammad Ali, Arthur Ashe, and Michael Jordan. When God wants to dazzle the world with dance, God comes through Judith Jamison, Alvin Ailey, Robert Mitchell, Hinton Battle, and Gregory Hines. When God wanted to give the world words, God came through Gwendolyn Brooks, Zora Neale Hurston, Langston Hughes, Maya Angelou, and Alice Walker.

Our Africanness is an instrumentality that God uses to enrich the world. God used Rosa Parks, Martin King, Adam Powell, Malcolm X, and Medgar Evers to remind the world that justice will well up like waters and righteousness like a mighty stream. God used Marcus Garvey to remind this world and us that we have one God, one aim, and one destiny. God used Randall Robinson to tell a U. S. President that your policy in Haiti is no good. God used Nelson Mandela to bring 350 years of apartheid to its knees and to tell Bill Clinton, "You run America, I run South Africa." And God wants to use *us* to make a contribution to this world. You see, we are a great people. This is our day. This is our time. This is our moment. This is our season.

Joshua said to the tribes of Ephraim and Manasseh and to us, "If thou be a great people get up to the hill country and make a place for yourselves there." Stop fighting over these petty plots of land. Stop fighting over insignificant positions and titles. Stop fighting over that which is trite. Stop waiting for someone else to make or open a door. You have a great work to do: churches to build, families to save, children to nurture, men to redeem, women to empower, marriages to mend, colleges to revitalize, businesses to open, churches to revive, visions to realize, a drug epidemic to rout out, an AIDS pandemic to cure, sin to conquer, salvation to gain, songs to sing, poems to write, hell to avoid, heaven to gain. If thou be a great people, the hill country awaits you.

Mind you, its not easy in the hill country. The Perizzites and the Canaanites are in the hill country with their vast weapons of irons and chariots. People who do not want you to be free, people who do not want you to succeed, people who do not want you to be educated, people who do not want you to make it. People who oppose God's dominion on earth. People who think that you know less than you know because you are female or male and because you are black. Establishment folk. Bound by tradition, custom, and habit. They tell you that it cannot be done. They tell you that your vision is too ambitious, that your dream is impossible. They say that we have never done it this way before. They have iron and chariots, money, methods, and means. They stand in direct opposition to your vision.

But I just stopped by to tell you that nothing can stop an idea whose time has come. Nothing can stop a people who are determined. Watch out for the opposition in the hill country. They are organized and determined. They are systematized and systemic. Sometimes it is hard to tell who they are and where they are. Sometimes they are white-collar businessmen messing with your financial institutions, health care, and social security. Sometimes it is a Democratic president who cuts the heart out of welfare and puts millions of children further into poverty. They can be the neighborhood drug dealers selling drugs to your sons and daughters. Sometimes they make you think that they are for you. All of our opposition is not from people who look different than we do. There are people in our communities who do us harm. We have leaders among us who violate our trust and destroy our integrity. We must cut them down, vote them out, and replace them!

There is even opposition among churches and in the churches. There are Christians who think that their church or denomination is the only ticket in town. They build themselves up by putting you down. But this is not a day for mealymouthed ministers, poorly prepared preachers, lackadaisical laypersons, and chicken-livered Christians. This world needs a strong word from the Lord, and we have been called to speak it. As we make this menacing, methodical march towards the next millennium, we need to put our game faces on. Step up to the plate and swing. We need to develop a Michael Jeffrey Jordan mentality. Michael loves to be twelve points behind with six minutes left to play in the fourth quarter of game seven of the championship series. The challenge brings out the best in Michael and this third millennium will bring out the best in us. We are not going to go tripping across the threshold of the third millennium.

The late Sandy F. Ray, that great Baptist preacher from the Cornerstone Church in Brooklyn, New York, called this the challenge of the wood country.[1] If it were easy to go into the hill country, everybody would be living there. Our challenge is to conquer the hill country in our lives, in our communities, and in our nation. Now it is your turn to make a name for yourselves. We are prepared for the challenges, changes, and

---

[1] Sandy F. Ray, *Journeying Through a Jungle* (Nashville: Broadman Press, 1979), 75–84.

crises of the third millennium. We have everything that we need in the hill country. God is for us. Emmanuel is with us. The Holy Spirit empowers us. Our ancestors are rooting for us. The next generation is depending on us.

You are a great people. You have an internal mechanism to help restore our families, save our babies, empower our women, and reclaim our men. More than that, we have an Eternal Motivator who is with us. I know somebody that knows all about the hill country because he's been there. Don't get nervous. You're not going into the hill country alone. God never sends us where God has not already been. God never sends us without first preparing the way. Jesus has already met the challenge. "On a hill far away stood an old rugged cross, the emblem of suffering and shame."[2] Jesus went into the hill country and made it a highway to heaven. He turned it into a gateway to eternity. He made it a roadway of reconciliation between God and humanity.

Jesus made a name for himself. At that name demons tremble, governments topple, blind folks can see, lame folks can walk, deaf folks can hear. At that name the dead shall live again. At that name every knee shall bow and every tongue shall confess that he is Lord to the glory of God.

Jesus Christ says to you and to me: If thou be a great people stand up, look up, get up into the hill country—not in your name, but in my name. Live your life. Realize your dreams. Let your light shine. Blow your trumpet. Sing your song. "All hail the power of Jesus' name! Let angels prostrate fall. Bring forth the royal diadem and crown Him Lord of all."[3]

---

[2] George Bennard, "The Old Rugged Cross," *Sing Joyfully* (Carol Stream, Illinois: Tabernacle, 1989), 247.

[3] Edward Perronet, "All Hail the Power of Jesus' Name!" *The Chalice Hymnal* (St. Louis: Chalice Press, 1995), 92.

32

Preaching from the Perspective of Postliberal Theology

The postliberal theologians contend that the church is to interpret its life and the world on the basis of its own sacred texts, presuppositions, doctrines, and practices. Postliberal preachers object to the Christian community measuring its worldview against standards outside of itself. Postliberals particularly protest submitting Christian narratives and claims to criteria derived from modernism. By modernity, postliberals mean that era in human history that began with the Enlightenment and continues in some quarters into the present. The moniker "postliberal" indicates this movement's attempt to go beyond modernity's liberalism, especially its reliance upon experience as a standard for truth and its claim that we can identify universal standards for truth.

Postliberals begin with the supposition that the Christian interpretation of the world especially as articulated in the Bible is normative for the Christian community. The church is to let the Bible and other orthodox Christian texts especially the Chalcedonian formulation describe the world. The church "is not to make the gospel credible to the modern world, but to make the world credible to the gospel.[1] The preacher is to narrate today's community into the story told by the scriptures and by Christian doctrine and practice. This truth is particular to the Christian community.

---

[1] Stanley Hauerwas and William Willimon, *Resident Aliens* (Nashville: Abingdon Press, 1989), 24.

The church is to read the Bible as it does every lifelike narrative. The community of faith acknowledges that some of the details in the Bible are not factually correct, but the description of life that comes to expression in the narrative is reliable because it tells the story of the divine character and purpose. The Christian community should not try to demonstrate the credibility of Christian belief and practice. Instead, the preacher teaches the congregation the language of the Bible and Christian tradition. This language can shape the church's view of God and the world so that the church is a contemporary extension of the Christian story. People who commit themselves to the vision of God and the world found in the Bible and in Christian tradition become a community. In fact, according to the postliberals, individualism was one of the most destructive outcomes of modernity. Preaching the biblical story is one means whereby community is created.

The major aim of preaching, then, is for the pastor to help the community name God and the world as narrated by the Bible and other orthodox Christian texts, doctrines, and practices. The sermon leads the church to understand how our story is absorbed into the biblical drama. The preacher does not interpret the Christian tradition as much as help the community understand how Christian tradition interprets life.

Postliberal preachers remind the church to retain a vivid sense of Christian identity at the core of the church's being. Postliberals caution the church against too quickly junking aspects of Christian tradition in the name of creating a faith that is "relevant." However, the postliberal approach has difficulties. The Bible and Christian tradition are not univocal. The Bible and Christian tradition contain a plurality of voices. Postliberalism sometimes finds it difficult to make sense of the pluralism of the Bible and Christian tradition. The postliberal preacher can have difficulty mediating among the authority of different narratives. Postliberals also wrestle to find a satisfactory notion of truth. Postliberal preachers struggle to help a community understand why a Christian interpretation of God and the world is commendable. Postliberal reasoning has a circular quality: The community should accept a Christian version of life because that version is at the center of Christian language and community. The postliberal's accent on narrating the contemporary community in the biblical story makes is hard for postliberals to help the church make Christian sense out of texts, doctrines, and practices that raise theological or moral difficulties.

In the Good Friday sermon below, Serene Jones helps the congregation understand the story of the death of Jesus as a story in which we have a place. We do not find our stories in the biblical text; to the contrary, the preacher invites us to let the story of the passion become the story that shapes our view of the world. The preacher leads the congregation to consider the church as a community through the eyes of Jesus crucified. We see ourselves as Jesus sees us. She preached the sermon in the midst of a community of seminary students, staff, and faculty in Marquand Chapel at Yale Divinity School. In the sermon she refers to a congregation, well-known to the worshiping community, located on public space in New Haven known as the Green. The sermon models one way that a preacher can deal with the major motifs in a long scripture reading (47 verses) in a single sermon.

SERENE JONES is associate professor of theology at The Divinity School, Yale University, in New Haven, Connecticut. Her *Calvin and the Rhetoric of Piety,* Columbia Series in Reformed Theology (Louisville: Westminster John Knox Press, 1995) is a groundbreaking study of the relationship between theological viewpoint and genre in preaching. She also edited, with Rita Nakashima Brock and Claudia Camp, *Setting the Table: Women in Theological Conversation* (St. Louis: Chalice Press, 1995). One can hear echoes of liberation theological motifs in this sermon.

SERENE JONES

A Church of Good Friday

Mark 15:1–47

The story we hear this morning on this day we call Good Friday is a horrifying one. It is a story of betrayal, of mockery, of mob hysteria, of cold, calculated brutality. It is a story of a slow, tortured, desolate, death. It is a story about the violent death of the One we call Savior, Redeemer, Lord, and Sovereign.

As I have moved through Lent and Holy Week this year, I have found the most profound catechetical direction offered to me not by the wisdom of one with years of ecclesial experience nor by one with a theological education. Instead, my Holy Week mentor has been a friend who only recently converted to Christianity. Raised as an activist and confirmed as a secularist university professor, she decided to become a Christian and join the church only two years ago. The questions she asks me in her freshness and her newness to the faith have been profoundly productive of theological insight.

This week, having read Mark's story of torture and execution, she asks: What does it mean to be part of a community with this image of horror at is center? What does it mean to be a church of Good Friday—a community that founds its identity upon a tale of gruesome murder? What does it mean to be the *ecclesia*—the gathered people—who stand on Golgotha, who come together around the cross, the ecclesia of the One whose body dies? What does it mean to for the church to be "the body" of this One whose flesh is mutilated?

There is a temptation, I believe, that haunts us as modern readers of scripture. It is the temptation to figure out where we are in this story. The reader, as the almighty, powerful subject makes meaning, enters this story by asking, "Where am I? What character-role do I play in the passion? Am I Pilate? Am I Barabbas? Am I one of the chief priests? Am I the criminal next to Jesus?" And even, at times, we ask, "Am I that one—the one who hangs on the cross?" In asking such questions, the temptation is to enter the story by deciding through which character's set of eyes I will view Jesus.

This morning, I ask that we pause and consider the possibility of seeing the story unfold not according to the different positions we take in looking at Jesus, but rather according to Jesus and his eyes as the focal point of meaning-making: *To look at Jesus looking at us.*

What does it mean to be a *church* when we look at church through the eyes of this story's central actor, Jesus? What does God see, looking down upon her people, as she hangs upon a tree and dies?

Let me lift up to you what seem to me to be three marks of this church—a church unfolding in the gaze of God.

Christ looks down upon a people who betray him. Thus, the first mark of this church is our identity as executioners. In the story we hear today, it is clear that those who finally abandon Jesus most profoundly, those who hand him over to be executed, those who say, "Kill him, kill him," are precisely the people with whom Jesus most closely identifies himself. His own people turn from him: the crowd, yes, but also his most intimate followers, the disciples. To be a church marked by this story is to be a community who sees itself starkly in terms of its ever-ready desire and action to kill God. It is to know the church as a community of sin and a community of sinners.

Who is this church? It is in its Presbyterian form the church that this week voted to exclude from its ordained leadership men and women to whom God has given the gift of gay and lesbian love. It is the church in its Roman Catholic form that excommunicated a Sri Lankan priest several times because he stood by his belief that women are equal to men in their ability to represent Christ in his priesthood. It is the church in its Congregational form that sits on a seven-million-dollar endowment on the middle of the New Haven Green in one of the nation's poorest cities and finds its primary conflict to be over the color of pew cushions. It is the church of each of us here who has sinned against God and our neighbors.

A second view of the church which we have from the cross is quite different from the first: a second mark held in tensive relation with our identity as executioners. Throughout the story, we find those who watch and, rather than abandoning Christ, stay faithful to him. We have the witness of the women, most particularly, who watch from a distance. In their distant vigil, we see the second mark of the church as witness to the execution of the God who loves us. It is a peculiar position to be in, for, as Mark tells us, the ones who watch are those who in Jesus life "provided for him in Galilee." These watchers are the ones who fed and clothed him in life and bathed his body in death. To be the church as witness is thus to be the community who tends the body of God.

But these women who watch from a distance are also in the peculiar position of being utterly powerless to save Jesus. Imagine Mary's wrenching grief. She refuses to abandon him, and yet, in watching his execution, she is powerless to stop it.

This church as tending witness is the church of Archbishop Romero, thousands of whom gathered to hear him celebrate a mass of liberation on the day of his execution. It is the church in its Reformed heritage that spoke a word that toppled apartheid. It is that church on the green that sent four elderly women on a bus to Hartford to protest the governor's budget. It is the church of each of us sitting here today, all saints who in our own way struggle to bear witness to God's mercy and to tend God's people.

Church as execution, church as tending witness—in addition to these two, there is yet a third mark we find in the story of Jesus on Golgotha: the mark of a church loved. And it is here, sisters and brothers, that we come to the heart of Jesus' death on the cross. He hangs there. He dies faster than the other two men at his sides—in a mere six hours (the others must have their legs broken so the full weight of their body is allowed to hasten their last breath). God, in taking human form, comes into our world to proclaim God's love for us. God desires to be with us—with a love so pure, so simple, so perfect that in fear we try to destroy it. And yet, even our violence does not cause God to turn from us. In God's oneness with us, the burden of torturous death is not lifted from Christ, but put upon him. God experiences even the most anguished death. Jesus Christ is shouting, "My God, my God, why hast thou forsaken me?" taking upon himself the horror of God's abandonment of us. Yet precisely in this paradoxical moment on the cross, God does not turn away from us, but joins us in the most profound way imaginable.

God takes wrath into Godself. God takes the reality of utter annihilation into the depths of God's being. Why is this good news?

It is good because we are a church of executioners, and yet there is no place that we can fall that God has not already redeemed. It is good news because the church who is called to witness the execution, the church of the women who watch, knows that it does not weep alone, but weeps with God. And it is good news because the church, both as saint and sinner, as both broken and healed, as both executioner and weeping mother, does not have given to it the task of saving the world. Christ has done that. God is with us. And there is no place for us to run. The One who looks down upon us from the cross is the One who knows the full weight of our sin—it is borne in his body—and who yet breathes his last in solidarity with us. This my friends, is the utterly horrifying, redemptive word of the cross.

As sinners, we are enabled to see our sin and to keep living. As saints, we are called to do justice in the freedom that comes from knowing our call is not to save the world.

33

Preaching from the Perspective of Revisionary Theology

The informal designation revisionary theology suggests a key characteristic of this movement. Theologians in this stream are open to revising their understandings of the contemporary world from the perspective of the gospel, and they are open to revising their interpretation of the Christian tradition (and its significance for today) from the perspective of the contemporary world.

Toward these ends, revisionary theology is distinguished by its method of mutual critical correlation. On the one hand, revisionary theologians seek to correlate the gospel with the contemporary world. That is, they seek to help the church name its current experience in the terms of the gospel. For instance, how does Christian tradition help us recognize distortions of God's purposes? How does Christian tradition help us perceive God's gracious, renewing presence and purposes? This correlation often leads the church to recognize that it has misperceived God's offer of love and God's call for justice. In order to be faithful to the gospel, we must enlarge our vision and witness. We must revise our interpretation of the world in response to the largess of God's love and God's call for justice in every relationship. For instance, some Christian communities effectively act as if God loves some people, and will justice for some, but not for all.

On the other hand, revisionary theologians also consider the degree to which today's experience may prompt the church to revise its understanding of Christian tradition. This pole of the correlation is powered by the recognition that God is always present and at work for the good of the community. However, because of human finitude, the Christian community is not always able to grasp the fullness of God's vision. All our interpretations of God are incomplete. Fresh awareness of God's presence and purpose may cause us to reframe our understanding of aspects of Christian tradition. Indeed, an occasional element of Christian tradition seems fundamentally to misrepresent God and God's intentions for the world. For instance, some revisionary theologians are troubled by biblical texts that picture God acting in ways that appear to be contrary to unconditional love.

The correlation is mutual in that we correlate the gospel with the contemporary setting even while we correlate aspects of the contemporary situation with the tradition. The correlation is critical in the sense that it calls for a careful evaluation of the adequacy of the community's understandings of both poles (tradition, today) and to be open to revising those understandings.

In a revisionary sermon, preacher and congregation explore the mutual critical correlation between the contemporary setting and some aspect of Christian tradition, e.g., the gospel, a biblical text, a doctrine, a Christian practice. The preacher seeks to determine the abiding values in the tradition that help the community interpret its present situation in gospel perspective. How does that perspective cause the community to understand itself? At the same time, the preacher considers the possibility that the contemporary setting raises questions about the adequacy of some aspects of Christian tradition.

In the sermon that follows, Marjorie Suchocki articulates a basic revisionary theme: God's presence and grace make it possible for the church to be open to fresh understandings of God, Christian community, and world. We may be uncertain, even fearful, when we consider giving up treasured notions of God, church, and world. However, our knowledge of God with us provides the security and continuity within which to recognize that fresh perspectives may be more adequate to our time than some former ones. A double motif is at work. Self and community can be transformed through interaction with the gospel; our perception of Christian tradition can be transformed through interaction with contemporary experience. Consequently, near the end of the sermon, the preacher bursts out, "Do not be afraid of knowledge!"

The sermon was prepared for a conference primarily attended by clergy on the subject of transformations in the church that are taking place (or that should take place) as we enter the postmodern era. The planning committee for the conference intended to organize the service of worship around water symbolism in connection with transformation. The preacher integrated this motif into the sermon so that the sermon and the larger service could work together. However, late in the preparations for the conference, the planning committee added fire symbolism to the service. In order to help the sermon and service work together in an optimum way, the preacher revised the sermon to include an image of fire. Many preachers can strengthen the relationship between their sermons and the service of worship in which a sermon comes to life by adapting their sermons after Suchocki's model.

The sermon is a noteworthy example of preaching from a whole book of the Bible in a single sermon. While the specific text is Romans 12:1–2, the preacher sets this text in its place in the development of Romans as a whole.

The sermon has a layered effect in that it can be heard on different levels. To newcomers to the Christian community, the sermon is a basic overview of Christian interpretation of life. To mature Christians, the themes and images of the sermon resonate within our deeper awareness of Christian theology and imagery.

MARJORIE HEWITT SUCHOCKI is dean and Ingraham Professor of Theology at Claremont School of Theology, Claremont, California. She is a leading relational (process) theologian whose major works include *The Whispered Word: A Theology of Preaching* (St. Louis: Chalice Press, 1999), *In God's Presence: Theological Reflections on Prayer* (St. Louis: Chalice Press, 1996), *The Fall to Violence: Original Sin in Relational Theology* (New York: Continuum, 1994), *God, Christ, Church*, revised edition (New York: Crossroad, 1989), *The End of Evil: Process Eschatology in Historical Perspective* (Albany: State University of New York Press, 1988), and *Coming Home: Wesley, Whitehead and Women* (Nashville: United Methodist Publishing House, 1987).

MARJORIE HEWITT SUCHOCKI

Do Not Be Afraid of Knowledge

Romans 12:1–2

In January I was standing on a pier in Ventura, California, looking down on waves as they built and crashed below me. It was the first time I saw that the foam on the crest of a breaking wave develops streaks, as if someone were combing the foam like hair! I watched in fascination as the waves below me grew—moving, swelling, breaking, foaming, streaking, crashing onto the shore in relentless grace, one following the other without end.

The book of Romans is like that, building throughout its first twelve chapters like mighty waves crashing upon its shore. Paul no sooner begins this letter than he draws us into a theological description of sin and its agonies, building a case that moves and expands until we, too, are caught in the rolling waters of sin. What are we to do? And he answers in crashing waves of law, guilt, and judgment in relentless succession, till we think those waves will drag us like a riptide to our death. But when all appears lost, the apostle calls forth a quite different wave that begins to reverse the riptide and to take us safely to the shore. It slowly swells and builds till finally it bursts with the great pronouncement of chapter 5, "Therefore, having been justified by faith, we have peace with God through our Lord Jesus Christ."

> The wave crashes on the shore
> and we are safe.

But another wave is inexorably building, completing the reversal. For whereas formerly we might have drowned in the waters of sin, now we are saved in the waters of baptism. One would think, then, the message is complete, but not so. This wave no sooner subsides than another builds, dealing with the perplexity of sin that still persists even in the baptized. We swim with Paul in those waters as he describes our own struggles with sin and grace, with the tension building and building like another mighty wave. Just when we think we will burst with the tension, he brings us to the breaking point of that great chapter 8: "There is therefore no condemnation for those which are in Christ Jesus!" and the wave swells yet further "for the Spirit bears witness to ours," and finally the crash comes. "For I am persuaded that neither death nor life nor angels nor rulers nor things present or things to come nor powers or height, nor depth, nor anything else in all creation will be able to separate from the love of God in Christ Jesus our Lord."

> And the wave crashes,
> while another builds.

Pluralism! What are we to do theologically about those who exhibit a righteous life but do not accept this particular faith of ours? Paul struggles with God's faithfulness to the Jewish people, even though they are not Christians. The wave builds till it finally crashes into Romans 11, as if it is sinking itself into the sands of mystery of God. "Oh the depth of the riches and wisdom and knowledge of God! How unsearchable are God's judgments and how inscrutable God's ways."

> And once more
> the wave comes crashing down.

Romans is the most theological of all the epistles, grand in its scope, lifting us with those waves into what it is to think about this Christian life we have been given. We move from struggling in those waves to soaring on them like a rider on a board, swooping into the troughs and experiencing the buildup until finally we land...on the shore! And what is this shore? What are these sands that these waves drive us to; what is the shape and contour of the shore created by such mighty waves of the Spirit?

Here is this strange thing about the book of Romans. It's divided, you see. Romans 1 through 11 takes us into the height and depth of doctrine, such that the images of waves echoes its majesty. But Romans 12 through 15 takes us into the most mundane practicalities of the Christian life. It's almost as if we were no longer feeling waves at the edge of a mighty ocean, but hearing instead the humbler sound made by waters lapping at a lakeside shore.

How mundane these humbler waters. Romans 12 gives injunctions for one's personal life, Romans 13 gives guidance for one's civic and political life, and Romans 14 and 15 suggest modes of conduct for our communal life together as church. Romans 16 finally concludes the letter with the most down-to-earth reality of all, the greetings to all those faithful women and women who together were leaders in the church. Phoebe, the deacon, and Junia, the apostle, Rufus and his mother, Philologus and Julia, Nereus and his sister, and others.

Such a book—such a division! Is it schizoid, this book, that it looks first at the theoretical and then at the practical? Are they so separated, the theological and the ethical, the thinking and the doing?

And it is just here that we go back to the turning point, to Romans 12:1 and 2—that tiny little pivotal, crucial, magnificent, connecting link. In my childhood I learned it almost thus: "I beseech you therefore brethren [and sisters!] by the mercies of God to present your bodies a living sacrifice, holy, acceptable unto God, which is your spiritual worship. And be not conformed to this world, but be ye transformed by the renewal of your minds, that you might prove what is the good and acceptable and perfect will of God."

Now, I was also taught, "Whenever you see a 'therefore,' look and see what it's there for."

I beseech you *therefore* brothers and sisters. All those waves, all that theology, all that soaring, that sailing on the crest of those waves, is there for one purpose: that it shall inform who we are, that being baptized into those waters, we shall become ourselves, immersed in the wonder of daring to think about who God is and what God has done for us in Christ! Knowledge is for the sake of being, of living, and doing.

But the wonder of all this is that this heady stuff is to infuse our bodies making us a living offering to God. With our whole embodied selves we are to plunge into these waters. And this embodiment of Christian identity is, in fact, a *spiritual* worship. Don't you love the forcing together of what we too often call opposites? The intellect is for our embodiment, and our embodiment is for our spirituality offered to God in worship. The whole of who we are in the dailiness of who we are is affected by this salvation. And all those women and men named at the end of Romans shout out this meaning, like a great culmination, for Paul shows us real people whose lives manifest the living implications of those magnificent waves of doctrine.

Having plunged us into embodied realization of this faith, Paul takes us back again to the life of the mind. Be not conformed to this world: "but be ye transformed by the renewal of your minds." In the midst of the world and its culture, transformed and renewed—but for what? To become great thinkers of thoughts? To be isolated theologians seeking out our towers? No! We are to be transformed for the sake of wisdom, so that, living our theologies, thinking our faiths, seeking ever deeper understanding, we shall discern right conduct in this world. We shall live in caring interpersonal relations. We shall exercise responsible citizenship. We shall tend to the care and nourishment and building up of the community of faith. We shall greet one another in peace.

There is a phrase "practical theology." I suggest that the book of Romans teaches us that all theology is practical, and that we are called to the living of our lives theologically informed.

We who are in church leadership dare not divorce these two. When we urge our sisters and brothers to Christian conduct, we can only do so responsibly when we recognize the truth of Romans: That all discernment is rooted in Christian knowledge turned to wisdom, and that true wisdom is the blending of knowledge with how we live.

"I beseech you, therefore, brothers and sisters, to present your bodies a living sacrifice. . . ." But just here in this moment of passage, does not the language of sacrifice call up yet another image, that of fire? We are bathed in waters that crash onto the shores of our lives, and a further wonder occurs: Those waters turn to the fires of transformation in living witness, living sacrifice, living worship.

I have used the image of water as an image of the Spirit. Is it so strange that it yields to this image of fire, also so frequently associated with the Spirit? If I have seen waves on the shores of California, I have also seen fires ablaze on the mountains of California. The mountains are covered with chaparral, an oily plant that is highly flammable—and which depends upon fire for its own vigor and growth. I watched one October as the fires danced over the mountains, leaping from one great peak to the next. The sparks flew, landed, ignited, setting the mountain ablaze. It was a fearsome thing to see, for the fires were frightening in their destructive power—but oddly enough it was also a beautiful thing to see, that dance of pure flame. I have seen the sun darkened at noonday with the smoke rising from that brightness. And when the mighty flames subsided, having devoured all in their path till there was nothing left to burn, the proud mountains were bent humble, naked, lowly in the charred remains of blackened earth. And I mourned their beauty. But in spring the rains came, and the miracle happened. The charred earth turned green as vegetation sprang once again wildly to life renewed by the fires of October.

The Spirit can seem like a destructive fire to us in the renewal of our minds. Sometimes our studies burn cherished suppositions, and we are confused, broken, charred by the loss. We can mourn what we think is the loss of the faith that once grew so greenly on the mountains of our spirits. Knowledge can be used by the Spirit not only like a wave that crashes, but like a fire that burns. Yet there comes a springtime of the Spirit—and the clearing of that old growth has made way for a deeper vigor, a greenness deep down in the heart of who we are. We are renewed, and in the renewal is our transformation.

Have you not seen? Do you not remember? I recall a time when my literalist faith in what I assumed to be the biblical story began to crack and tremble against what seemed to me to be the destructive onslaught of a quite different understanding of how God reveals Godself and that which we need for our salvation. I remember how fearsome it was to let it go, to stop trusting my faith, and to begin trusting God. Ah, how the fire of the Spirit burns. And ah! How green is the Spirit's springtime.

Do not be afraid of knowledge, whether it be the crashing waves of God's work newly understood or the burning fires of transformation. Rather, let the Spirit do its work, and you will find it a work that deepens your spiritual service of worship in the church and in the world. Its renewal of your minds brings the gift of discernment for daily living; your own life is to be a miniature of that amazing book of Romans. Godly knowing is for the sake of godly living. Knowing God, you will discover the very practical and challenging and daunting and glorious and mundane will of God.

"I beseech you, therefore, brothers and sisters, by the mercies of God, to present your bodies a living sacrifice...and be not conformed to this world, but be transformed by the renewal of your minds...that you might prove what is the good and acceptable and perfect will of God."

34

Preaching in a Postmodern Perspective

Writers in the field of preaching are struggling to understand the relationship between preaching and the emerging postmodern situation. Most authors who consider this matter focus on preaching in an ethos that is increasingly postmodern. John S. McClure is among the first preachers to articulate an approach to preaching that is postmodern in character. McClure makes postmodern assumptions in formulating the nature, purpose, and norms of preaching.

One of the most permeating insights of postmodernism is the recognition that every perception is an act of interpretation. Because individuals and communities are different, all interpretations differ. Therefore, according to McClure, the preacher must recognize that all statements and claims are negotiations of positions within a larger communicative field. We negotiate with one another with respect to meaning. No person or community has an absolute grasp of truth. Communities that think they have the whole truth are idolatrous, for they have treated their relative notions as absolute.

Preachers who are postmodern seek to subvert conventional understandings of the world in order to help a congregation name its own negotiation of reality and to engage the views of others. The preacher unmasks a community's understanding of what is real (ontology), of the stories and values that the community uses to interpret itself and the world (metanarrative), and the philosophies it uses to make sense of the world (metaphysics). Postmodern preachers also subvert the authorities that ground preaching in order to reopen preaching to the other.

The following sermon is a *collaborative* effort to open preaching to its human others, particularly its hearers. The preacher seeks to accomplish this task by letting the sermon grow out of the biblical and theological reflections of a small group of the sermon's hearers called the Sermon Roundtable. This process is designed, among other things, to unmask (and transgress) the cultural and ecclesial assumption that the clerical elite's particular configuration of authorities (e.g., scripture, tradition, experience, reason) is primary in preaching. It assumes that others have genuine insight into the divine nature and purpose. It makes explicit what is tacitly known: that the practice of Christian being and living in a pluralistic postmodern context are not simply given but result from conversation.

The sermon that follows was preached at Louisville Presbyterian Theological Seminary on the Friday before Passion Sunday. A week prior to the sermon, the preacher met with the Sermon Roundtable comprised of eight members of the seminary community—faculty, students, staff, administration. The sermon grows out of conversation on the biblical text, and on ideas, experiences, insights into culture, theological reflections. The sermon arises from a collaborative negotiation of Christian memory, meaning, experience, and worldview in one North American seminary. The preacher says, "The sermon is very different from the one I would have preached prior to collaboration with the hearers." Collaborative preaching makes conversation about authority itself central to the sermon.

How does the preacher organize the insights from the conversation into a sermon? As McClure sees it, the postmodern preacher works with four fields within which people communicate. Each field is an ongoing conversation that corresponds to one of the four codes that relate to the four authorities that inform Christian faith and preaching: (1) what we remember as the foundational events of faith and how we remember them (*scriptural code*); (2) what is Christian truth and how we hold it to be true (*semantic code*); (3) the experience of faith and how it is experienced (*cultural code*); (4) the theological worldview that informs the community (*theo-symbolic code*). Each field and each code are coextensive. This chart shows the relationship between the codes and the fields of communication.

Sermon	Roundtable	Congregation
Theo-symbolic Code	<coming to terms with>	Worldview
Semantic Code	<coming to terms with>	Truth (meaning)
Cultural Code	<coming to terms with>	Experience
Scriptural Code	<coming to terms with>	Anamnesis (memory)

The collaborative conversation helps the preacher encode in the sermon the ways that the preacher and the congregation are coming to terms with each other within each communicative field. The roundtable helps the preacher discern how to discuss in the sermon the congregation's ongoing negotiations concerning worldview, truth, experience, and memory.

For instance, in a roundtable conversation on a miracle story from one of the Synoptic Gospels, the group might spend several minutes discussing what happened in Galilee in the days of Jesus. This conversation might include an exchange regarding "what happened" between Bob, a young college student who participates in a conservative spiritual life group on campus, and Milder, who arrived at the discussion with a commentary influenced by a reversionary theologian tucked under her arm. The two go back and forth over whether the miracle happened as described or whether the story was the writer's way of helping an ancient congregation understand the power of faith. The preacher could then decide to encode this part of the negotiation and its results, as a part of the section of the sermon processing the Scripture Code. The sermon might report each argument and accentuate how the disagreement was resolved (or not resolved) in the congregation.

The conversation about the miracle story is multifaceted. At the semantic (truth) level, the group negotiates the degree to which Christian faith is dependent upon a historical event that reveals the supernatural power of God or results from an experience of understanding the world through the eyes of faith. At another level, the conversation negotiates how faith is experienced. Is it a power "over" me or a power "within" me? At still another level, the roundtable jockies for position as to which parts of our theological worldview are most significant for the community's life together—the omnipotence of God or the reception of grace in human life. The preacher, typically, will not just choose sides, but will encode the actual negotiation into the sermon so that the congregation can overhear itself coming to terms with these important matters.

Sermons in this mode will have several sequences of movement. A sequence is a segment that contributes to the development of the sermon as a whole. A sequence is an interweaving of idea (semantic code), experience, image, and feeling (cultural code), theological symbols (theo-symbolic code), and the community's memory of the foundational events of their faith (scriptural code). In each sequence, the preacher should deal with all four codes.

Within a given sequence, *each of the codes deals with the same subject matter but addresses a different communicative field.* The preacher unfolds all four codes within each sequence. McClure intends, therefore, that the following sermon is not to be read or preached in a linear fashion—from the top of the page down. Rather, the goal is to complete each sequence by moving back and forth among the four codes.

This interweaving could be accomplished in a number of ways. As an illustration, you might try reading the sermon below several ways. If you are in a context in which you are working with hearers who expect biblical exposition to be the center of the sermon, you might begin each sequence with the scriptural code. If the culture has raised a question that is the focus of the sermon, you might begin with the cultural code. Reading back and forth among the codes within each sequence allows you feel how best to deliver the sermon.

This sermon is also thematically postmodern. It makes use of the postmodern decentering of the self to reinterpret Paul's language of self-emptying in Philippians 2. The ethic gleaned from this text resembles one articulated by Emmanuel Levinas and others.[1] In this ethic, the self recognizes its own relativity and steps outside of itself in order to open a space in life that makes possible a profound experience of the other as one with whom the self is related. McClure believes that this precarious encounter is the beginning of compassion and has the power to heal the festering wounds of church and society.

JOHN S. McCLURE is Frank H. Caldwell Professor of Preaching and Worship at Louisville Presbyterian Theological Seminary, Louisville, Kentucky. He is the author of the influential *The Roundtable Pulpit* (Nashville: Abingdon Press, 1995) and *The Four Codes of Preaching: Rhetorical Strategies* (Minneapolis: Fortress Press, 1991). He is also editor of *Best Advice for Preaching* (Minneapolis: Fortress Press, 1998) and, with Nancy Ramsay, *Telling the Truth: Preaching About Sexual and Domestic Violence* (Cleveland: United Church Press, 1998).

---

[1] Emmanuel Levinas, *Otherwise Than Being or Beyond Essence*, trans. by Alphonso Lingis (Boston: Martinus Nijhoff, 1981); cf. Edward Farley, *Good and Evil: Interpreting a Human Condition* (Minneapolis: Fortress, 1990), 31–62.

JOHN S. McCLURE

Alienation>Emptying>Compassion
Philippians 2:5–11

Sequence One

Theo-symbolic Code

We are different. This is the human condition. It is both beautiful and tragic. It is beautiful because it opens spaces for endless varieties of creative relationships. It is tragic because the simple, beautiful differences between us can become a door through which evil can enter—an evil that turns benign difference into malignant alienation.

How does this happen? It happens as we lose sight of the face of the other. We lose sight of the other person as vulnerable and fragile—as we are.

Semantic Code

Relationships are conflicts waiting to happen.
The conflicts among us can turn to violence.

Cultural Code

A young married couple begin their marriage with different views about money. For her enjoyment and mental health, she wants to maintain a horse at an expensive stable ($1,000 per month). He wants to save for a bigger house and more substantial retirement. Ten years later, they file for divorce.

After years of steadily deepening conflict in Kosovo, heavily armed Serb police surrounded four villages and opened fire with machine guns, grenades, rocket launchers.

In Uganda, adults are afraid of their own children whom rebels have abducted by the thousands and turned into heartless killers.

The Christian church continues to fragment into interest groups. Differences of theology, gender, sexual orientation, social and political outlook have deepened into entrenched opposition.

Scriptural Code

We are naturally conflicted people. That is our "mind" (to use Paul's language)—our "mindset."

The Philippian church is becoming more and more conflicted. From Epaphroditus, Paul has heard about deepening divisions and disunity.

Sequence Two

Theo-symbolic Code

The only way to stop benign indifference from turning into malignant alienation is through self-emptying love.

Emptying means *not exploiting* the powers that we have. In other words, Christ *emptied himself of power as domination.*

By emptying himself of the desire to use his power to dominate, control, or use others for his own ends, Jesus comes close, close enough to see our faces, and for us to see God's face; close enough to experience our vulnerability and to show us God's.

Semantic Code

The answer is self-emptying, self-giving love.

This is not self-abnegation, but a different way to use the powers that constitute the self: in mutual, self-giving ways rather than in cycles of submission, domination, coercion, abuse, or violence.

Cultural Code

When an abused spouse says, "The Bible says I should empty myself," and "Go one more mile with my abuser," our response is, "No! You must empty yourself of this nonrelationship. Empty yourself of this abusive, dominating-submitting way of using the different powers that you and your spouse each have. Empty yourself of this cycle of deepening alienation. There is a better way to be in relationships.

In Northern Ireland and Bosnia, people are trying to *leave* the cycle of violence, abandon the only selves they have known for years—selves caught up in power serving alienation and unholy separation. It is time for them to exit, deconstruct, yes—"empty"—themselves of the very culture of malignant violence that has defined them.

In our church, we also confront the need for an emptying—an exiting—of the pattern of relating to each other by using our powers to dominate (and submit) to one another—men and women, young and old, straight and gay.

Scriptural Code

Paul turns a metaphysical doxology about how God and Jesus are related to each other into an ethical vision for the church and all of humanity. Christ Jesus "did not regard equality with God (his power) as something to be exploited (used to dominate others), but emptied himself...."

Sequence Three

Theo-symbolic Code

Once we begin to empty ourselves of our enmeshment in patterns of power as domination, the vulnerable faces of others begin to emerge on the horizon of our lives. This is the beginning of compassion.

On the one hand, this is great joy. On the other hand, it makes us frightfully aware of the distance that still exists between us—the gap created by the long history of the exploitation of the power that still pervades our lives. Love, as Dante points out, shows us the gates of hell. We are then confronted with another, painful emptying: We begin to empty ourselves of the assurance that we can fully love.

Semantic Code

Once we begin to love, *we empty ourselves of any assurance that we can ultimately empty ourselves.*

We have no assurance that we can ever become authentic Christians—in whom authenticity means congruence between what we are committed to, and who we are. We are disqualified even as we run the race, and yet love requires that we run.

Cultural Code

In the documentary film *Family Name*, Mackie Alston, whose family owned thousands of slaves, goes in search of his soul. As he interviews children of former slaves and relatives, seeing their faces and experiencing their wounds, he realizes that he is trying to purge himself of something, to rid himself of part of himself that haunts him, gnaws at him, and continues to work its evil magic in him in ways that he cannot seem to shake. Midway through the movie, he begins to realize that he has no assurance that this huge documentary project will succeed in emptying him of his racism—of its pervasive power in and over him. He alternates between the painful realization that he is disqualified from ever becoming free of prejudice and the profound commitment to continuing running the race toward reconciliation with his black family members—many of whom share his name, "Alston," and some, probably, are his actual blood relatives.

Scriptural Code

Being "born in human likeness," Jesus had no assurance that he could empty himself of these evil patterns of dominating power. Resisting the power of this evil was his vocation, from his temptation to his final moments on the cross. Most scholars believe that Paul added the words "even death on a cross." These words seem to emphasize that Jesus himself knew no victory in his journey of love.

Sequence Four

Theo-symbolic Code

Christ's passion is a profound laying aside of dominating, instrumental power.

Christ's passion shows us the way into the only kind of love that can resist and ultimately heal the malignant conflicts and violence in our midst.

Christ's passion is a journey with no assurance of success. As far as we know, all of our struggles for liberation, inclusivity, salvation, wholeness, and reconciliation will ultimately fail As far as we know, the reality of Christian faith will forever be marginal—exist only in the margins—of our own lives and of the world in which we live.

Yet, Christ's passion is the only journey that can salvage the tragic beauty of human difference from the violent wreckage of human alienation.

Semantic Code

Today, the Friday before Passion/Palm Sunday, we recommit our lives to Christ's journey to the cross.

Cultural Code

The Lord's supper today binds us together with Christ. It puts us into deepest solidarity with him on his journey of domination-emptying love. Here, more than anywhere else, we experience the depths of this love and the insecurity of this commitment.

Scriptural Code

Let the same mind be in you that was in Christ Jesus, who, though he was in the form of God, did not regard the power that he had as something to be exploited, but emptied himself of dominating power...to the point of death, even death on a cross.

Index of Sermon Texts

This index cites the major Bible passages on which the sermons in this volume are based. The index notes days on which the texts appear in the Revised Common Lectionary.

Printed in the United States
201257BV00003B/301-453/A